Lecture Notes in Computer Science

Lecture Notes in Computer Science

Edited by G. Goos and J. Hartmanis

51

B. S. Garbow   J. M. Boyle
J. J. Dongarra   C. B. Moler

Matrix Eigensystem Routines –
EISPACK Guide Extension

Springer-Verlag
Berlin · Heidelberg · New York 1977

Author

Burton S. Garbow
Applied Mathematics Division
Argonne National Laboratory
9700 South Cass Avenue
Argonne, Illinois 60439 USA

Library of Congress Cataloging in Publication Data

Main entry under title:

Matrix eigensystem routines.

   (Lecture notes in computer science ; 51)
   Supplements the 2d. ed of Matrix eigensystem routines :
EISPACK guide.
   1. EISPACK (Computer program) I. Garbow, B. S.,
1930-   II. Series.
QA193.M38   001.6'425   77-2802

AMS Subject Classifications (1970): 15 A 18, 65 F 15
CR Subject Classifications (1974):   5.14

ISBN 3-540-08254-9 Springer-Verlag Berlin · Heidelberg · New York
ISBN 0-387-08254-9 Springer-Verlag New York · Heidelberg · Berlin

© by Springer-Verlag Berlin · Heidelberg 1977
Printed in Germany

Printing and binding: Beltz Offsetdruck, Hemsbach/Bergstr.
2145/3140-543210

PREFACE

This volume supplements the earlier Volume 6 in this series [10]; together they provide guidance for the complete second release of the EISPACK Eigensystem Package. The stress in this book is on four additional problem classes: the symmetric band eigenproblem, the generalized symmetric eigenproblem, the generalized real eigenproblem, and the singular value decomposition of a rectangular matrix and solution of an associated linear least squares problem.

The organization of material in this volume follows closely that of [10]. Several of the newer problems transform to problems covered earlier in [10]; reference should be made there for details that apply after the problem has been transformed. Towards achieving a certain degree of self-sufficiency, however, the documentation for seven earlier subroutines that recur here in the various recommended paths of Section 2 has been recopied in Section 7.1 of this volume.

The EISPAC control program, available with the IBM version of EISPACK, extends to each of the newer problem classes except Singular Value Decomposition; the discussion of its usage, where applicable, is integrated into the various sections of this volume. Its documentation, earlier provided in [10], has been recopied in Section 7.2 of this volume.

EISPACK is a product of the NATS (National Activity to Test Software) Project ([3],[4],[5]) which has been guided by the principle that the effort to produce high quality mathematical software is justified by the wide use of that software in the scientific community. EISPACK has been distributed to several hundred computer centers throughout the world since the package was first released in May, 1972, and now the second release is available as described in Section 5.

Building a systematized collection of mathematical software is necessarily
a collaborative undertaking demanding the interplay of a variety of skills;
we wish to acknowledge a few whose roles were especially crucial during the
preparation of the second release. J. Wilkinson persisted in his encourage-
ment of the project and his counsel was often sought during his frequent
visits to North America. Organization and direction came from W. Cowell and
J. Pool. B. Smith and V. Klema provided highly valued consultation. The
field testing was carried out at the installations listed in Section 5 through
the sustained efforts of M. Berg, A. Cline, D. Dodson, B. Einarsson, S. Eisenstat,
I. Farkas, P. Fox, F. Fritsch, C. Frymann, G. Haigler, H. Happ, L. Harding,
M. Havens, H. Hull, D. Kincaid, P. Messina, M. Overton, R. Raffenetti, J. Stein,
J. Walsh, and J. Wang. Additional assistance in providing the timing information for the tables of Section 4 was given by T. Pinter. Appreciation is also
expressed for the very important feedback received from users not formally
associated with the testing effort. Finally, we acknowledge the skill and
cooperation of our typist, J. Beumer.

Work performed under the auspices of the United States Energy Research and
Development Administration and the National Science Foundation.

TABLE OF CONTENTS

SECTION 1

SECTION 2

LIST OF TABLES

Section 1

INTRODUCTION

The subset of the EISPACK package of Fortran IV programs included within this volume is a systematized collection of subroutines which compute the eigenvalues and/or eigenvectors for three special classes of matrix problems and the singular value decomposition of an arbitrary matrix. The three problem classes are real symmetric band, generalized real symmetric, and generalized real. The singular value decomposition, in turn, enables the solution of certain linear least squares problems. The subroutines are based mainly upon Algol procedures published in the Handbook series of Springer-Verlag by Wilkinson and Reinsch [1] and the QZ algorithm of Moler and Stewart [8] as extended by Ward [9]. They have been adapted and thoroughly tested on several different machines, and have been certified and are supported by the NATS project [3,4,5]. The machines for which they are certified include IBM 360-370, CDC 6000-7000, Univac 1110, Honeywell 6070, DEC PDP-10, and Burroughs 6700.

This manual is a user guide to these newer capabilities of EISPACK (complementing [10]) and to a control program EISPAC available with the IBM version of the package. It contains program segments which illustrate each of the basic computations with EISPACK and discusses variants of these that provide mild tradeoffs of efficiency, storage, and accuracy. Other sections of the guide discuss the validation procedures used for testing EISPACK, report execution times of the EISPACK subroutines on several machines, advertise the certified status and availability of EISPACK, and describe the major differences between the published Algol procedures in [1] and their Fortran counterparts. The final section includes detailed documentation with Fortran listings of each EISPACK subroutine referenced herein and the document for the control program.

Section 1.1

ORGANIZATION OF THE GUIDE

This guide is organized for the convenience, hopefully, of the user. Material most pertinent to the basic uses of the package and the control program appears in the early sections and references the more detailed and specific information in later sections. Here follows a brief description of the organization of the guide.

The remaining subsection of this introduction is a general statement with regard to the expected accuracy of the results from EISPACK. This statement is based upon the careful and detailed analyses of Wilkinson and others. Only a brief overview is provided in this subsection and the interested reader is directed to [1] and [2] for more detailed statements of accuracy.

Section 2 is divided into a prologue and four major subsections. The prologue introduces the concept of an EISPACK path, discusses the economies that can be realized with the use of the control program if available, and instructs on the selection among the 10 basic paths of this volume. The first subsection establishes several conventions that are useful in clarifying the discussions of the paths. It then details the 10 basic paths and associated control program calls in the form of program segments. Each program segment is introduced by a brief description of the problem it solves and any specific considerations needed for the path, and is followed by a summary of array storage requirements for the path and sample execution times on the IBM 370/195 computer. The next subsection describes possible variants of the 10 basic paths, focusing on those conditions for which the variants are to be preferred. The third subsection provides further information about specific details of EISPACK and the control program and

2

suggests several additional applications of the package. Complete sample programs illustrating the use of EISPACK and EISPAC to solve a specified eigenproblem appear at the end of this subsection. The last subsection describes the EISPACK capabilities to compute the singular value decomposition of a matrix and to solve an associated linear least squares problem.

Section 3 outlines the validation procedures for EISPACK that led to the certification of the package. Section 4 reports sample execution times of the individual subroutines and of several of the program segments of Section 2 and also discusses such considerations as the dependence of the execution times upon the matrix and the computer. The statement of certification for EISPACK, the machines and operating systems on which it has been certified, and its availability appear in Section 5. Section 6 itemizes the principal differences between the referenced Fortran subroutines and their Algol antecedents published in [1]. Finally, the documentation and Fortran listing for each subroutine appear in edited form in Section 7.

Section 1.2

ACCURACY OF THE EISPACK SUBROUTINES

The most useful statement that can be made with regard to the accuracy

of the EISPACK subroutines is that they are based on algorithms which are

numerically stable; that is, for every computed eigenpair (λ, z) associated

with a matrix A, there exists a matrix E with norm small compared to that

of A for which λ and z are an exact eigenpair of A+E. For generalized

problems, the corresponding claim can be made after associating also with

B a matrix of small relative norm. This backward or inverse approach in

describing the accuracy of the subroutines is necessitated by the inherent

properties of the problem which, in general, preclude the more familiar

forward approach. However, for real symmetric band matrices the forward

approach also applies, and indeed is a consequence of the backward analysis.

For these problems the eigenvalues computed by EISPACK must be close to the

exact ones, but a similar claim for the eigenvectors is not possible. What

is true in this case is that the computed eigenvectors will be closely ortho-

gonal if the subroutines that accumulate the transformations are used.

The size of E, of course, is crucial to a meaningful statement of

accuracy, and the reader is referred to the detailed error analyses of

Wilkinson and others ([1],[2]). In our many tests of EISPACK, we have sel-

dom observed an E with norm larger than a small multiple of the product of

the order of the matrix or system, an appropriate norm, and the precision

of the machine.

Section 2

HOW TO USE EISPACK

This section is designed to provide, in readily accessible form, the basic information you need to correctly use subroutines from EISPACK to solve an eigenproblem. The way in which this information is presented is influenced by the design of the eigensystem package; hence we will first consider briefly the global structure of EISPACK.

EISPACK is capable of performing 32 different basic computations (22 of them described in [10]), plus several variations of them. If each of these computations (and variations) were performed completely within a single EISPACK subroutine, the package would be unwieldy indeed. It also would be highly redundant, since the same steps appear in many of the computations. To avoid these problems, the subroutines in EISPACK are designed so that each performs a basic step which appears in one or more of the computations. (See [7] for an introduction to the modularization of EISPACK.) Consequently, the redundancy (hence the size) of the package is minimized.

Another consequence is that, in general, more than one subroutine from EISPACK is required to perform a given computation. These subroutines must of course be called in the correct order and with the proper parameters; in addition, some computations also require certain auxiliary actions, e.g., initializing parameters and testing for errors. Throughout the remainder of this book such an ordered set of subroutine calls and associated auxiliary actions will be called an EISPACK *path*.

As a result of this structure the documentation for the use of EISPACK comprises two main parts: a description of the basic paths and their variations, and a description of the individual subroutines in EISPACK. The information about the paths constitutes the remainder of this section

5

while the subroutine documentation is collected in Section 7.

The path descriptions are divided into three parts. Section 2.1 describes the 10 basic paths and includes a table to facilitate reference to them. Section 2.2 describes some of the variations of these paths and suggests when such variations might be useful. Section 2.3 contains certain additional information about and examples of the use of EISPACK. To keep the descriptions of the basic paths and their variants simple, we have omitted much of the detailed information (e.g., the meanings of non-zero error indicators and the descriptions of certain parameters) and collected it in Section 2.3. Detailed information about each subroutine may be obtained from the documentation for the individual subroutines in Section 7. We hope, however, that the information given in this section will be sufficient to permit you to correctly solve most eigenproblems.

The detail of path information that you must know to solve certain basic eigenproblems can be reduced by using an appropriate driver subroutine to build the desired path from other EISPACK members. Applicability of the driver subroutines is limited to those problems where all eigenvalues and eigenvectors or all eigenvalues only are desired. There is a driver subroutine for each class of problems handled by the package; driver subroutine calls corresponding to six of the 10 basic paths are given as part of the discussion of the paths in this section.

Substantial further reduction in the detail of path information that you must know to solve an eigenproblem, with wider applicability, can be achieved by use of a control program, called EISPAC, which is available with the IBM version of the eigensystem package [6]. (It is only practical to implement this control program on those computing systems which adequately support execution-time loading of subroutines.) EISPAC accepts a relatively straightforward problem description stated in terms of the properties of the input matrix or system and the kinds of results required. It checks this description for consistency, automatically selects and executes the appropriate path, and then returns the results to your program. Thus EISPAC not only simplifies the use of the eigensystem package, but also enhances its robustness by eliminating the possibility of making errors in transcribing a path.

To use EISPAC, you call it with a set of parameters which describes the problem you wish to solve, and which enables EISPAC to choose the appropriate path. EISPAC calls corresponding to the 10 basic paths (and most of their variations) are given as a further part of the discussion of the paths in this section. Note that in order to use EISPAC, you must provide system control cards defining the file from which the EISPACK subroutines are to be loaded; this and other detailed information on the use of EISPAC can be found in its subroutine document in Section 7.2.

Section 2.1

RECOMMENDED BASIC PATHS IN EISPACK

This section describes how to use EISPACK to compute some or all of
the eigenvalues, or some or all of the eigenvalues and their corresponding eigenvectors, for the three classes of problems mentioned in Section 1.
The paths recommended here provide accurate solutions for their respective
eigenproblems using a minimum of storage. Under some circumstances,
variations of these paths (using different subroutines) may provide
slightly more accurate or speedier solutions; these variations are discussed in Section 2.2.

To determine the recommended path to solve your particular eigenproblem, consult Table 1 at the end of this section. First, decide to
which of the three classes listed across the top of the table your problem
belongs. In general, the computation will be more accurate and efficient
if you use any known special properties of the matrix or system to place
it in the most specialized applicable class. Thus a generalized problem
which is real symmetric (both A and B symmetric and B positive definite)
is better classified so, than as just real (but see Section 2.3.4). On
the other hand, some special properties cannot be utilized; for example,
advantage cannot be taken of the band form of a matrix unless it is symmetric
as well.

Next, determine which of the problem classifications listed down the
left side of Table 1 most closely matches the subset of eigenvalues and
eigenvectors you wish to find. The table entry so determined indicates
the subsection which describes the recommended path for your problem. (If
variations of the path exist, the subsection will refer you to Section
2.2 for them or to the corresponding section of [10].) For example, if

you have a real symmetric band matrix and you wish to find all its eigenvalues and their corresponding eigenvectors, the table directs you to Section 2.1.1.

Each subsection to which the table refers provides just the information you need to use the described path correctly. It begins with a statement of the problem and an identification of the main input and result variables. The subroutine calls and auxiliary statements consttuting the path are given and are followed by the corresponding driver subroutine call, if applicable, and the EISPAC call. Next is a description of additional parameters (if any) appearing in the path and a brief summary of the disposition of the results of the computation. Dimension information for the arrays appearing in the path and a summary of the total amount of array storage used is then given. These are followed by indicative timing results. (Timing considerations are discussed more fully in Section 4.) The subsection concludes with references to applicable subsections of Section 2.2 (or to [10]).

We have employed a few conventions in these subsections to streamline the presentation of information. One of these concerns the types of the parameters. All parameters have their Fortran implied type: those beginning with I, J, K, L, M, or N are type INTEGER, and the others are what will be called *working precision*, which denotes either type REAL or type DOUBLE PRECISION depending on the version of EISPACK being used.

A second convention concerns certain parameters which are used only to pass intermediate results from one subroutine to another. The roles of these parameters are not described in the subsections, since only their type and dimension need be known to execute a path correctly. To facilitate recognition of these parameters, they are written in lower case, employing a systematic nomenclature. Their names are composed of f or i

to indicate type (working precision or integer), s, v, or m to indicate dimensionality (scalar, vector, or matrix), and a serial number. Thus $fv1$ is used for the first working precision temporary vector to appear in a given path.

A third convention is used to indicate how the array parameters in a path are dimensioned. It employs three "variables" nm, mm, and mb, which must be replaced in array declarator statements by Fortran integer constants. The parameters NM, MM, and MB communicate the values of these constants to array declarator statements in the EISPACK subroutines; therefore NM must be set to the constant used for nm, MM set to that used for mm, and MB to that used for mb. It is of utmost importance that whenever a path is executed, N and, if used, M, satisfy $N \leq nm$ and $M \leq mm$; otherwise unpredictable errors will occur.

An example may help clarify the use of nm and mm. Suppose you are using the path described in Section 2.1.7. Considering only the parameters A, B, W, and Z, the dimension information is stated there as $A(nm,nm)$, $B(nm,nm)$, $W(mm)$, and $Z(nm,mm)$. If the largest system for which you intend to use this path is of order 50, and if you do not expect to compute more than 10 eigenvalues and eigenvectors, you might use the array declarator statement

    DIMENSION A(50,50),B(50,50),W(10),Z(50,10)

together with

    NM = 50
    MM = 10

You would, of course, set N to the actual order of the system for each execution of the path; it must satisfy $N \leq 50$. Similarly, M will be set (by the path) to the number of eigenvalues determined; it must satisfy $M \leq 10$.

The summary of the total amount of array storage used by a path is given in terms of the order parameters N and M, rather than in terms of nm and mm. Thus it represents the minimum array storage required to execute the path for a given order matrix or system, achieved when nm is equal to N and mm is equal to M. Note that when using the EISPAC control program you need not dimension any parameters which do not appear in the call to EISPAC (i.e., those named according to the second convention above) since it allocates them for you. This does not, however, reduce the minimum storage required, which remains as indicated in the summary.

A fourth convention relates to the calls to subroutines that have an eigenvector option, when eigenvalues only are computed. In such a case the formal parameter corresponding to the eigenvector matrix Z, although required, is not referenced in the subroutine; the variable name DUMMY will appear instead at the corresponding position in the calling statement.

A final convention concerns the handling of execution errors in a path. Certain EISPACK subroutines may fail to satisfactorily perform their step of the computation; in this case an error parameter, universally denoted by IERR, is set to a non-zero value indicating the type of error which occurred. In many cases the execution of a path must not be allowed to continue after such an error; hence a conditional branch to statement number 99999 is inserted in each path after each subroutine call which may set the parameter IERR. Appropriate action at statement 99999 might be to print IERR and stop. Each distinct error that can occur in EISPACK produces one of a unique set of values for IERR. The possible values of IERR and their meanings, together with an indication of whether or not any partial results have been correctly computed, are summarized in

11

Section 2.3.8; more detailed information on IERR can be obtained by consulting the documents for the individual subroutines. If you are using EISPAC, it will print a message describing any errors which occur and terminate execution, unless you elect to examine IERR as discussed in Section 2.3.7 and in the EISPAC document.

In summary, to select the recommended EISPACK path to solve your eigenproblem, consult Table 1 and then read the subsection to which it refers in light of the above conventions. Note that in order to ensure correct execution of the path, you must, in addition to providing input data and result storage, do the following: provide arrays for storage of intermediate or temporary results, call the subroutines in the path in the correct order, pass parameters from one call to the next exactly as described, and perform certain auxiliary actions. Alternatively, if the control program EISPAC is included in your version of EISPACK, you may simply call it and let it perform these tasks for you.

TABLE 1

SECTIONS DESCRIBING THE RECOMMENDED BASIC PATHS IN EISPACK

Problem Classification \ Class of Matrix or System	Real Symmetric Band	Real Symmetric Generalized	Real Generalized
All Eigenvalues & Corresponding Eigenvectors	2.1.1	2.1.5	2.1.9
All Eigenvalues	2.1.2	2.1.6	2.1.10
Some Eigenvalues & Corresponding Eigenvectors	2.1.3	2.1.7	--
Some Eigenvalues	2.1.4	2.1.8	--

Section 2.1.1

ALL EIGENVALUES AND CORRESPONDING EIGENVECTORS OF A REAL SYMMETRIC BAND MATRIX

A real symmetric band matrix of order N and (half) band width MB can be presented to EISPACK as an MB-column array, with the lowest subdiagonal stored in the last N+1-MB positions of the first column, the next higher subdiagonal in the last N+2-MB positions of the second column, further subdiagonals similarly, and finally the principal diagonal in the last column. Contents of storage locations not part of the matrix are arbitrary. For example, when N = 5 and MB = 3, the array (designated A) should contain

$$\begin{bmatrix} * & * & A(1,1) \\ * & A(2,1) & A(2,2) \\ A(3,1) & A(3,2) & A(3,3) \\ A(4,2) & A(4,3) & A(4,4) \\ A(5,3) & A(5,4) & A(5,5) \end{bmatrix}$$

where the subscripts for each element refer to the row and column of the element in the standard two-dimensional representation, and '*' denotes an arbitrary value.

To determine all the eigenvalues W and their corresponding eigenvectors Z of a real symmetric band matrix A of order N and (half) band width MB, the recommended EISPACK path is:

    CALL BANDR(NM,N,MB,A,W,$fv1$,$fv1$,.TRUE.,Z)

    CALL TQL2(NM,N,W,$fv1$,Z,IERR)

    IF (IERR .NE. 0) GO TO 99999

or, using driver subroutine RSB:

    CALL RSB(NM,N,MB,A,W,1,Z,$fv1$,$fv1$,IERR)

    IF (IERR .NE. 0) GO TO 99999

13

or, using EISPAC:

CALL EISPAC(NM,N,MATRIX('REAL',A,'SYMMETRIC'),BAND(MB),VALUES(W),VECTOR(Z))

This path returns the eigenvalues in ascending order and a set of ortho-normal eigenvectors; A is destroyed except for its last two columns which retain a copy of the tridiagonal matrix produced in the initial reduction.

Note that if the band matrix is already tridiagonal (MB = 2), EISPAC selects the more specialized tridiagonal path and may return slightly differ-ent eigenvalues and eigenvectors than the EISPACK path or driver subroutine RSB.

Suitable dimensions for the arrays are: $A(nm,mb)$, $W(nm)$, $Z(nm,nm)$, and $fv1(nm)$.

The array storage required to execute this path is $N^2 + N(MB+2)$ working precision words.

Indicative execution times for this path (run on an IBM 370/195) are .006, .033, .22, and 1.5 seconds for sample matrices of order and (half) band width (10,3), (20,6), (40,12), and (80,24) respectively. Extrapolation of these execution times for matrices of different (half) band widths is discussed in Section 4.5.

A variant of this path substitutes the implicit for the explicit QL shift; see Section 2.2.3 of [10].

Section 2.1.2

ALL EIGENVALUES OF A REAL SYMMETRIC BAND MATRIX

A real symmetric band matrix of order N and (half) band width MB can
be presented to EISPACK as an MB-column array, with the lowest subdiagonal
stored in the last N+1-MB positions of the first column, the next higher
subdiagonal in the last N+2-MB positions of the second column, further
subdiagonals similarly, and finally the principal diagonal in the last
column. Contents of storage locations not part of the matrix are arbitrary.
For example, when N = 5 and MB = 3, the array (designated A) should contain

$$\begin{bmatrix} * & * & A(1,1) \\ * & A(2,1) & A(2,2) \\ A(3,1) & A(3,2) & A(3,3) \\ A(4,2) & A(4,3) & A(4,4) \\ A(5,3) & A(5,4) & A(5,5) \end{bmatrix}$$

where the subscripts for each element refer to the row and column of the
element in the standard two-dimensional representation, and '*' denotes an
arbitrary value.

To determine all the eigenvalues W of a real symmetric band matrix A
of order N and (half) band width MB, the recommended EISPACK path is:

    CALL BANDR(NM,N,MB,A,W,*fv1*,*fv2*,.FALSE.,DUMMY)
    CALL TQLRAT(N,W,*fv2*,IERR)
    IF (IERR .NE. 0) GO TO 99999

or, using driver subroutine RSB:

    CALL RSB(NM,N,MB,A,W,0,DUMMY,*fv1*,*fv2*,IERR)
    IF (IERR .NE. 0) GO TO 99999

15

or, using EISPAC:

    CALL EISPAC(NM,N,MATRIX('REAL',A,'SYMMETRIC'),BAND(MB),VALUES(W))

This path returns the eigenvalues in ascending order; A is destroyed except for its last two columns which retain a copy of the tridiagonal matrix produced in the initial reduction.

Note that if the band matrix is already tridiagonal (MB = 2), EISPAC selects the more specialized tridiagonal path and may return slightly different eigenvalues than the EISPACK path or driver subroutine RSB.

Suitable dimensions for the arrays are: $A(nm,mb)$, $W(nm)$, $fv1(nm)$, and $fv2(nm)$.

The array storage required to execute this path is N(MB+3) working precision words.

Indicative execution times for this path (run on an IBM 370/195) are .002, .011, .061, and .38 seconds for sample matrices of order and (half) band width (10,3), (20,6), (40,12), and (80,24) respectively. Extrapolation of these execution times for matrices of different (half) band widths is discussed in Section 4.5.

Variants of this path substitute the explicit or implicit for the rational QL shift; see Section 2.2.3 of [10].

Section 2.1.3

SOME EIGENVALUES AND CORRESPONDING EIGENVECTORS OF A REAL SYMMETRIC BAND MATRIX

A real symmetric band matrix of order N and (half) band width MB can
be presented to EISPACK as an MB-column array, with the lowest subdiagonal
stored in the last N+1-MB positions of the first column, the next higher
subdiagonal in the last N+2-MB positions of the second column, further
subdiagonals similarly, and finally the principal diagonal in the last
column. Contents of storage locations not part of the matrix are arbitrary.
For example, when N = 5 and MB = 3, the array (designated A) should contain

$$
\begin{bmatrix}
* & * & A(1,1) \\
* & A(2,1) & A(2,2) \\
A(3,1) & A(3,2) & A(3,3) \\
A(4,2) & A(4,3) & A(4,4) \\
A(5,3) & A(5,4) & A(5,5)
\end{bmatrix}
$$

where the subscripts for each element refer to the row and column of the
element in the standard two-dimensional representation, and '*' denotes an
arbitrary value.

To determine the eigenvalues W in an interval extending from RLB to
RUB, together with their corresponding eigenvectors Z, of a real symmetric
band matrix A of order N and (half) band width MB, the recommended EISPACK
path is:

```
    DO 100 J = 1, MB

      DO 50 I = 1, N

        fm1(I,J) = A(I,J)

 50    CONTINUE

100 CONTINUE

    CALL BANDR(NM,N,MB,A,fv1,fv2,fv3,.FALSE.,DUMMY)

    EPS1 = 0.0

    CALL BISECT(N,EPS1,fv1,fv2,fv3,RLB,RUB,MM,M,W,iv1,IERR,fv4,fv5)

    IF (IERR .NE. 0) GO TO 99999

    CALL BANDV(NM,N,MB,fm1,0.0,M,W,Z,IERR,NV,fv6,fv5)

    IF (IERR .NE. 0) GO TO 99999
```

or, using EISPAC:

```
    CALL EISPAC(NM,N,MATRIX('REAL',A,'SYMMETRIC'),
      BAND(MB),VALUES(W,MM,M,RLB,RUB),VECTOR(Z))
```

NV communicates the dimension of the scratch array $fv6$ and must be at least $N(2\overline{MB}-1)$.

The parameter EPS1 is used to control the accuracy of the eigenvalue computation. Setting it to zero or calling EISPAC without supplying it causes the use of a default value suitable for most matrices. Further information about the use of EPS1 can be found in Section 2.3.3 and in the BISECT and EISPAC documents. Upon completion of the path, M is set to the number of eigenvalues determined to lie in the interval defined by RLB and RUB and, provided $M \leq MM$, the eigenvalues are in ascending order in W and their corresponding orthonormal eigenvectors are in the first M columns of Z. Note that, should the computed M be greater than MM, BISECT sets IERR non-zero and does not compute any eigenvalues. This path destroys A except for its last two

18

columns which retain a copy of the tridiagonal matrix produced in the initial reduction.

Note that if the band matrix is already tridiagonal (MB = 2), EISPAC selects the more specialized tridiagonal path and may return slightly different eigenvalues and eigenvectors than the EISPACK path.

Suitable dimensions for the arrays are: A(nm,mb), W(mm), Z(nm,mm), $fm1$(nm,mb), $fv1$(nm), $fv2$(nm), $fv3$(nm), $fv4$(nm), $fv5$(nm), $fv6$(nv), and $iv1$(mm).

The array storage required to execute this path is 4N(MB+1) + M(N+1) working precision words and M integer words. (N working precision words could be saved by transmitting $fv6$ to BISECT in place of $fv4$.)

Indicative execution times for this path (run on an IBM 370/195), when computing all N eigenvalues and eigenvectors, are .025, .13, 1.1, and 11 seconds for sample matrices of order and (half) band width (10,3), (20,6), (40,12), and (80,24) respectively. Extrapolation of these execution times for cases where M is less than N or for matrices of different (half) band widths is discussed in Sections 4.1 and 4.5.

A variant of this path substitutes the band symmetric QR algorithm for the tridiagonalization and bisection steps of BANDR and BISECT; see Section 2.2.1. Other variants substitute the rational QR method for the bisection process or allow the specification of boundary eigenvalue indices instead of an interval to the bisection process; see Sections 2.2.4 and 2.2.8 of [10].

19

Section 2.1.4

SOME EIGENVALUES OF A REAL SYMMETRIC BAND MATRIX

A real symmetric band matrix of order N and (half) band width MB can be presented to EISPACK as an MB-column array, with the lowest subdiagonal stored in the last N+1-MB positions of the first column, the next higher subdiagonal in the last N+2-MB positions of the second column, further subdiagonals similarly, and finally the principal diagonal in the last column. Contents of storage locations not part of the matrix are arbitrary. For example, when N = 5 and MB = 3, the array (designated A) should contain

$$
\begin{bmatrix}
* & * & A(1,1) \\
* & A(2,1) & A(2,2) \\
A(3,1) & A(3,2) & A(3,3) \\
A(4,2) & A(4,3) & A(4,4) \\
A(5,3) & A(5,4) & A(5,5)
\end{bmatrix}
$$

where the subscripts for each element refer to the row and column of the element in the standard two-dimensional representation, and '*' denotes an arbitrary value.

To determine the eigenvalues W in an interval extending from RLB to RUB of a real symmetric band matrix A of order N and (half) band width MB, the recommended EISPACK path is:

    CALL BANDR(NM,N,MB,A,$fv1$,$fv2$,$fv3$,.FALSE.,DUMMY)

    EPS1 = 0.0

    CALL BISECT(N,EPS1,$fv1$,$fv2$,$fv3$,RLB,RUB,MM,M,W,$iv1$,IERR,$fv4$,$fv5$)

    IF (IERR .NE. 0) GO TO 99999

or, using EISPAC:

```
CALL EISPAC(NM,N,MATRIX('REAL',A,'SYMMETRIC'),
     BAND(MB),VALUES(W,MM,M,RLB,RUB))
```

The parameter EPS1 is used to control the accuracy of the eigenvalue computation. Setting it to zero or calling EISPAC without supplying it causes the use of a default value suitable for most matrices. Further information about the use of EPS1 can be found in Section 2.3.3 and in the BISECT and EISPAC documents. Upon completion of the path, M is set to the number of eigenvalues determined to lie in the interval defined by RLB and RUB and, provided M $\leq$ MM, the eigenvalues are in ascending order in W. Note that, should the computed M be greater than MM, BISECT sets IERR non-zero and does not compute any eigenvalues. This path destroys A except for its last two columns which retain a copy of the tridiagonal matrix produced in the initial reduction.

Suitable dimensions for the arrays are: $A(nm,mb)$, $W(mm)$, $fv1(nm)$, $fv2(nm)$, $fv3(nm)$, $fv4(nm)$, $fv5(nm)$, and $iv1(mm)$.

The array storage required to execute this path is N(MB+5) + M working precision words and M integer words.

Indicative execution times for this path (run on an IBM 370/195), when computing all N eigenvalues, are .017, .061, .25, and 1.0 seconds for sample matrices of order and (half) band width (10,3), (20,6), (40,12), and (80,24) respectively. Extrapolation of these execution times for cases where M is less than N or for matrices of different (half) band widths is discussed in Sections 4.1 and 4.5.

A variant of this path substitutes the band symmetric QR algorithm for the tridiagonalization and bisection steps of BANDR and BISECT; see Section 2.2.1. Other variants substitute the rational QR method for the bisection process or allow the specification of boundary eigenvalue indices instead of an interval to the bisection process; see Sections 2.2.4 and 2.2.8 of [10].

Section 2.1.5

ALL EIGENVALUES AND CORRESPONDING EIGENVECTORS OF A GENERALIZED REAL
SYMMETRIC MATRIX SYSTEM

The real generalized eigenproblem $Az = \lambda Bz$ is further characterized as
symmetric if both A and B are symmetric and B is positive definite (all
positive eigenvalues). To determine all the eigenvalues W and their corresponding eigenvectors Z for the real symmetric generalized eigenproblem
$Az = \lambda Bz$ of order N, the recommended EISPACK path is:

```
CALL REDUC(NM,N,A,B,fv2,IERR)
IF (IERR .NE. 0) GO TO 99999
CALL TRED2(NM,N,A,W,fv1,Z)
CALL TQL2(NM,N,W,fv1,Z,IERR)
IF (IERR .NE. 0) GO TO 99999
CALL REBAK(NM,N,B,fv2,N,Z)
```

or, using driver subroutine RSG:

```
CALL RSG(NM,N,A,B,W,1,Z,fv1,fv2,IERR)
IF (IERR .NE. 0) GO TO 99999
```

or, using EISPAC:

```
CALL EISPAC(NM,N,MATA('REAL',A,'SYMMETRIC'),MATB('REAL',B,'SYMMETRIC',
    'POSITIVE DEFINITE'),VALUES(W),VECTOR(Z))
```

This path returns the eigenvalues in ascending order and a set of eigenvectors normalized so that $Z^T BZ = I$; it preserves the full upper triangle of
B and the strict upper triangle of A.

Suitable dimensions for the arrays are: $A(nm,nm)$, $B(nm,nm)$, $W(nm)$,
$Z(nm,nm)$, $fv1(nm)$, and $fv2(nm)$.

22

The array storage required to execute this path is $3N^2 + 3N$ working precision words. However, for this particular path the eigenvectors can overwrite the A matrix if the same array parameter is used for both A and Z, thereby reducing the storage required to $2N^2 + 3N$ working precision words.

Indicative execution times for this path (run on an IBM 370/195) are .009, .049, .30, and 2.0 seconds for sample systems of order 10, 20, 40, and 80 respectively.

A variant of this path substitutes the implicit for the explicit QL shift; see Section 2.2.3 of [10]. Variants of the problem itself are discussed in Section 2.2.2 of this volume.

Section 2.1.6

ALL EIGENVALUES OF A GENERALIZED REAL SYMMETRIC MATRIX SYSTEM

The real generalized eigenproblem $Az = \lambda Bz$ is further characterized as symmetric if both A and B are symmetric and B is positive definite (all positive eigenvalues). To determine all the eigenvalues W for the real symmetric generalized eigenproblem $Az = \lambda Bz$ of order N, the recommended EISPACK path is:

```
CALL REDUC(NM,N,A,B,fv2,IERR)
IF (IERR .NE. 0) GO TO 99999
CALL TRED1(NM,N,A,W,fv1,fv2)
CALL TQLRAT(N,W,fv2,IERR)
IF (IERR .NE. 0) GO TO 99999
```

or, using driver subroutine RSG:

```
CALL RSG(NM,N,A,B,W,0,DUMMY,fv1,fv2,IERR)
IF (IERR .NE. 0) GO TO 99999
```

or, using EISPAC:

```
CALL EISPAC(NM,N,MATA('REAL',A,'SYMMETRIC'),MATB('REAL',B,'SYMMETRIC',
   'POSITIVE DEFINITE'),VALUES(W))
```

This path returns the eigenvalues in ascending order; it preserves the full upper triangle of B and the strict upper triangle of A.

Suitable dimensions for the arrays are: $A(nm,nm)$, $B(nm,nm)$, $W(nm)$, $fv1(nm)$, and $fv2(nm)$.

The array storage required to execute this path is $2N^2 + 3N$ working precision words.

Indicative execution times for this path (run on an IBM 370/195) are .004, .019, .11, and .64 seconds for sample systems of order 10, 20, 40, and 80 respectively.

Variants of this path substitute the explicit or implicit for the rational QL shift; see Section 2.2.3 of [10]. Variants of the problem itself are discussed in Section 2.2.2 of this volume.

Section 2.1.7

SOME EIGENVALUES AND CORRESPONDING EIGENVECTORS OF A GENERALIZED REAL
SYMMETRIC MATRIX SYSTEM

The real generalized eigenproblem $Az = \lambda Bz$ is further characterized as
symmetric if both A and B are symmetric and B is positive definite (all
positive eigenvalues). To determine the eigenvalues W in an interval extending from RLB to RUB, together with their corresponding eigenvectors Z,
for the real symmetric generalized eigenproblem $Az = \lambda Bz$ of order N, the
recommended EISPACK path is:

    CALL REDUC(NM,N,A,B,$fv9$,IERR)

    IF (IERR .NE. 0) GO TO 99999

    CALL TRED1(NM,N,A,$fv1$,$fv2$,$fv3$)

    EPS1 = 0.0

    CALL BISECT(N,EPS1,$fv1$,$fv2$,$fv3$,RLB,RUB,MM,M,W,$iv1$,IERR,$fv4$,$fv5$)

    IF (IERR .NE. 0) GO TO 99999

    CALL TINVIT(NM,N,$fv1$,$fv2$,$fv3$,M,W,$iv1$,Z,IERR,$fv4$,$fv5$,$fv6$,$fv7$,$fv8$)

    IF (IERR .NE. 0) GO TO 99999

    CALL TRBAK1(NM,N,A,$fv2$,M,Z)

    CALL REBAK(NM,N,B,$fv9$,M,Z)

or, using EISPAC:

    CALL EISPAC(NM,N,MATA('REAL',A,'SYMMETRIC'),MATB('REAL',B,'SYMMETRIC',
      'POSITIVE DEFINITE'),VALUES(W,MM,M,RLB,RUB),VECTOR(Z))

The parameter EPS1 is used to control the accuracy of the eigenvalue
computation. Setting it to zero or calling EISPAC without supplying it
causes the use of a default value suitable for most matrices. Further information about the use of EPS1 can be found in Section 2.3.3 and in the
BISECT and EISPAC documents. Upon completion of the path, M is set to the

number of eigenvalues determined to lie in the interval defined by RLB and RUB and, provided M $\leq$ MM, the eigenvalues are in ascending order in W and their corresponding eigenvectors, normalized so that $z^T Bz = 1.0$, are in the first M columns of Z. Note that, should the computed M be greater than MM, BISECT sets IERR non-zero and does not compute any eigenvalues. This path preserves the full upper triangle of B and the strict upper triangle of A.

Suitable dimensions for the arrays are: A(nm,nm), B(nm,nm), W(mm), Z(nm,mm), $fv1(nm)$, $fv2(nm)$, $fv3(nm)$, $fv4(nm)$, $fv5(nm)$, $fv6(nm)$, $fv7(nm)$, $fv8(nm)$, $fv9(nm)$, and $iv1(mm)$.

The array storage required to execute this path is $2N^2 + 9N + M(N+1)$ working precision words and M integer words.

Indicative execution times for this path (run on an IBM 370/195), when computing all N eigenvalues and eigenvectors, are .023, .088, .41, and 2.1 seconds for sample systems of order 10, 20, 40, and 80 respectively. Extrapolation of these execution times for cases where M is less than N is discussed in Section 4.1.

Variants of this path substitute the rational QR method or the implicit QL method for the bisection process, allow the specification of boundary eigenvalue indices instead of an interval to the bisection process, or combine the determination of the eigenvalues and eigenvectors of the tridiagonal form into a single subroutine; see Sections 2.2.4, 2.2.7, 2.2.8, and 2.2.5 of [10]. Variants of the problem itself are discussed in Section 2.2.2 of this volume.

Section 2.1.8

SOME EIGENVALUES OF A GENERALIZED REAL SYMMETRIC MATRIX SYSTEM

The real generalized eigenproblem $Az = \lambda Bz$ is further characterized as symmetric if both A and B are symmetric and B is positive definite (all positive eigenvalues). To determine the eigenvalues W in an interval extending from RLB to RUB for the real symmetric generalized eigenproblem $Az = \lambda Bz$ of order N, the recommended EISPACK path is:

CALL REDUC(NM,N,A,B,*fv2*,IERR)

IF (IERR .NE. 0) GO TO 99999

CALL TRED1(NM,N,A,*fv1*,*fv2*,*fv3*)

EPS1 = 0.0

CALL BISECT(N,EPS1,*fv1*,*fv2*,*fv3*,RLB,RUB,MM,M,W,*iv1*,IERR,*fv4*,*fv5*)

IF (IERR .NE. 0) GO TO 99999

or, using EISPAC:

CALL EISPAC(NM,N,MATA('REAL',A,'SYMMETRIC'),MATB('REAL',B,'SYMMETRIC',
'POSITIVE DEFINITE'),VALUES(W,MM,M,RLB,RUB))

The parameter EPS1 is used to control the accuracy of the eigenvalue computation. Setting it to zero or calling EISPAC without supplying it causes the use of a default value suitable for most matrices. Further information about the use of EPS1 can be found in Section 2.3.3 and in the BISECT and EISPAC documents. Upon completion of the path, M is set to the number of eigenvalues determined to lie in the interval defined by RLB and RUB and, provided $M \leq MM$, the eigenvalues are in ascending order in W. Note that, should the computed M be greater than MM, BISECT sets IERR non-zero and does not compute any eigenvalues. This path preserves the full upper triangle of B and the strict upper triangle of A.

Suitable dimensions for the arrays are: $A(nm,nm)$, $B(nm,nm)$, $W(mm)$, $fv1(nm)$, $fv2(nm)$, $fv3(nm)$, $fv4(nm)$, $fv5(nm)$, and $iv1(mm)$.

The array storage required to execute this path is $2N^2 + 5N + M$ working precision words and M integer words.

Indicative execution times for this path (run on an IBM 370/195), when computing all N eigenvalues, are .019, .069, .29, and 1.3 seconds for sample systems of order 10, 20, 40, and 80 respectively. Extrapolation of these execution times for cases where M is less than N is discussed in Section 4.1.

Variants of this path substitute the rational QR method for the bisection process or allow the specification of boundary eigenvalue indices instead of an interval to the bisection process; see Sections 2.2.4 and 2.2.8 of [10]. Variants of the problem itself are discussed in Section 2.2.2 of this volume.

Section 2.1.9

ALL EIGENVALUES AND CORRESPONDING EIGENVECTORS OF A GENERALIZED
REAL MATRIX SYSTEM

To determine all the eigenvalues (ALFR,ALFI,BETA) and their corresponding eigenvectors Z for the real generalized eigenproblem $Az = \lambda Bz$ of order
N, the recommended EISPACK path is:

    CALL QZHES(NM,N,A,B,.TRUE.,Z)

    CALL QZIT(NM,N,A,B,EPS1,.TRUE.,Z,IERR)

    CALL QZVAL(NM,N,A,B,ALFR,ALFI,BETA,.TRUE.,Z)

    IF (IERR .NE. 0) GO TO 99999

    CALL QZVEC(NM,N,A,B,ALFR,ALFI,BETA,Z)

or, using driver subroutine RGG:

    CALL RGG(NM,N,A,B,ALFR,ALFI,BETA,1,Z,IERR)

    IF (IERR .NE. 0) GO TO 99999

or, using EISPAC:

    CALL EISPAC(NM,N,MATA('REAL',A),MATB('REAL',B),
       VALUES(ALFR,ALFI,BETA),VECTOR(Z))

BETA is always non-negative. The triplet (ALFR,ALFI,BETA) returned by
the path can be transformed to the eigenvalue itself by two divisions,
ALFR/BETA to produce the real part and ALFI/BETA to produce the imaginary
part. The divisions are not performed within the programs because of the
possible loss of information content in those situations where B or both A
and B are nearly singular or even singular (see Section 2.3.1).

The parameter EPS1 is used to control the accuracy of the eigenvalue
computation. Setting it to zero or calling EISPAC without supplying it

causes the use of a default value suitable for most systems. Further information about the use of EPS1 can be found in Section 2.3.3 and in the QZIT and EISPAC documents.

Pairs of complex eigenvalues are stored in consecutive elements of (ALFR,ALFI,BETA) with that member of the pair with positive imaginary part first. The corresponding columns of Z contain the real and imaginary parts, respectively, of the eigenvector associated with the eigenvalue of positive imaginary part. See Section 2.3.2 for a discussion of the eigenvector packing into Z.

Each eigenvector of Z is normalized so that the modulus of its largest component is 1.0. This path destroys A and B.

Suitable dimensions for the arrays are: A(nm,nm), B(nm,nm), ALFR(nm), ALFI(nm), BETA(nm), and Z(nm,nm).

The array storage required to execute this path is $3N^2 + 3N$ working precision words.

Indicative execution times for this path (run on an IBM 370/195) are .026, .17, 1.0, and 7.0 seconds for sample systems of order 10, 20, 40, and 80 respectively.

Section 2.1.10

ALL EIGENVALUES OF A GENERALIZED REAL MATRIX SYSTEM

To determine all the eigenvalues (ALFR,ALFI,BETA) for the real generalized eigenproblem $Az = \lambda Bz$ of order N, the recommended EISPACK path is:

```
CALL QZHES(NM,N,A,B,.FALSE.,DUMMY)
CALL QZIT(NM,N,A,B,EPS1,.FALSE.,DUMMY,IERR)
CALL QZVAL(NM,N,A,B,ALFR,ALFI,BETA,.FALSE.,DUMMY)
IF (IERR .NE. 0) GO TO 99999
```

or, using driver subroutine RGG:

```
CALL RGG(NM,N,A,B,ALFR,ALFI,BETA,0,DUMMY,IERR)
IF (IERR .NE. 0) GO TO 99999
```

or, using EISPAC:

```
CALL EISPAC(NM,N,MATA('REAL',A),MATB('REAL',B),VALUES(ALFR,ALFI,BETA))
```

BETA is always non-negative. The triplet (ALFR,ALFI,BETA) returned by the path can be transformed to the eigenvalue itself by two divisions, ALFR/BETA to produce the real part and ALFI/BETA to produce the imaginary part. The divisions are not performed within the programs because of the possible loss of information content in those situations where B or both A and B are nearly singular or even singular (see Section 2.3.1).

The parameter EPS1 is used to control the accuracy of the eigenvalue computation. Setting it to zero or calling EISPAC without supplying it causes the use of a default value suitable for most systems. Further information about the use of EPS1 can be found in Section 2.3.3 and in the QZIT and EISPAC documents.

Pairs of complex eigenvalues are stored in consecutive elements of (ALFR, ALFI,BETA) with that member of the pair with positive imaginary part first. This path destroys A and B.

Suitable dimensions for the arrays are: A(nm,nm), B(nm,nm), ALFR(nm), ALFI(nm), and BETA(nm).

The array storage required to execute this path is $2N^2 + 3N$ working precision words.

Indicative execution times for this path (run on an IBM 370/195) are .020, .11, .63, and 4.2 seconds for sample systems of order 10, 20, 40, and 80 respectively.

Section 2.2

VARIATIONS OF THE RECOMMENDED EISPACK PATHS

This section describes variants of the recommended paths given in Section 2.1. These variants are obtained by modifying one or more of the call or ancillary statements in the recommended paths; they provide some additional or alternate capability. The variant paths are related to: the use of the QR algorithm for finding a few eigenvalues of real symmetric band matrices; and the capacity for solving alternate representations of the real symmetric generalized eigenproblem. The variant paths are described in terms of modifications to the recommended paths; to illustrate the modifications, examples of each of the variant paths are given.

Section 2.2.1

THE QR ALGORITHM FOR REAL SYMMETRIC BAND MATRICES

The recommended paths of Sections 2.1.1-2.1.4 for real symmetric band
matrices all employ subroutine BANDR to first reduce the matrix to tridiagonal
form, followed by an iterative step to determine the eigenvalues. When the
problem requires only the determination of the eigenvalue nearest to a prescribed number and possibly a few neighbors, it may be advantageous to use
subroutine BQR which applies the QR algorithm directly to the input matrix,
thus telescoping the otherwise separate reduction and iterative steps.

Subroutine BQR determines exactly one eigenvalue when called, but in so
doing deflates the problem such that a further call can easily be made to
determine another value. In fact, the only action that the user needs to
take after storing the returned eigenvalue is to decrement the parameter
specifying the order of the matrix and call BQR again.

BQR will usually find the eigenvalue of smallest modulus of the input
matrix. If, more generally, the eigenvalue nearest to a prescribed number
T is desired, BQR can be presented an input matrix derived from the original
matrix by shifting (diminishing) the diagonal elements by T; when T is added
back to the eigenvalue of smallest modulus of the shifted matrix, one obtains
the eigenvalue of the original matrix nearest to T. In the execution of BQR,
further shifting is done, with accumulation of the shift into T, until the
resultant matrix has a zero eigenvalue -- indeed has a zero final row and
column, thus simultaneously isolating an eigenvalue and deflating to next
lower order.

As an example of the use of BQR, to find the two eigenvalues W(1) and
W(2) nearest to 4.0 of a real symmetric band matrix A of order N and (half)
band width MB, the following program segment might be used:

```
      T = 4.0
      DO 100 I = 1, N
100 A(I,I) = A(I,I) - T
      R = 0.0
      CALL BQR(NM,N,MB,A,T,R,IERR,NV,fv1)
      W(1) = T
      CALL BQR(NM,N-1,MB,A,T,R,IERR,NV,fv1)
      W(2) = T
```

R is used to decide when the last row and column of the current transformed band matrix can be regarded as negligible. It should be set to zero
for the initial call and is reset in BQR to a value suitable for the subsequent call.

NV communicates the dimension of the temporary array $fv1$ which must be
at least $2\overline{MB}^2 + 4\overline{MB} - 3$.

Suitable dimensions for the arrays are A(nm,mb) and $fv1(2\overline{mb}^2+4\overline{mb}-3)$.

The array storage required to execute this path is MB(N+2$\overline{MB}$+4) - 3 working precision words.

Indicative execution times for this subroutine (run on an IBM 370/195),
when computing the single eigenvalue of a random matrix nearest to T = 0.0
are .011, .055, .30, and 2.0 seconds for sample matrices of order and (half)
band width (10,3), (20,6), (40,12), and (80,24) respectively. Extrapolation
of these execution times for matrices of different (half) band widths is discussed in Section 4.5.

If eigenvectors corresponding to the computed eigenvalues are desired,
subroutine BANDV can be called exactly as in the recommended path of
Section 2.1.3. Here also the input matrix would have to be saved initially,
since BQR destroys it.

The control program EISPAC does not use BQR.

Section 2.2.2

VARIANTS OF THE REAL SYMMETRIC GENERALIZED EIGENPROBLEM

The real symmetric generalized eigenproblem $Az = \lambda Bz$, for which the recommended basic paths of Sections 2.1.5-2.1.8 apply, has two variants that can be solved with EISPACK; namely, the problems $ABz = \lambda z$ and $BAz = \lambda z$. Indeed, only two additional EISPACK members are invoked as can be seen from the following discussion.

Since B is symmetric and positive definite, its Cholesky factorization $B = LL^T$ exists, enabling the problem $Az = \lambda Bz$ to be rewritten $Az = \lambda LL^T z$ and then transformed to an equivalent standard symmetric problem $A_1 y = \lambda y$ with $A_1 = L^{-1} A L^{-T}$ and $y = L^T z$. Thus, given the capacity to solve the standard problem, the generalized problem can be solved with two additional subroutines, one to determine and compose $L^{-1} A L^{-T}$ and the other to solve $L^T z = y$ for z. In EISPACK these subroutines are REDUC and REBAK, respectively, employed in the paths of Sections 2.1.5-2.1.8.

If the problem arises instead in the form $ABz = \lambda z$, then again proceeding from the Cholesky factorization of B, it can be transformed to the standard problem $A_2 y = \lambda y$ with $A_2 = L^T A L$ and y, although different, related to z by $y = L^T z$ as before. The additional EISPACK subroutine REDUC2 forms $L^T A L$ and thus, with REBAK, enables the solution of this variant problem.

Finally, the problem $BAz = \lambda z$ can be transformed to the standard problem $A_2 x = \lambda x$ with $A_2 = L^T A L$ as for the variant $ABz = \lambda z$, and $x = L^{-1} z$. The one further EISPACK subroutine REBAKB forms $z = Lx$ and thus, with REDUC2, enables the solution of this variant problem.

Corresponding to each of the paths of Sections 2.1.5-2.1.8, there are explicit subroutine, driver subroutine (RSGAB and RSGBA), and control program calls for these variant problems. For example, to determine all the eigenvalues

W and their corresponding eigenvectors Z for the real symmetric generalized eigenproblem $ABz = \lambda z$ of order N, the recommended EISPACK path is (cf. Section 2.1.5):

```
CALL REDUC2(NM,N,A,B,fv2,IERR)
IF (IERR .NE. 0) GO TO 99999
CALL TRED2(NM,N,A,W,fv1,Z)
CALL TQL2(NM,N,W,fv1,Z,IERR)
IF (IERR .NE. 0) GO TO 99999
CALL REBAK(NM,N,B,fv2,N,Z)
```

or, using driver subroutine RSGAB:

```
CALL RSGAB(NM,N,A,B,W,1,Z,fv1,fv2,IERR)
IF (IERR .NE. 0) GO TO 99999
```

or, using EISPAC:

```
CALL EISPAC(NM,N,MATA('REAL',A,'SYMMETRIC'),MATB('REAL',B,'SYMMETRIC',
    'POSITIVE DEFINITE','ABX=LX'),VALUES(W),VECTOR(Z))
```

The eigenvectors here, as in the path of Section 2.1.5, are normalized so that $Z^T BZ = I$.

As a second example, to determine the eigenvalues W in an interval extending from RLB to RUB, together with their corresponding eigenvectors Z, for the real symmetric generalized eigenproblem $BAz = \lambda z$ of order N, the recommended EISPACK path is (cf. Section 2.1.7):

```
CALL REDUC2(NM,N,A,B,fv9,IERR)

IF (IERR .NE. 0) GO TO 99999

CALL TRED1(NM,N,A,fv1,fv2,fv3)

EPS1 = 0.0

CALL BISECT(N,EPS1,fv1,fv2,fv3,RLB,RUB,MM,M,W,iv1,IERR,fv4,fv5)

IF (IERR .NE. 0) GO TO 99999

CALL TINVIT(NM,N,fv1,fv2,fv3,M,W,iv1,Z,IERR,fv4,fv5,fv6,fv7,fv8)

IF (IERR .NE. 0) GO TO 99999

CALL TRBAK1(NM,N,A,fv2,M,Z)

CALL REBAKB(NM,N,B,fv9,M,Z)
```

or, using EISPAC:

```
CALL EISPAC(NM,N,MATA('REAL',A,'SYMMETRIC'),MATB('REAL',B,'SYMMETRIC',
   'POSITIVE DEFINITE','BAX=LX'),VALUES(W,MM,M,RLB,RUB),VECTOR(Z))
```

The eigenvectors here are normalized so that $z^T B^{-1} z = 1.0$.

The paths for the variant problems share the characteristics of the corresponding paths of Sections 2.1.5-2.1.8 with respect to extent of input array preservation, suitable array dimensions, and required array storage. The indicative execution times of Sections 2.1.5-2.1.8 extend to the paths for the variant problems as well; more precise timing information is provided in Section 4.

39

Section 2.3

ADDITIONAL INFORMATION AND EXAMPLES

This section contains additional information about and examples of the use of EISPACK and the control program which are either too detailed to be included in the discussion of a particular path, or which apply to more than one path. The specific topics covered include the representation of the eigenvalues of generalized real matrix systems; the packing of the eigenvectors of generalized real matrix systems; considerations regarding the user-supplied error tolerance in the computation of the eigenvalues; possible ill-condition of the generalized real symmetric eigenproblem paths; higher degree eigenvalue problems; the solution of band systems of linear equations; the examination of the IERR parameter and intermediate results when using the control program EISPAC; and a summary of the possible values of IERR and their meanings. The section concludes with two complete example driver programs illustrating the use of EISPACK and the control program EISPAC.

Section 2.3.1

THE REPRESENTATION OF THE EIGENVALUES OF A GENERALIZED REAL MATRIX SYSTEM

The EISPACK routines which compute the eigenvalues for the generalized real matrix problem $Az = \lambda Bz$ do not return the λ's directly; possible singularity or near singularity of A and B dictate a different representation of the eigenvalues that maximizes their informational content.

No special problems are posed when A is singular with B non-singular; the eigenvalues are all finite with some of them zero. But when B is singular with A non-singular, some of the eigenvalues must be thought of as infinite. And finally, when both A and B are singular there may again be infinite eigenvalues, and in some extreme situations, for example when A and B have a common null space (non-zero vectors z for which $Az = 0$ and $Bz = 0$), the matrix $A - \lambda B$ will be singular for any choice of λ.

In practice with inexact data and imprecise arithmetic, it is desirable to avoid making decisions about exact singularity. Consequently the problem is reformulated to find pairs of scalars α and β for which

$$\beta Az = \alpha Bz .$$

The algorithm used in EISPACK determines two unitary matrices Q and Z such that QAZ and QBZ are both upper triangular. Then the desired α_j and β_j are simply the diagonal elements of the two triangular matrices, and it is these quantities which are returned by the subroutine.

Because the algorithm uses only unitary transformations, there is more information in the individual α_j and β_j than there is in the ratios $\lambda_j = \alpha_j/\beta_j$. The errors in α_j and β_j are all about the same absolute size, namely the size of the errors in the input data (or of roundoff errors in the computation). Consequently, if an α_j or β_j is obtained which is about the same size as the original matrix elements, it can be regarded as accurately determined by the data and the computation. If, however, it is smaller than the input data, it must be regarded as having a correspondingly higher relative error.

For example, suppose the general size of the elements in A and B is about 1.0. If $\alpha_j = 1.0$ and $\beta_j = 2.0$, then $\lambda_j \simeq 0.5$ to about the accuracy of the data; if instead $\alpha_j = 1.0 \cdot 10^{-6}$ and $\beta_j = 2.0 \cdot 10^{-6}$, then again $\lambda_j \simeq 0.5$ but this time to six fewer figures of accuracy. In the extreme case where α_j and β_j are both about the size of the errors in the data or of roundoff errors in the computation, then any value of λ makes $A - \lambda B$ singular to working accuracy. If β_j is very small but α_j is not, then λ_j should be regarded as infinite.

These statements about accuracy are further complicated in the presence of multiple eigenvalues. If λ_j is a zero of $\det(A-\lambda B)$ of multiplicity m or if it is an element of a cluster of m nearly equal zeros, and if ε is the relative accuracy of the data, then α_j and β_j may have relative errors on the order of $\varepsilon^{1/m}$. For example, if λ_j is a double eigenvalue, then perturbations on the order of 10^{-6} in the data may cause perturbations on the order of 10^{-3} in the corresponding α_j and β_j.

Section 2.3.2

UNPACKING THE EIGENVECTORS OF A GENERALIZED REAL MATRIX SYSTEM

Since for a generalized real matrix system the complex eigenvalues and their corresponding eigenvectors occur as conjugate pairs and therefore both members of such a pair are determined once the real and imaginary parts of one member are known, only N^2 real numbers are required to recover all the eigenvectors of such a system. The EISPACK routines which compute the eigenvectors of generalized real matrix systems take advantage of this fact (and so save storage) by packing both real and complex eigenvectors into one N by N matrix.

In order to determine whether a given column of the matrix of eigenvectors represents a real eigenvector, the real part of a complex eigenvector, or the imaginary part of a complex eigenvector, the imaginary part of the corresponding eigenvalue must be examined. Perhaps the clearest way to describe how this packing is done is to present a program segment which unpacks the matrix of eigenvectors into two separate matrices representing the real and imaginary parts of the eigenvectors.

First, suppose that you have computed all the eigenvalues and eigenvectors of a generalized real matrix system according to Section 2.1.9. The following program segment unpacks the matrix Z of eigenvectors into matrices ZR and ZI, dimensioned ZR(nm,nm) and ZI(nm,nm). Note that this program segment utilizes the property of the EISPACK programs that for generalized real matrix systems the eigenvalues of each complex conjugate pair are ordered so that the eigenvalue of positive imaginary part appears first in (ALFR,ALFI,BETA).

```
      DO 150 K = 1, N

         IF (ALFI(K) .NE. 0.0) GO TO 110

         DO 100 J = 1, N

            ZR(J,K) = Z(J,K)

            ZI(J,K) = 0.0

100      CONTINUE

         GO TO 150

110      IF (ALFI(K) .LT. 0.0) GO TO 130

         DO 120 J = 1, N

            ZR(J,K) = Z(J,K)

            ZI(J,K) = Z(J,K+1)

120      CONTINUE

         GO TO 150

130      DO 140 J = 1, N

            ZR(J,K) = ZR(J,K-1)

            ZI(J,K) = -ZI(J,K-1)

140      CONTINUE

150 CONTINUE
```

Note that this program segment has been designed so that Z and ZR can be the same matrix; if they are, then the fourth and tenth statements can be omitted.

Section 2.3.3

THE EPS1 PARAMETER

As discussed in Section 1, the various versions of the subroutines in EISPACK are designed to provide the best accuracy possible given the working precisions of the particular machines for which they are available. For most of the subroutines, accuracy is controlled by an internal variable, MACHEP ("machine epsilon"), whose value reflects the precision of the machine arithmetic and should not be altered. However, user control of accuracy is possible with subroutines BISECT and QZIT. This accuracy control is provided by the parameter EPS1, which principally affects the precision of the eigenvalues, and thus the eigenvectors as well, but which also has some effect on computation time. Some of the considerations helpful in choosing EPS1 are discussed briefly below; further information can be found in the respective documents for the subroutines and in the Handbook ([1], pp. 249-256).

In subroutine BISECT, the computation of an eigenvalue is considered to have converged when the refined interval [XU,XO] known to contain the eigenvalue satisfies the condition:

$$XO - XU \leq 2 \times MACHEP \times (|XO| + |XU|) + EPS1$$

This condition has the character of a relative accuracy test for eigenvalues whose magnitudes are large with respect to EPS1/MACHEP, and that of an absolute accuracy test for eigenvalues of small magnitude. EPS1 is thus an *absolute* error tolerance.

When the input value of EPS1 is zero (or negative) as in the recommended paths, BISECT automatically resets it to an appropriate default value for each submatrix; this default value is MACHEP times the larger (in magnitude)

Gerschgorin bound for the eigenvalues of that submatrix. This value prevents the above termination criterion from requiring "unreasonably" high accuracy in the eigenvalues which are near zero. (In the implementation of BISECT, EPS1 is actually set negative when the default value is requested. This serves as a flag to cause the recomputation of the default value for each submatrix; the returned value of EPS1 is this negative default value for the final submatrix.)

A positive input value for EPS1 will not be reset in BISECT. When the positive input value of EPS1 exceeds the default value, the convergence test is less stringent for eigenvalues of smaller magnitude, and computation time tends to be reduced. If EPS1 is smaller than its default value, the convergence test becomes more stringent and computation time tends to increase. Care should be taken, however, not to specify a smaller value for EPS1 unless the small eigenvalues are known to be insensitive to perturbations in the input matrix; otherwise the additional precision will be meaningless. Although computation time tends to increase with decreasing EPS1, the exact relationship is highly dependent on the particular matrix.

When eigenvectors are computed by the method of inverse iteration, the success of the computation depends critically on the accuracy of the computed eigenvalues. Thus, when TINVIT follows BISECT, use of an EPS1 larger than the default value may result in failure of the eigenvector calculation to converge.

In subroutine QZIT, an element of either A or B is considered negligible if it is smaller than the product of EPS1 and the respective matrix norm. In particular, an eigenvalue has converged when the lowest subdiagonal element of A becomes negligible. As with BISECT, a zero or negative value of EPS1 requests the default; in QZIT, however, EPS1 itself is not reset.

To use a value of EPS1 other than the default, the statement

EPS1 = 0.0

in the paths should be replaced by a statement setting EPS1 to the desired value. When using the control program EISPAC, EPS1 can be supplied for the recommended paths only by adding EPS1 as the last subparameter to the VALUES parameter. Thus the VALUES parameter becomes:

...VALUES(W,MM,M,RLB,RUB,EPS1),... or ...VALUES(ALFR,ALFI,BETA,EPS1),...

as appropriate. With EISPAC, the input value of EPS1 is not altered, even though the default value may be used in the computation.

Section 2.3.4

POSSIBLE ILL-CONDITION OF THE GENERALIZED REAL SYMMETRIC EIGENPROBLEM PATHS

The solution of the generalized real symmetric eigenproblem $Az = \lambda Bz$ by the paths of Sections 2.1.5-2.1.8 demands that the matrix B be positive definite and proceeds from the Cholesky factorization $B = LL^T$. The problem is then reduced to the standard symmetric problem $A_1 y = \lambda y$, where $A_1 = L^{-1} A L^{-T}$ and $y = L^T z$. The computed eigenvalues are obtained with an accuracy which is measured relative to the size of the elements of A_1. Consequently if L^{-1} and hence A_1 have large elements, the small eigenvalues may have high relative errors. This occurs when B is close to an indefinite matrix and is indicated by the presence of eigenvalues λ which are much larger than the elements of A and B.

The alternative approach in this situation is to ignore the symmetry and simply use the paths of Sections 2.1.9-2.1.10 for the generalized real eigenproblem. In addition to increased costs, this approach produces eigenvectors which are normalized in a different way and may produce eigenvalues with non-zero imaginary parts. However, the small eigenvalues will usually be more accurate than those produced in the symmetric paths. Furthermore, the size of the α_j and β_j give some indication of the accuracy obtained.

It is difficult to give precise guidelines for the choice among these two approaches. The symmetric path is certainly preferable if B is well conditioned with respect to inversion and hence there are no large eigenvalues. If B is badly conditioned, or its properties are unknown, then the real path is safer since it always produces accurate eigenvalues. It requires little additional programming, but the increase in execution time and the fact that it may produce eigenvalues with non-zero imaginary parts means that it should probably be used only for small problems or as a check on the accuracy of the symmetric path.

Section 2.3.5

HIGHER DEGREE EIGENVALUE PROBLEMS

EISPACK can be used to solve problems of the form

$$(\lambda^r C_0 + \lambda^{r-1} C_1 + \ldots + \lambda C_{r-1} + C_r)x = 0$$

where $C_0, \ldots, C_r$ are given real matrices of order m. It is desired to find the scalars λ_j which make the matrix in parentheses singular and possibly to find the corresponding null vectors x_j. In general, the approach to this problem involves forming two matrices A and B of order n = m·r, illustrated for the case r = 3, by

$$A = \begin{pmatrix} -C_1 & -C_2 & -C_3 \\ I & 0 & 0 \\ 0 & I & 0 \end{pmatrix}$$

$$B = \begin{pmatrix} C_0 & 0 & 0 \\ 0 & I & 0 \\ 0 & 0 & I \end{pmatrix} .$$

The original problem is then equivalent to the generalized real eigenproblem

$$Az = \lambda Bz$$

where

$$z = \begin{pmatrix} \lambda^2 x \\ \lambda x \\ x \end{pmatrix} .$$

This can be solved using the paths of Sections 2.1.9–2.1.10. In general, there will be n values of λ, counting multiplicities. However, if C_0 is singular, some of these values will be infinite (see Section 2.3.1).

In particular, if C_0 is the identity matrix, then the problem is equivalent to the standard problem

$$Az = \lambda z$$

which can be solved using the EISPACK subroutines and paths described in Sections 2.1.8-2.1.10 of [10].

Section 2.3.6

THE USE OF BANDV IN SOLVING BAND SYSTEMS OF LINEAR EQUATIONS

Subroutine BANDV has appeared earlier in the recommended path of
Section 2.1.3 that determines some eigenvalues and corresponding eigenvectors
of a real symmetric band matrix. BANDV can also be used to solve systems of
linear equations in band form -- in this usage the coefficient matrix may be
either symmetric or non-symmetric. (The symmetry requirement towards the use
of BANDV for determining eigenvectors is not fundamental; no allowance for
non-symmetric band matrices is made simply because no capability exists in
EISPACK for determining the corresponding eigenvalues.)

The extendibility of BANDV to systems of linear equations derives from
an awareness that the determination of an eigenvector associated with a specified eigenvalue itself depends on the solution of a linear system, in this
case a homogeneous system. That is, BANDV solves the linear system $(A-\lambda I)x = b$,
where λ is an approximate eigenvalue and b the zero vector in the determination
of an eigenvector, and where λ is a parameter (commonly zero) and b a prescribed constant vector in the solution of a system of linear equations.

To signal the usage of BANDV to solve band systems of linear equations,
set parameter E21 to 1.0 if the matrix is symmetric and to -1.0 if not (for
eigenvectors, E21 is set to 0.0 or 2.0), and transmit the band coefficient
matrix, the constant matrix, and parameters λ as described in the documentation for BANDV in Section 7.1. The solution matrix overwrites the constant
matrix; the input band matrix is unaltered. The error parameter, if set,
indicates that near singularity of the input matrix has been detected.
Execution time for BANDV in solving systems of linear equations should closely
approximate the time for its use in eigenvector determination, reported in
Section 4.

Section 2.3.7

ADDITIONAL FACILITIES OF THE EISPAC CONTROL PROGRAM

The EISPAC control program has two facilities which increase its flexi-
bility and range of application. The first provides the opportunity to
examine the IERR parameter values returned by the EISPACK subroutines; the
second provides the opportunity to examine intermediate results as the
computation proceeds, much as can be done when the EISPACK subroutines are
called explicitly.

The facility to examine the value of IERR is invoked by setting an
integer variable, say IERROR, to zero and supplying it as the subparameter
of the keyword parameter ERROR in the call to EISPAC. For example, the path
of Section 2.1.10 becomes

```
IERROR = 0

CALL EISPAC(NM,N,MATA('REAL',A),MATB('REAL',B),
   VALUES(ALFR,ALFI,BETA),ERROR(IERROR))
```

To understand the effect of supplying the ERROR keyword, consider the behavior
of EISPAC when it is not supplied. When one of the subroutines returns a
non-zero value of IERR, EISPAC prints a message describing the error and
terminates execution of your program. When ERROR(IERROR) is supplied,
EISPAC behaves instead as follows: If no execution errors occur, EISPAC
returns to your program after execution of the path, and IERROR is still
equal to zero. If one of the routines returns a positive value of IERR
(a "fatal error), EISPAC terminates the path, prints the error message
(unless suppressed by initializing IERROR to a machine dependent value as
described in Section 7.2), and then returns to your program with IERROR
equal to IERR. Finally, if one of the routines returns a negative value
of IERR (a "non-fatal" error), EISPAC completes execution of the path in

order to produce some useful results, prints the error message, and returns
to your program with IERROR equal to IERR. Thus the principal use of the
IERR examination facility is to enable you to retrieve useful partial
results when a non-fatal error occurs; which results are useful is described in the discussion of the particular path in Section 2.1 or 2.2 and
is summarized in Table 3 of Section 2.3.8.

The EISPAC facility to examine intermediate results is provided by a
mode of operation in which EISPAC calls a user-supplied subroutine just
before execution of the path begins, and again after execution of each subroutine and auxiliary action in it. You are free to choose the name of the
subroutine, say USUB, but the parameter list and declaration statements must
correspond to:

```
      SUBROUTINE USUB(ISUBNO,NM,N,AR,AI,WR,WI,ZR,ZI,MM,M,RLB,RUB,EPS1,
     X    SELECT,IDEF,TYPE,IERR,LOW,IGH,BND,D,E,E2,IND,INT,ORTR,SCALE,
     X    TAU,ORTI,M11,NV,MB,BR,DL,ALFR,ALFI,BETA)
      REAL*8 AR(NM,NM),AI(NM,NM),WR(NM),WI(NM),ZR(NM,NM),ZI(NM,NM),
     X    RLB,RUB,EPS1,BND(N),D(N),E(N),E2(N),ORTR(N),SCALE(N),
     X    TAU(2,N),ORTI(N),BR(NM,NM),DL(N),ALFR(NM),ALFI(NM),BETA(NM)
      INTEGER ISUBNO,NM,N,MM,M,IDEF,IERR,LOW,IGH,IND(N),INT(N),M11,NV,MB
      LOGICAL SELECT(NM),TYPE
```

In order to avoid Fortran errors it is important that the array parameters be
dimensioned as indicated (except that MM may be used for the last dimension
of WR and of ZR and ZI, where appropriate), even though some arrays might
not appear relevant to a particular path.

You inform EISPAC that you wish to use the intermediate result examination facility by inserting the keyword parameter SUBR with subparameter USUB

in the EISPAC call. Note that the statement EXTERNAL USUB must also appear
in your calling program.

When USUB is called by EISPAC, the value of the integer parameter
ISUBNO is set to indicate which EISPACK subroutine call or auxiliary action
has just been completed. It is zero when USUB is called just before execution of the path begins. ISUBNO values in the range 100-299 signify that
the preceding action allocated or freed temporary storage, those in the
range 300-499 indicate auxiliary actions (initializing or copying arrays,
for example), and those beyond 500 correspond to calls to the EISPACK subroutines as indicated in Table 2. Thus the value of ISUBNO indicates where
in the execution of a path USUB has been called, and can be used to determine what action USUB is to take in examining the intermediate results.
Table 2 also indicates which of the parameters passed to USUB appeared in
the just-completed call to the EISPACK subroutine.

As an example of the use of this facility, suppose you wish to inter-
rupt the path of Section 2.1.2 and use a subroutine TRDIAG to print the
tridiagonal matrix produced from the first step in the determination of the
eigenvalues of a real symmetric band matrix. Your driver program must contain the statements

```
EXTERNAL TRDIAG
   :
   :
CALL EISPAC(NM,N,MATRIX('REAL',A,'SYMMETRIC'),BAND(MB),VALUES(W),SUBR(TRDIAG)
```

To determine how to write TRDIAG, consult the definition of the path in
Section 2.1.2 in conjunction with Table 2. The tridiagonal matrix is returned
from BANDR and is overwritten in the subsequent execution of TQLRAT, so the
interruption must be made immediately after the call to BANDR. Table 2 indicates that this call in this path has an associated ISUBNO of 545, and

inspection of the parameters in the BANDR call (see BANDR documentation in Section 7) shows that the diagonal elements are in WR and the subdiagonal elements are in E. Hence the subroutine might be written as follows:

```
      SUBROUTINE TRDIAG(ISUBNO,NM,N,AR,AI,WR,WI,ZR,ZI,MM,M,RLB,RUB,EPS1,
     X    SELECT,IDEF,TYPE,IERR,LOW,IGH,BND,D,E,E2,IND,INT,ORTR,SCALE,
     X    TAU,ORTI,M11,NV,MB,BR,DL,ALFR,ALFI,BETA)
      REAL*8 AR(NM,NM),AI(NM,NM),WR(NM),WI(NM),ZR(NM,NM),ZI(NM,NM),
     X    RLB,RUB,EPS1,BND(N),D(N),E(N),E2(N),ORTR(N),SCALE(N),
     X    TAU(2,N),ORTI(N),BR(NM,NM),DL(N),ALFR(NM),ALFI(NM),BETA(NM)
      INTEGER ISUBNO,NM,N,MM,M,IDEF,IERR,LOW,IGH,IND(N),INT(N),M11,NV,MB
      LOGICAL SELECT(NM),TYPE
      IF (ISUBNO .NE. 545) RETURN
      WRITE(6,1000) (WR(I),E(I),I=1,N)
 1000 FORMAT(19H1TRIDIAGONAL MATRIX//(1X,1P2D16.8))
      RETURN
      END
```

TRDIAG immediately returns after every call from EISPAC except when ISUBNO is 545 (after BANDR); then it writes out the diagonal and subdiagonal elements of the reduced tridiagonal matrix from BANDR.

TABLE 2

ISUBNO VALUES AND PARAMETER NAMES FOR
SUBROUTINE CALLS FROM EISPAC

ISUBNO Value	Subroutine Call*
544	BANDR (NM,N,MB,AR,WR,E,E,.TRUE.,ZR) in path for all values and vectors (2.1.1)
545	BANDR (NM,N,MB,AR,WR,E,E2,.FALSE.,-) in path for all values, no vectors (2.1.2)
546	BANDR (NM,N,MB,AR,D,E,E2,.FALSE.,-) in paths for some values (2.1.3, 2.1.4)
547	BANDV (NM,N,MB,-,E2(1),M,WR,ZR,IERR,NV,-,-)
526	BISECT (N,EPS1,D,E,E2,RLB,RUB,MM,M,WR,IND,IERR,-,BND)
(not used)	BQR
(not used)	MINFIT
568	QZHES (NM,N,AR,BR,.TRUE.,ZR) in path for all values and vectors (2.1.9)
572	QZHES (NM,N,AR,BR,.FALSE.,-) in path for all values, no vectors (2.1.10)
569	QZIT (NM,N,AR,BR,EPS1,.TRUE.,ZR,IERR) in path for all values and vectors (2.1.9)
573	QZIT (NM,N,AR,BR,EPS1,.FALSE.,-,IERR) in path for all values, no vectors (2.1.10)
570	QZVAL (NM,N,AR,BR,ALFR,ALFI,BETA,.TRUE.,ZR) in path for all values and vectors (2.1.9)
574	QZVAL (NM,N,AR,BR,ALFR,ALFI,BETA,.FALSE.,-) in path for all values, no vectors (2.1.10)
571	QZVEC (NM,N,AR,BR,ALFR,ALFI,BETA,ZR)
551	REBAK (NM,N,BR,DL,M,ZR)
550	REBAKB (NM,N,BR,DL,M,ZR)
548	REDUC (NM,N,AR,BR,DL,IERR)

TABLE 2 (Contd.)

ISUBNO VALUES AND PARAMETER NAMES FOR
SUBROUTINE CALLS FROM EISPAC

ISUBNO Value	Subroutine Call*
549	REDUC2 (NM,N,AR,BR,DL,IERR)
(not used)	SVD
528	TINVIT (NM,N,D,E,E2,M,WR,IND,ZR,IERR,-,-,-,-,BND)
543	TQLRAT (N,WR,E2,IERR)
542	TQL2 (NM,N,WR,E,ZR,IERR)
536	TRBAK1 (NM,N,AR,E,M,ZR)
534	TRED1 (NM,N,AR,WR,E,E2) in path for all values, no vectors (2.1.6)
535	TRED1 (NM,N,AR,D,E,E2) in paths for some values (2.1.7, 2.1.8)
533	TRED2 (NM,N,AR,WR,E,ZR)

---

*
A dash at some position in a parameter list indicates a temporary
storage array which is not passed to the user subroutine by EISPAC.

Section 2.3.8

NON-ZERO VALUES OF IERR

This section summarizes the non-zero values of the error parameter
IERR that can be returned by the EISPACK subroutines, either directly or
via the control program (see Section 2.3.7), when an execution error is
detected. Such execution errors are classified into two categories: first,
path-terminating errors, indicated by positive values of IERR and signifying
that although some possibly useful results have been obtained, continued
execution of the path is meaningless; second, non-terminating errors, indicated by negative values of IERR and signifying that although errors have
already occurred, some further meaningful results may be obtained if the
remaining part of the path is executed. Each distinct error that can occur
in EISPACK corresponds to one of a unique set of values for IERR, that one
being a function of the order of the matrix.

The non-zero values of IERR are summarized in Table 3 at the end of
this section. To determine the significance of a particular value of IERR,
scan the column headed IERR for the expression with the value of your
particular error. The name of the subroutine that set the error parameter
is included in the list to the right; also given is the EISPAC error message
number and a brief description of the significance of the error. More detailed information may be obtained from the documentation for the particular
subroutine in Section 7.

TABLE 3

SUMMARY OF VALUES OF IERR

IERR	SUBROUTINES	EISPAC MESSAGE	SIGNIFICANCE OF THE ERROR
i, $1 \leq i \leq N$	MINFIT,QZIT, RGG,RSB,RSG, RSGAB,RSGBA, SVD,TQLRAT, TQL2	00	The calculation of the ith eigenvalue or singular value failed to converge. If MINFIT, QZIT (with QZVAL), RGG, or SVD was being used, the eigenvalues or singular values $i+1, i+2, \ldots, N$ should be correct; otherwise, the eigenvalues $1, 2, \ldots, i-1$ should be correct. In neither case are any eigenvectors correct.
N	BQR	--	The calculation of the eigenvalue failed to converge.
$3N+1$	BISECT	03	The parameter MM specified insufficient storage to hold all the eigenvalues in the interval (RLB, RUB). The only useful result is M, which is set to the number of eigenvalues in this interval.
$7N+1$	REDUC,REDUC2, RSG,RSGAB, RSGBA	07	The matrix BR is not positive definite as required in the real symmetric generalized paths. No useful results are produced.
$-i$, $1 \leq i \leq N$	BANDV,TINVIT	50	The calculation of one or more of the eigenvectors including the ith vector failed to converge; these vectors are set to zero. These failures may be caused by insufficient accuracy of the corresponding eigenvalues. All non-zero eigenvectors and their corresponding eigenvalues should be correct.
$10N$	RGG,RSB,RSG, RSGAB,RSGBA	--	The parameter N specifying the order of the input matrix or system exceeds the dimension parameter NM. No results are produced.
$12N$	RSB	--	Either the parameter MB specifying the (half) band width is non-positive or it exceeds the matrix order N. No results are produced.

Section 2.3.9

EXAMPLES ILLUSTRATING THE USE OF THE EISPACK SUBROUTINES AND THE CONTROL PROGRAM

We illustrate the use of Section 2 in preparing two programs to solve
the same eigenproblems, one program calling the EISPACK subroutines directly
and the other using the control program EISPAC. The problems are to find the
eigenvalues in the interval (0,3) and the corresponding eigenvectors of two
generalized real symmetric matrix systems of orders 3 and 4, chosen to exhibit,
respectively, normal and abnormal path termination. The purpose of choosing
these problems is to illustrate the use of this publication in following
a somewhat complicated path; in practice, for such low order systems, it
is probably easier to use the paths that compute the complete eigensystem.

The two sample programs are complete in that they contain input and output statements; the data for each case and the computed results accompany the
program listing. For both programs, it is assumed that the EISPACK subroutines
are available in compiled form and that appropriate control cards are provided.
Note that the EISPAC sample program also assumes that the compiled form of
EISPAC is available, and may require additional control statements that point
to EISPAC and the EISPACK subroutines.

The EISPACK sample program is written in standard single precision
Fortran IV, while the EISPAC sample program is written in IBM's long precision
Fortran IV. Both programs use Fortran logical unit 5 for input and Fortran
logical unit 6 for output.

For these sample programs, we assume more generally that the order of
the input system will not exceed 20 and that the number of eigenvalues in the
interval (0,3) will not exceed 3. Thus the integer constants *nm* and *mm* discussed in Section 2.1 have the values 20 and 3 respectively.

Given the above eigenproblems, we are directed by Table 1 to Section 2.1.7. There, the appropriate calls to the EISPACK subroutines and to EISPAC are displayed. Dimensions for the array variables in the sample programs depend upon *nm* and *mm* and hence from the above discussion, the declaration statements must be

> *working precision* A(20,20),B(20,20),W(3),Z(20,3)
> *working precision* FV1(20),FV2(20),FV3(20),FV4(20),FV5(20),FV6(20),
>   FV7(20),FV8(20),FV9(20)
> INTEGER   IV1(3)

To communicate these dimensions to the EISPACK subroutines and to EISPAC, the parameters NM and MM are set to 20 and 3 respectively. Finally, variables RLB and RUB are set to 0.0 and 3.0 respectively, specifying the interval to be searched for the eigenvalues.

The matrices of the system are read row-wise from unit 5 and printed row-wise on unit 6. The first sample system has one eigenvalue in the interval (0,3), which with its corresponding eigenvector are printed on unit 6. The second sample system has more than three eigenvalues in (0,3) and the path is terminated after BISECT with IERR set to 13 = 3N+1. For this system, the EISPACK sample program distinguishes this error at statement 99999 from other possible errors, prints the appropriate message on unit 6 and continues execution (until a system of order zero is specified on unit 5). The EISPAC sample program also distinguishes this error value from other possible error values, prints a message numbered 03 on unit 6 and terminates execution. (See Section 2.3.7 for use of the ERROR keyword parameter to continue execution.)

LISTING OF THE EISPACK SAMPLE PROGRAM

```
C      SAMPLE PROGRAM ILLUSTRATING THE USE OF THE EISPACK SUBROUTINES.
C
C      THIS PROGRAM READS REAL SYMMETRIC MATRICES  A  AND  B  FROM
C      FORTRAN LOGICAL UNIT 5 AND COMPUTES EIGENVALUES  W  IN THE
C      INTERVAL (0,3) AND THE ASSOCIATED EIGENVECTORS  Z  FOR THE
C      GENERALIZED PROBLEM AZ = WBZ.  SEE SECTION 2.1.7.
C
C      REAL SYMMETRIC MATRICES  A  AND  B, NO LARGER THAN ORDER  20.
C      REAL EIGENVALUES  W, AT MOST  3  OF THEM.
C      EIGENVECTORS  Z, AT MOST  3  OF THEM.
C
       REAL   A(20,20),B(20,20),W(3),Z(20,3)
       REAL      RLB,RUB,EPS1
C
C      TEMPORARY STORAGE ARRAYS.
C
       REAL    FV1(20),FV2(20),FV3(20),FV4(20),FV5(20),FV6(20),
      +        FV7(20),FV8(20),FV9(20)
       INTEGER IV1(3)
C
C      ROW AND COLUMN DIMENSION PARAMETERS ASSIGNED.
C
       NM = 20
       MM = 3
C
C      READ IN THE REAL SYMMETRIC MATRICES OF ORDER  N  ROW-WISE.
C
    10 READ(5,20) N
    20 FORMAT(I4)
       IF (N .LE. 0) STOP
C
       DO 40 I = 1, N
          READ(5,30) (A(I,J),J=1,N)
    30    FORMAT(4E16.8)
    40 CONTINUE
C
       DO 45 I = 1, N
          READ(5,30) (B(I,J),J=1,N)
    45 CONTINUE
C
       WRITE(6,50) N
    50 FORMAT(///23H ORDER OF THE SYSTEM IS,I4//16H MATRIX ELEMENTS)
C
       DO 70 I = 1, N
          WRITE(6,60) (A(I,J),J=1,N)
    60    FORMAT(1X,1P4E16.8)
    70 CONTINUE
C
       WRITE(6,60)
C
       DO 75 I = 1, N
          WRITE(6,60) (B(I,J),J=1,N)
    75 CONTINUE
```

LISTING OF THE EISPACK SAMPLE PROGRAM (CONTD.)

```
C
C     INITIALIZE THE INTERVAL (RLB,RUB).
C
      RLB = 0.0
      RUB = 3.0
C
C     THE FOLLOWING PATH IS COPIED FROM SECTION 2.1.7.
C
      CALL REDUC(NM,N,A,B,FV9,IERR)
      IF (IERR .NE. 0) GO TO 99999
      CALL TRED1(NM,N,A,FV1,FV2,FV3)
      EPS1 = 0.0
      CALL BISECT(N,EPS1,FV1,FV2,FV3,RLB,RUB,MM,M,W,IV1,IERR,FV4,FV5)
      IF (IERR .NE. 0) GO TO 99999
      CALL TINVIT(NM,N,FV1,FV2,FV3,M,W,IV1,Z,IERR,FV4,FV5,FV6,FV7,FV8)
      IF (IERR .NE. 0) GO TO 99999
      CALL TRBAK1(NM,N,A,FV2,M,Z)
      CALL REBAK(NM,N,B,FV9,M,Z)
C
C     PRINT THE  M  EIGENVALUES AND CORRESPONDING EIGENVECTORS.
C
      IF (M .EQ. 0) GO TO 88888
      WRITE(6,90) M
   90 FORMAT(/47H NUMBER OF EIGENVALUES IN THE INTERVAL (0,3) IS,I4)
C
      DO 110 I = 1, M
         WRITE(6,100) W(I),(Z(J,I),J=1,N)
  100    FORMAT(/11H EIGENVALUE/1X,1PE16.8//14H CORRESPONDING,
     +           12H EIGENVECTOR/(1X,3E16.8))
  110 CONTINUE
C
      GO TO 10
C
C     THERE ARE NO EIGENVALUES IN (0,3).
C
88888 WRITE(6,88100)
88100 FORMAT(48H0NO EIGENVALUES OF SYSTEM IN THE INTERVAL (0,3).)
      GO TO 10
C
C     HANDLING OF IERR PARAMETER
C
99999 IF (IERR .GT. 0) GO TO 99200
      IERR = -IERR
      WRITE(6,99100) IERR
99100 FORMAT(52H0AT LEAST ONE EIGENVECTOR FAILED TO CONVERGE, NAMELY,I5)
      GO TO 10
C
99200 IF (IERR .EQ. 7*N+1) WRITE(6,99250)
99250 FORMAT(/35H MATRIX B IS NOT POSITIVE DEFINITE.)
      IF (IERR .EQ. 3*N+1) WRITE(6,99300) M
99300 FORMAT(/35H NOT ENOUGH SPACE ALLOCATED FOR THE,I4,
     +           35H EIGENVALUES IN THE INTERVAL (0,3).)
      GO TO 10
      END
```

LISTING OF THE EISPAC SAMPLE PROGRAM

```
C     SAMPLE PROGRAM ILLUSTRATING THE USE OF THE CONTROL PROGRAM EISPAC.
C
C     THIS PROGRAM READS REAL SYMMETRIC MATRICES A  AND  B  FROM
C     FORTRAN LOGICAL UNIT 5 AND COMPUTES EIGENVALUES  W  IN THE
C     INTERVAL (0,3) AND THE ASSOCIATED EIGENVECTORS  Z  FOR THE
C     GENERALIZED PROBLEM  AZ = WBZ.  SEE SECTION 2.1.7.
C
C     REAL SYMMETRIC MATRICES  A  AND  B, NO LARGER THAN ORDER  20.
C     REAL EIGENVALUES  W, AT MOST  3  OF THEM.
C     EIGENVECTORS  Z, AT MOST  3  OF THEM.
C
      REAL*8    A(20,20),B(20,20),W(3),Z(20,3)
      REAL*8    RLB,RUB,EPS1
C
C     ROW AND COLUMN DIMENSION PARAMETERS ASSIGNED.
C
      NM = 20
      MM = 3
C
C     READ IN THE REAL SYMMETRIC MATRICES OF ORDER  N  ROW-WISE.
C
   10 READ(5,20) N
   20 FORMAT(I4)
      IF (N .LE. 0) STOP
C
      DO 40 I = 1, N
         READ(5,30) (A(I,J),J=1,N)
   30    FORMAT(4D16.8)
   40 CONTINUE
C
      DO 45 I = 1, N
         READ(5,30) (B(I,J),J=1,N)
   45 CONTINUE
C
      WRITE(6,50) N
   50 FORMAT(///23H ORDER OF THE SYSTEM IS,I4//16H MATRIX ELEMENTS)
C
      DO 70 I = 1, N
         WRITE(6,60) (A(I,J),J=1,N)
   60    FORMAT(1X,1P4D16.8)
   70 CONTINUE
C
      WRITE(6,60)
C
      DO 75 I = 1, N
         WRITE(6,60) (B(I,J),J=1,N)
   75 CONTINUE
```

LISTING OF THE EISPAC SAMPLE PROGRAM (CONTD.)

```
C
C      INITIALIZE THE INTERVAL (RLB,RUB).
C
       RLB = 0.0D0
       RUB = 3.0D0
C
C      THE FOLLOWING CALL IS COPIED FROM SECTION 2.1.7.
C
       CALL EISPAC(NM,N,MATA('REAL',A,'SYMMETRIC'),
      +            MATB('REAL',B,'SYMMETRIC','POSITIVE DEFINITE'),
      +            VALUES(W,MM,M,RLB,RUB),VECTOR(Z))
C
C      PRINT THE  M  EIGENVALUES AND CORRESPONDING EIGENVECTORS.
C
C          ARE THERE ANY EIGENVALUES IN (0,3)?
C
           IF (M .NE. 0) GO TO 90
C
C          NO.
C
       WRITE(6,80)
   80 FORMAT(48H0NO EIGENVALUES OF SYSTEM IN THE INTERVAL (0,3).)
       GO TO 10
C
C      YES.
C
   90 WRITE(6,100) M
  100 FORMAT(/47H NUMBER OF EIGENVALUES IN THE INTERVAL (0,3) IS,I4)
C
       DO 120 I = 1, M
          WRITE(6,110) W(I),(Z(J,I),J=1,N)
  110     FORMAT(/11H EIGENVALUE/1X,1PD16.8//14H CORRESPONDING,
      +           12H EIGENVECTOR/(1X,3D16.8))
  120 CONTINUE
C
       GO TO 10
       END
```

DATA FOR THE SAMPLE PROGRAMS READ FROM UNIT 5

3			
-1.0	1.0	-1.0	
1.0	1.0	-1.0	
-1.0	-1.0	1.0	
2.0	1.0	0.0	
1.0	2.0	1.0	
0.0	1.0	2.0	
4			
1.875	-0.5	0.375	-0.25
-0.5	2.25	-0.25	-0.375
0.375	-0.25	2.125	-0.125
-0.25	-0.375	-0.125	2.125
6.0	3.0	0.0	0.0
3.0	6.0	3.0	0.0
0.0	3.0	6.0	3.0
0.0	0.0	3.0	6.0
0			

OUTPUT FROM THE EISPACK SAMPLE PROGRAM PRINTED ON UNIT 6

ORDER OF THE SYSTEM IS   3

MATRIX ELEMENTS
```
 -1.00000000E 00   1.00000000E 00  -1.00000000E 00
  1.00000000E 00   1.00000000E 00  -1.00000000E 00
 -1.00000000E 00  -1.00000000E 00   1.00000000E 00

  2.00000000E 00   1.00000000E 00   0.0
  1.00000000E 00   2.00000000E 00   1.00000000E 00
  0.0              1.00000000E 00   2.00000000E 00
```

NUMBER OF EIGENVALUES IN THE INTERVAL (0,3) IS   1

EIGENVALUE
```
  1.99999905E 00
```

CORRESPONDING EIGENVECTOR
```
  4.21468599E-07   7.07105637E-01  -7.07107246E-01
```


ORDER OF THE SYSTEM IS   4

MATRIX ELEMENTS
```
  1.87500000E 00  -5.00000000E-01   3.75000000E-01  -2.50000000E-01
 -5.00000000E-01   2.25000000E 00  -2.50000000E-01  -3.75000000E-01
  3.75000000E-01  -2.50000000E-01   2.12500000E 00  -1.25000000E-01
 -2.50000000E-01  -3.75000000E-01  -1.25000000E-01   2.12500000E 00

  6.00000000E 00   3.00000000E 00   0.0              0.0
  3.00000000E 00   6.00000000E 00   3.00000000E 00   0.0
  0.0              3.00000000E 00   6.00000000E 00   3.00000000E 00
  0.0              0.0              3.00000000E 00   6.00000000E 00
```

NOT ENOUGH SPACE ALLOCATED FOR THE   4 EIGENVALUES IN THE INTERVAL (0,3).

OUTPUT FROM THE EISPAC SAMPLE PROGRAM PRINTED ON UNIT 6

ORDER OF THE SYSTEM IS . 3

MATRIX ELEMENTS
```
 -1.00000000D 00   1.00000000D 00  -1.00000000D 00
  1.00000000D 00   1.00000000D 00  -1.00000000D 00
 -1.00000000D 00  -1.00000000D 00   1.00000000D 00

  2.00000000D 00   1.00000000D 00   0.0
  1.00000000D 00   2.00000000D 00   1.00000000D 00
  0.0              1.00000000D 00   2.00000000D 00
```

NUMBER OF EIGENVALUES IN THE INTERVAL (0,3) IS   1

EIGENVALUE
```
  2.00000000D 00
```

CORRESPONDING EIGENVECTOR
```
  2.94392336D-17   7.07106781D-01  -7.07106781D-01
```


ORDER OF THE SYSTEM IS   4

MATRIX ELEMENTS
```
  1.87500000D 00  -5.00000000D-01   3.75000000D-01  -2.50000000D-01
 -5.00000000D-01   2.25000000D 00  -2.50000000D-01  -3.75000000D-01
  3.75000000D-01  -2.50000000D-01   2.12500000D 00  -1.25000000D-01
 -2.50000000D-01  -3.75000000D-01  -1.25000000D-01   2.12500000D 00

  6.00000000D 00   3.00000000D 00   0.0              0.0
  3.00000000D 00   6.00000000D 00   3.00000000D 00   0.0
  0.0              3.00000000D 00   6.00000000D 00   3.00000000D 00
  0.0              0.0              3.00000000D 00   6.00000000D 00
```

**** **** **** **** **** **** **** **** **** **** **** **** ****

EISPAC EXECUTION PHASE ERROR(S)...
03 IF PARAMETER MM WAS USED, MM SPECIFIED INSUFFICIENT STORAGE
    TO HOLD ALL EIGENVALUES IN THE INTERVAL RLB TO RUB.
      IF PARAMETER M11 WAS USED, MULTIPLE EIGENVALUES
      AT INDEX M11 MAKE UNIQUE SELECTION IMPOSSIBLE.

EXECUTION TERMINATED.

**** **** **** **** **** **** **** **** **** **** **** **** ****

Section 2.4

SINGULAR VALUE DECOMPOSITION WITH EISPACK

This section discusses the Singular Value Decomposition, a matrix
factorization that involves eigenvalues but which has applications to many
problems that do not explicitly refer to eigenvalues. Two subroutines, SVD
and MINFIT, provide the EISPACK capability for singular value decomposition.
The two subroutines overlap to a certain extent, but in their respective
principal applications they complement each other in much the same way as
matrix inversion and linear equation solving subroutines do.

The first subsection of this section defines the singular value decomposition and describes how it provides information for estimating the rank of a
matrix. The next subsection describes the use of subroutines SVD and MINFIT
in computing selected elements of the decomposition. The final three subsections identify the related applications of the decompositions from SVD
and MINFIT to the determination of the pseudo-inverse of a rectangular matrix
and to the minimal norm least squares solution of an associated set of linear
equations, respectively, and their joint applicability to the solution of
homogeneous systems of equations.

Section 2.4.1

THE SINGULAR VALUE DECOMPOSITION AND RANK ESTIMATION

The Singular Value Decomposition proceeds from a real rectangular matrix A with M rows and N columns. M and N are not constrained but the primary applications of the decomposition have $M \geq N$. The decomposition is commonly written

$$A = U \Sigma V^T$$

where Σ is an N by N diagonal matrix with non-negative entries σ_j, $j=1,\ldots,N$, and U and V are matrices with orthonormal columns of dimensions M by N and N by N, respectively. Note that U has the same dimensions as A and that V has as many columns as A but is square. The elements σ_j of Σ are denoted the singular values of A, and the columns of U and V are the left and right singular vectors, respectively.

Theoretically, the singular value decomposition can be characterized by the fact that the singular values are the square roots of the eigenvalues of $A^T A$, the columns of V are the corresponding eigenvectors, and the columns of U are a certain subset of the eigenvectors of AA^T. However, this is not a satisfactory basis for computation because roundoff errors in the formation of $A^T A$ often destroy pertinent information.

Most applications of the singular value decomposition require the specification of a tolerance or zero threshold τ. In problems involving experimental or other inexact data, this tolerance should reflect the absolute accuracy of the matrix elements. Thus if Δ_{ij} are the errors in a_{ij}, then an appropriate value for τ satisfies

$$\tau \geq \max_{i,j} |\Delta_{ij}| .$$

70

In problems where the matrix elements are known exactly or are contaminated only by roundoff error, an appropriate τ is

$$\tau \geq \sqrt{M \cdot N} \cdot \varepsilon \cdot \max_{j} \sigma_{j}$$

where ε is the relative accuracy of the floating point arithmetic (called MACHEP in the EISPACK subroutines). Although this tolerance is important, its exact value is not critical; in many situations it is useful to test the effect of using several different values. In particular, Sections 2.4.3-2.4.5 describe applications of the singular value decomposition each of which can be affected by the choice of τ.

One fundamental application of the singular value decomposition is the determination of the effective or numerical rank of a matrix whose elements are not known exactly. Roughly, the effective rank is the largest number of columns of the matrix which are linearly independent to within the threshold τ. Since the orthogonal transformations of U and V preserve linear independence, the ranks of A and Σ are the same, and the effective rank can be precisely defined to be the number of singular values which are greater than τ. A matrix with $M \geq N$ is said to have "full rank" if its effective rank is N.

Section 2.4.2

SUBROUTINES SVD AND MINFIT

Subroutine SVD computes the singular value decomposition $A = U \Sigma V^T$ of an arbitrary rectangular matrix A (see Section 2.4.1); it stores the diagonal matrix Σ as a vector W, and optionally accumulates the orthogonal transformations into U and/or V. To determine, for example, the singular values W and the transformation matrices U and V associated with the singular value decomposition of the M by N matrix A, the call to SVD is:

CALL SVD(NM,M,N,A,W,.TRUE.,U,.TRUE.,V,IERR,*fv1*)

To avoid accumulating U or V, replace .TRUE. by .FALSE. in the calling sequence position ahead of the corresponding array identifier; note that the V array is not referenced if preceded by .FALSE. but that the U array must be provided for use as intermediate storage even when the transformations are not accumulated. SVD returns the singular values unordered; it leaves A unaltered.

Suitable dimensions for the arrays are: A(*nm*,*nm*), W(*nm*), U(*nm*,*nm*), V(*nm*,*nm*), and *fv1*(*nm*). (Note that $N \leq nm$ and $M \leq nm$ must both be satisfied.)

The array storage required for SVD is $2N + \max(M,N) \cdot 3N$ working precision words, reducible to $2N(M+1)$ if V is not requested. Furthermore, either U or V may overwrite A, thereby reducing storage correspondingly.

SVD executes properly when either $M \geq N$ or $M < N$; it is generally more efficient, however, when a matrix is proposed with $M < N$ to present its transpose instead to SVD and interchange the roles of U and V.

Indicative execution times for SVD (run on an IBM 370/195) are .011, .065, .43, and 3.0 seconds for sample problems with M = N of order 10, 20, 40, and 80 respectively, where both U and V are requested. Extrapolation of these execution times for cases where M differs from N is discussed in Section 4.5.

Subroutine MINFIT computes the elements Σ and V of the singular value decomposition of A, but instead of U forms $U^T B$ where B is a prescribed matrix with the same number of rows as A (anticipating the application described in Section 2.4.4). It stores the diagonal matrix Σ as a vector W, and overwrites A with V and B with $U^T B$. To determine the singular values W and the transformation matrix V associated with the singular value decomposition of the M by N matrix A and to form $U^T B$ atop the M by IP matrix B, the call to MINFIT is:

CALL MINFIT(NM,M,N,A,W,IP,B,IERR,$fv1$)

IP can be 0 in which case B is not referenced. MINFIT returns the singular values unordered (exactly as from SVD); as described above, A is overwritten by V and B by $U^T B$.

Suitable dimensions for the arrays are: A(nm,nm), W(nm), B(nm,ip), and $fv1$(nm). (Note that N $\leq nm$ and M $\leq nm$ must both be satisfied.)

The array storage required for MINFIT is $2N + \max(M,N) \cdot (N+IP)$ working precision words.

Indicative execution times for MINFIT (run on an IBM 370/195) are .009, .047, .29, and 2.0 seconds for sample problems with M = N and IP = 1 of order 10, 20, 40, and 80 respectively. Extrapolation of these execution times for cases where M differs from N and IP is other than 1 is discussed in Section 4.5.

The control program EISPAC does not use SVD and MINFIT. For more information on SVD and MINFIT, consult their respective subroutine documents in Section 7.

Section 2.4.3

THE PSEUDO-INVERSE OF A RECTANGULAR MATRIX

If A is an M by N matrix and τ is a threshold chosen as described in Section 2.4.1, then the N by M matrix A^+ is defined to be the effective pseudo-inverse of A if it has the following properties:

1) AA^+ is symmetric

2) A^+A is symmetric

3) $A^+AA^+ = A^+$

4) $\|(AA^+A - A)\| \leqslant \tau$

5) $\|(A^+)\| < 1/\tau$

where the norm in 4) and 5) is the Euclidean matrix norm. If τ is smaller than all the non-zero singular values of A, then A^+ becomes the Moore-Penrose pseudo-inverse; if A is square and non-singular and τ is smaller than all its singular values, then $A^+ = A^{-1}$.

If $A = U \Sigma V^T$, then $A^+ = V \Sigma^+ U^T$ where Σ^+ is the diagonal matrix with elements

$$\sigma_j^+ = \begin{cases} 1/\sigma_j & \text{if } \sigma_j \geq \tau \\ 0 & \text{otherwise.} \end{cases}$$

Since V, Σ, and U are all available from subroutine SVD, what is further required to compute A^+ is to determine Σ^+ based on the selected τ and combine the matrix operands into the required product. Sample coding for this matrix product is provided in the document for SVD in Section 7.

74

Section 2.4.4

LEAST SQUARES SOLUTIONS OF MINIMAL NORM

If A is an M by N matrix and b is a given column vector with M components, then the N-component vector x is defined to be the least squares
solution of the linear system Ax = b if it minimizes the Euclidean norm of
the residual vector b - Ax. If τ is a threshold chosen as described in
Section 2.4.1, and if A is of full rank relative to τ, then the solution x
is unique. If A is not of full rank, then the solution is not unique; in
the absence of other criteria, it is common to specify that from all vectors
x for which $\|b - Ax\|$ is within τ of the minimum, the one which minimizes
$\|x\|$ is to be chosen. This is known as the minimal norm least squares solution of Ax = b.

If $A = U \Sigma V^T$, then the desired solution x can be written $x = V \Sigma^+ U^T b$
where Σ^+ (as in the pseudo-inverse determination of Section 2.4.3) is the
diagonal matrix with elements

$$\sigma_j^+ = \begin{cases} 1/\sigma_j \text{ if } \sigma_j \geq \tau \\ 0 \text{ otherwise.} \end{cases}$$

Since V, Σ, and $U^T b$ are all available from subroutine MINFIT, what is
further required to compute x is to determine Σ^+ based on the selected τ
and combine the matrix operands into the required product. Sample coding
for this matrix product is provided in the document for MINFIT in Section 7.

The minimal norm solution x depends upon the choice of τ. If τ is
increased to a value which causes one or more additional singular values to
be neglected, then $\|b - Ax\|$ will be increased and $\|x\|$ will be decreased.

MINFIT admits more generally of a B matrix with IP columns in which
case the solution matrix X also has IP columns. If b is a single column
vector, then IP should be set to 1.

Section 2.4.5

HOMOGENEOUS LINEAR EQUATIONS

In Section 2.4.1, the determination of the effective rank of the M by N matrix A for a threshold τ was described. If the effective rank is not N, then the dependencies of the columns can be expressed as non-trivial approximate solutions of the homogeneous system of equations $Az = 0$. If $A = U \Sigma V^T$, then $Av_j = \sigma_j u_j$, and therefore for those columns v_j which correspond to singular values σ_j less than the threshold τ, $\|Av_j\| < \tau$. If a linear combination of these v_j with otherwise arbitrary coefficients α_j except that $\Sigma \alpha_j^2 \leq 1$ be designated z, then $\|Az\| < \tau$. Any such z can be regarded as a solution of $Az = 0$ to within the threshold. Furthermore, any such z can be added to the minimal norm least squares solution x of Section 2.4.4 without increasing $\|b - Ax\|$ by more than τ.

Either SVD or MINFIT can be used for this application with equal efficiency. With SVD, U need not be accumulated, while MINFIT can be called with IP = 0.

Section 3

VALIDATION OF EISPACK

As part of its original development, EISPACK was subjected to careful testing designed to thoroughly exercise each subroutine in the package. Before a version of EISPACK is declared certified, however, it must also be validated at one or more test sites not involved in the adaptation. This validation has two important goals. One is to insure that the adaptation has been carried out successfully and that EISPACK performs as anticipated on that computer system. The second has been of major importance in the development of EISPACK; it is to provide feedback on the ease of use of EISPACK and its documentation. The procedures included in and the philosophy behind this validation are discussed in further detail in ([3],[5]).

Thus, validation at test sites includes two kinds of testing. The first employs test drivers and a collection of 156 matrices supplied with EISPACK; its purpose is to verify that the subroutines have been adapted to the machine and system properly, and to obtain data which can later be used as a check at other locations having the same computer system. These test drivers and matrices are included on the tape from the distribution center as described in Section 5.

The second kind of testing is the more informal; it seeks to employ EISPACK in actual scientific computations to measure the ease of use of the routines and their documentation. By its very nature, of course, this informal testing is not repeatable.

In order to simplify the communication of the results of the formal testing, a measure of performance for EISPACK, based on the backward error analysis of Wilkinson and Reinsch ([1],[2]), was defined. It is computed variously, depending on the problem class, as:

$$\mu = \max_{1 \leq i \leq N} \frac{||Az_i - \lambda_i z_i||}{10 \cdot N \cdot \varepsilon \cdot ||A|| \cdot ||z_i||}$$ for standard (full or band) eigenproblems,

$$\mu = \max_{1 \leq i \leq N} \frac{||Az_i - \lambda_i Bz_i||}{10 \cdot N \cdot \varepsilon \cdot ||A|| \cdot ||z_i||}$$ for the real symmetric generalized eigenproblem $Az = \lambda Bz$,

$$\mu = \max_{1 \leq i \leq N} \frac{||ABz_i - \lambda_i z_i||}{10 \cdot N \cdot \varepsilon \cdot ||A|| \cdot ||B|| \cdot ||z_i||}$$ for the real symmetric generalized eigenproblem $ABz = \lambda z$,

$$\mu = \max_{1 \leq i \leq N} \frac{||BAz_i - \lambda_i z_i||}{10 \cdot N \cdot \varepsilon \cdot ||B|| \cdot ||A|| \cdot ||z_i||}$$ for the real symmetric generalized eigenproblem $BAz = \lambda z$,

$$\mu = \max_{1 \leq i \leq N} \frac{||\beta_i Az_i - \alpha_i Bz_i||}{10 \cdot N \cdot \varepsilon \cdot (\beta_i \cdot ||A|| + |\alpha_i| \cdot ||B||) \cdot ||z_i||}$$ for the real generalized eigenproblem $\beta Az = \alpha Bz$ (see Section 2.3.1),

$$\mu = \max_{1 \leq i \leq N} \frac{||Av_i - \sigma_i u_i|| + ||A^T u_i - \sigma_i v_i||}{10 \cdot \max(M,N) \cdot \varepsilon \cdot ||A|| \cdot (||u_i|| + ||v_i||)}$$ for the singular value decomposition $A = U\Sigma V^T$,

$$\mu = \max_{1 \leq i \leq M} \frac{||Ax_i - b_i||}{N \cdot \varepsilon \cdot ||A|| \cdot ||x_i||}$$ for the band linear system $Ax = b$ (with M column vectors b_i),

where A and B are matrices of order N (A is M by N for singular value decomposition), and where ε is the precision of arithmetic on the test machine (called MACHEP in the subroutines).

The factor 10 in the formulas for μ was chosen empirically to obtain the following criterion for the performance of EISPACK:

If μ is less than 1, EISPACK has performed satisfactorily (as well as can be expected according to the backward error analysis for the particular precision of arithmetic). If μ is greater than 100, the performance is

deemed poor. Finally, if μ is between 1 and 100, the performance is pro-
gressively marginal, and further investigation might be in order to verify
that no error has occurred.

This measure of performance is also useful as a check on the correct
installation of EISPACK; the residuals are very sensitive to small perturbations in the eigenvalues or singular values, and hence so is μ. μ may thus
reflect small changes in the performance of EISPACK caused either by changes
in the subroutines themselves or by the hardware, operating system, compiler,
or library with which they are used. Hence it provides an excellent "quick
check" of the correct installation of EISPACK on a hardware-software system.
If the values of μ obtained from the test cases are similar to those obtained
at the test site, it is virtually certain that EISPACK has been correctly
installed. If, however, some values of μ are distinctly larger, an error may
have occurred in the transmission or implementation of EISPACK, or the
hardware-software system may differ from that on which it was tested; such
instances should probably be investigated.

The collection of 156 test matrices has been accumulated from various
sources and provides a wide spectrum of test cases from trivial to patho-
logical. Most values of the performance index μ for these test cases were
less than 1 for the systems on which EISPACK has been certified.

Section 4

EXECUTION TIMES FOR EISPACK

In this section we display approximate execution times of the individual
subroutines and various paths in EISPACK covered in this volume, measured
with sample matrices on many of the computer systems for which the subroutines have been certified. The elements of the sample matrices are random
numbers sampled from uniform distributions. Tables of execution times appear
in the first subsection, and considerations regarding the reliability of the
timing measurements, their dependence upon the elements of the matrices, and
the extrapolation of these results to other machines are discussed in later
subsections. A further subsection discusses timing considerations for band
problems and singular value decomposition with coefficient matrices of different shapes. The section concludes with listings of the program segments that
generate the sample matrices.

Section 4.1

TABLES OF EXECUTION TIMES

For each of 17 computer systems there follow two tables displaying sample
execution times respectively for real symmetric band matrices and generalized
real symmetric matrix systems jointly, and for generalized real matrix systems
and singular value decomposition jointly. A further table follows comparing
the performance of the computer systems with each other. Finally, one additional table is included reporting path timings on the IBM 370/195 when the
control program EISPAC is used.

For timing of band matrices over the various machines, the (half) band
width MB has been chosen uniformly as MB = 3N/10 where N is the order of the
matrix. For singular value decomposition the matrices are square (M = N)
with one constant vector (IP = 1) furnished to MINFIT. See Section 4.5 for
a discussion of the effects of matrix shape on timing for these problem
classes.

The tables report execution times both for the individual subroutines and
for the recommended paths of Section 2.1. Each column of a table reports
times for a matrix or matrix system of different order. The entries in any
column are expressed as multiples of the time unit that appears at the head
of the column. The time unit chosen is the absolute time for subroutine
TRED1 in one table and for subroutine ELMHES in the other. (ELMHES itself
does not appear in a path, but normalizing to the time for ELMHES (and TRED1)
enables more convenient comparison of the tables in this volume with those
that appeared earlier in [10].) A dash appears in place of an entry representing an execution time too small to be measured within the resolution of
the clock.

For those subroutines that compute some eigenvalues or eigenvectors, the tabulated time for BISECT or TINVIT represents that required for the subroutine to compute <u>all</u> eigenvalues or eigenvectors, while that for BQR or BANDV is for <u>one</u> eigenvalue or eigenvector. The times for the eigenvector subroutines TINVIT and BANDV are measured when the eigenvalues are provided by the subroutines BISECT and BQR respectively; these times could be significantly longer if less accurate eigenvalue subroutines were substituted.

Extrapolation of the BANDV times is approximately linear with the number of requested vectors. BQR times are not easy to extrapolate owing to the iterative nature of the algorithm with its speed dependent at each call on the closeness of an eigenvalue to the input parameter T. Actually the question of extrapolation here is pretty much academic; it appears rare that BQR can compete with the combination of BANDR and BISECT if more than one eigenvalue is desired, or even for a single eigenvalue unless a close approximation is known.

In several of the eigensystem subroutines the accumulation of transformations is an option. For these subroutines the tables report both possible times, the subroutine name being followed by '(Z)' in the case where the transformations are accumulated. With subroutine SVD there exist options to accumulate the U matrix, V matrix, or both. Three of the four different SVD times have been measured -- those identified as SVD(U), SVD(V), and SVD. The time for SVD(U,V) can be approximated as $[SVD(U) + SVD(V) - SVD]$.

For the paths, the entries are built by summing the times for the separate subroutines. The entries for those paths that compute partial eigensystems are expressed as the sum of two terms: the first term is the base time for the path and the second term is that part which depends upon the number of eigenvalues and eigenvectors computed. This latter term is either the product

of the estimated time to compute one eigenvalue-eigenvector pair and M, the
number of pairs computed, or the product of the estimated time to compute
one eigenvalue and M, the number of eigenvalues computed. Program segments
that generate the sample matrices and matrix systems are listed in Section 4.6.

TABLE 4

SUMMARY OF EXECUTION TIMES FOR THE
EISPACK SUBROUTINES INCLUDED IN THE PATHS FOR
REAL SYMMETRIC BAND MATRICES AND
GENERALIZED REAL SYMMETRIC MATRIX SYSTEMS

MACHINE: IBM 370/195, Fortran H, OPT=2
ARGONNE NATIONAL LABORATORY

SUBROUTINE	ORDER OF MATRIX OR SYSTEM				
	N=10	N=20	N=40	N=60	N=80
Time Unit (Sec)	.001	.007	.042	.12	.27
TRED1	1	1	1	1	1
TRED2	1.7	1.9	2.0	2.1	2.2
TRBAK1	1.2	1.4	1.6	1.7	1.8
BANDR(Z)	.87	1.4	1.9	2.1	2.3
BANDR	.52	.86	1.1	1.2	1.2
BQR	8	8	7	8	6
BANDV	.64	.52	.48	.46	.48
REDUC	1.2	1.1	1.1	1.2	1.2
REDUC2	1.2	1.1	1.1	1.1	1.1
REBAK	.66	.71	.73	.76	.76
REBAKB	.68	.78	.89	.96	1.0
TQL2	3.4	3.4	3.3	3.2	3.2
TQLRAT	1.3	.72	.36	.25	.17
BISECT	12	8.1	4.9	3.5	2.8
TINVIT	.97	.66	.40	.32	.31

PATHS

RSB (BANDR(Z),TQL2)	4.3	4.9	5.2	5.4	5.4
RSB (BANDR,TQLRAT)	1.8	1.6	1.4	1.4	1.4
BANDR,BISECT,BANDV	.52+1.9M	.86+.92M	1.1+.60M	1.2+.52M	1.2+.51M
BANDR,BISECT	.52+1.2M	.86+.40M	1.1+.12M	1.2+.06M	1.2+.03M
RSG (REDUC,TRED2,TQL2,REBAK)	6.9	7.1	7.1	7.3	7.3
RSG (REDUC,TRED1,TQLRAT)	3.4	2.8	2.5	2.4	2.3
REDUC,TRED1,BISECT,TINVIT, TRBAK1,REBAK	2.2+1.5M	2.1+.54M	2.1+.19M	2.2+.11M	2.2+.07M
REDUC,TRED1,BISECT	2.2+1.2M	2.1+.40M	2.1+.12M	2.2+.06M	2.2+.03M

TABLE 5

SUMMARY OF EXECUTION TIMES FOR THE
EISPACK SUBROUTINES INCLUDED IN THE PATHS FOR
GENERALIZED REAL MATRIX SYSTEMS AND
SINGULAR VALUE DECOMPOSITION

MACHINE: IBM 370/195, Fortran H, OPT=2
ARGONNE NATIONAL LABORATORY

	ORDER OF MATRIX OR SYSTEM				
SUBROUTINE	N=10	N=20	N=40	N=60	N=80
Time Unit (Sec)	.001	.006	.048	.16	.36
ELMHES	1	1	1	1	1
QZHES(Z)	6.5	5.9	5.6	5.5	5.6
QZHES	5.7	5.1	4.7	4.6	4.7
QZIT(Z)	20	18	14	13	13
QZIT	16	12	8.5	7.1	7.0
QZVAL(Z)	.55	.18	.05	.02	.01
QZVAL	.54	.17	.05	.02	.01
QZVEC	2.6	1.9	1.5	1.4	1.3
SVD(U)	11	7.6	5.8	5.4	5.2
SVD(V)	11	7.8	5.9	5.6	5.2
SVD	7.5	4.4	2.9	2.4	2.2
MINFIT	11	7.6	5.9	5.4	5.2
PATHS					
RGG (QZHES(Z),QZIT(Z), QZVAL(Z),QZVEC)	29	26	21	20	19
RGG (QZHES,QZIT,QZVAL)	22	17	13	12	12

TABLE 6

SUMMARY OF EXECUTION TIMES FOR THE
EISPACK SUBROUTINES INCLUDED IN THE PATHS FOR
REAL SYMMETRIC BAND MATRICES AND
GENERALIZED REAL SYMMETRIC MATRIX SYSTEMS

MACHINE: IBM 360/75, Fortran H, OPT=2
UNIVERSITY OF ILLINOIS

SUBROUTINE	ORDER OF MATRIX OR SYSTEM			
	N=20	N=40	N=60	N=80
Time Unit (Sec)	.077	.46	1.5	3.5
TRED1	1	1	1	1
TRED2	1.7	2.1	2.0	2.1
TRBAK1	1.3	1.5	1.5	1.6
BANDR(Z)	1.3	1.8	1.8	2.0
BANDR	.73	.89	.87	.93
BQR	5	4	4	5
BANDV	.31	.30	.28	.29
REDUC	.96	1.1	1.0	1.1
REDUC2	.99	1.1	1.0	1.1
REBAK	.62	.75	.72	.71
REBAKB	.64	.79	.76	.80
TQL2	4.6	5.3	4.8	5.0
TQLRAT	.51	.33	.20	.15
BISECT	4.7	2.9	1.8	1.4
TINVIT	.47	.33	.25	.26

PATHS

	N=20	N=40	N=60	N=80
RSB (BANDR(Z),TQL2)	5.9	7.1	6.6	7.0
RSB (BANDR,TQLRAT)	1.2	1.2	1.1	1.1
BANDR,BISECT,BANDV	.73+.54M	.89+.37M	.87+.31M	.93+.31M
BANDR,BISECT	.73+.23M	.89+.07M	.87+.03M	.93+.02M
RSG (REDUC,TRED2,TQL2,REBAK)	7.9	9.2	8.5	8.9
RSG (REDUC,TRED1,TQLRAT)	2.5	2.4	2.2	2.2
REDUC,TRED1,BISECT,TINVIT, TRBAK1,REBAK	2.0+.35M	2.1+.14M	2.0+.07M	2.1+.05M
REDUC,TRED1,BISECT	2.0+.23M	2.1+.07M	2.0+.03M	2.1+.02M

TABLE 7

SUMMARY OF EXECUTION TIMES FOR THE
EISPACK SUBROUTINES INCLUDED IN THE PATHS FOR
GENERALIZED REAL MATRIX SYSTEMS AND
SINGULAR VALUE DECOMPOSITION

MACHINE: IBM 360/75, Fortran H, OPT=2
UNIVERSITY OF ILLINOIS

SUBROUTINE	ORDER OF MATRIX OR SYSTEM			
	N=20	N=40	N=60	N=80
Time Unit (Sec)	.07	.50	1.7	4.1
ELMHES	1	1	1	1
QZHES(Z)	7.0	7.3	7.0	6.8
QZHES	6.0	6.1	5.8	5.8
QZIT(Z)	21	18	17	15
QZIT	13	10	8.8	7.2
QZVAL(Z)	.23	.06	.01	.01
QZVAL	.23	.05	.02	.01
QZVEC	1.6	1.5	1.4	1.3
SVD(U)	8.1	7.1	6.5	6.1
SVD(V)	8.2	7.2	6.6	6.2
SVD	3.7	2.7	2.3	2.0
MINFIT	8.7	7.4	6.7	6.3
PATHS				
RGG (QZHES(Z),QZIT(Z), QZVAL(Z),QZVEC)	29	27	26	23
RGG (QZHES,QZIT,QZVAL)	20	16	15	13

TABLE 8

SUMMARY OF EXECUTION TIMES FOR THE
EISPACK SUBROUTINES INCLUDED IN THE PATHS FOR
REAL SYMMETRIC BAND MATRICES AND
GENERALIZED REAL SYMMETRIC MATRIX SYSTEMS

MACHINE: IBM 360/65, Fortran H, OPT=2
AMES LABORATORY

SUBROUTINE	ORDER OF MATRIX OR SYSTEM				
	N=10	N=20	N=40	N=60	N=80
Time Unit (Sec)	.017	.12	.86	2.5	5.9
TRED1	1	1	1	1	1
TRED2	2	1.8	1.8	2.0	2.0
TRBAK1	1	1.4	1.5	1.6	1.5
BANDR(Z)	1	1.4	1.7	1.9	1.9
BANDR	-	.76	.84	.94	.91
BQR	7	5	4	4	4
BANDV	-	.31	.30	.29	.30
REDUC	2	1.0	.91	1.0	1.0
REDUC2	1	.98	1.0	.98	.96
REBAK	1	.62	.65	.70	.69
REBAKB	1	.71	.67	.75	.75
TQL2	6	5.4	5.2	5.3	5.0
TQLRAT	2	.71	.35	.23	.17
BISECT	11	5.6	3.2	2.1	1.6
TINVIT	1	.61	.31	.26	.26

PATHS

	N=10	N=20	N=40	N=60	N=80
RSB (BANDR(Z),TQL2)	7	6.8	6.9	7.2	6.9
RSB (BANDR,TQLRAT)	2	1.5	1.2	1.2	1.1
BANDR,BISECT,BANDV	1.5M	.76+.59M	.84+.38M	.94+.32M	.91+.32M
BANDR,BISECT	1.1M	.76+.28M	.84+.08M	.94+.03M	.91+.02M
RSG (REDUC,TRED2,TQL2,REBAK)	10	8.8	8.6	9.0	8.7
RSG (REDUC,TRED1,TQLRAT)	4	2.7	2.3	2.3	2.2
REDUC,TRED1,BISECT,TINVIT, TRBAK1,REBAK	3+1.4M	2.0+.41M	1.9+.14M	2.0+.08M	2.0+.05M
REDUC,TRED1,BISECT	3+1.1M	2.0+.28M	1.9+.08M	2.0+.03M	2.0+.02M

TABLE 9

SUMMARY OF EXECUTION TIMES FOR THE
EISPACK SUBROUTINES INCLUDED IN THE PATHS FOR
GENERALIZED REAL MATRIX SYSTEMS AND
SINGULAR VALUE DECOMPOSITION

MACHINE: IBM 360/65, Fortran H, OPT=2
AMES LABORATORY

SUBROUTINE	N=10	N=20	N=40	N=60	N=80
Time Unit (Sec)	.015	.11	.89	3.1	7.2
ELMHES	1	1	1	1	1
QZHES(Z)	7	7.3	7.4	6.9	6.9
QZHES	7	6.3	6.0	5.7	5.7
QZIT(Z)	24	22	18	16	15
QZIT	18	14	9.7	8.6	7.3
QZVAL(Z)	-	.17	.03	.02	.01
QZVAL	-	.13	.03	.02	.01
QZVEC	2	1.7	1.4	1.2	1.2
SVD(U)	11	8.6	6.9	6.3	6.0
SVD(V)	11	8.4	7.0	6.1	6.0
SVD	6	3.9	2.6	2.1	2.0
MINFIT	12	8.6	7.0	6.2	6.0

ORDER OF MATRIX OR SYSTEM

PATHS

	N=10	N=20	N=40	N=60	N=80
RGG (QZHES(Z),QZIT(Z), QZVAL(Z),QZVEC)	34	31	27	24	23
RGG (QZHES,QZIT,QZVAL)	25	20	16	14	13

TABLE 10

SUMMARY OF EXECUTION TIMES FOR THE
EISPACK SUBROUTINES INCLUDED IN THE PATHS FOR
REAL SYMMETRIC BAND MATRICES AND
GENERALIZED REAL SYMMETRIC MATRIX SYSTEMS

MACHINE: IBM 370/165, Fortran H Extended, OPT=2
THE UNIVERSITY OF TORONTO

SUBROUTINE	ORDER OF MATRIX OR SYSTEM				
	N=10	N=20	N=40	N=60	N=80
Time Unit (Sec)	.002	.020	.12	.41	.93
TRED1	1	1	1	1	1
TRED2	3	1.7	1.7	1.8	2.0
TRBAK1	1	1.4	1.5	1.7	1.6
BANDR(Z)	1	1.4	2.1	2.0	2.2
BANDR	1	.85	.95	.89	.94
BQR	10	6	4	4	5
BANDV	1	.41	.39	.37	.43
REDUC	2	1.1	1.1	1.1	1.1
REDUC2	1	1.0	.99	1.0	1.1
REBAK	1	.68	.82	.80	.79
REBAKB	1	.64	.69	.75	.84
TQL2	6	4.2	4.7	4.4	4.3
TQLRAT	2	.73	.39	.27	.19
BISECT	14	6.2	3.6	2.6	1.9
TINVIT	2	.64	.41	.33	.28

PATHS

	N=10	N=20	N=40	N=60	N=80
RSB (BANDR(Z),TQL2)	8	5.6	6.9	6.5	6.6
RSB (BANDR,TQLRAT)	3	1.6	1.3	1.2	1.1
BANDR,BISECT,BANDV	1+2.1M	.85+.72M	.95+.48M	.89+.41M	.94+.45M
BANDR,BISECT	1+1.4M	.85+.31M	.95+.09M	.89+.04M	.94+.02M
RSG (REDUC,TRED2,TQL2,REBAK)	11	7.7	8.4	8.2	8.2
RSG (REDUC,TRED1,TQLRAT)	4	2.8	2.5	2.4	2.3
REDUC,TRED1,BISECT,TINVIT, TRBAK1,REBAK	3+1.8M	2.1+.44M	2.1+.16M	2.1+.09M	2.1+.06M
REDUC,TRED1,BISECT	3+1.4M	2.1+.31M	2.1+.09M	2.1+.04M	2.1+.02M

TABLE 11

SUMMARY OF EXECUTION TIMES FOR THE
EISPACK SUBROUTINES INCLUDED IN THE PATHS FOR
GENERALIZED REAL MATRIX SYSTEMS AND
SINGULAR VALUE DECOMPOSITION

MACHINE: IBM 370/165, Fortran H Extended, OPT=2
THE UNIVERSITY OF TORONTO

	ORDER OF MATRIX OR SYSTEM				
SUBROUTINE	N=10	N=20	N=40	N=60	N=80
Time Unit (Sec)	.003	.015	.13	.46	1.2
ELMHES	1	1	1	1	1
QZHES(Z)	6	7.6	7.2	7.1	6.4
QZHES	5	6.7	5.9	5.9	5.1
QZIT(Z)	19	24	18	17	13
QZIT	15	15	9.6	8.6	6.3
QZVAL(Z)	-	.20	.06	.03	.01
QZVAL	-	.24	.06	.02	.01
QZVEC	2	2.0	1.5	1.5	1.3
SVD(U)	9	9.6	7.1	6.2	5.2
SVD(V)	10	9.7	7.2	6.4	5.4
SVD	7	4.8	2.8	2.3	2.1
MINFIT	10	9.4	7.2	6.5	5.4
PATHS					
RGG (QZHES(Z),QZIT(Z), QZVAL(Z),QZVEC)	28	33	27	26	21
RGG (QZHES,QZIT,QZVAL)	21	22	16	14	11

TABLE 12

SUMMARY OF EXECUTION TIMES FOR THE
EISPACK SUBROUTINES INCLUDED IN THE PATHS FOR
REAL SYMMETRIC BAND MATRICES AND
GENERALIZED REAL SYMMETRIC MATRIX SYSTEMS

MACHINE: IBM 370/168 Mod 3, Fortran H Extended, OPT=2
STANFORD UNIVERSITY

	ORDER OF MATRIX OR SYSTEM				
SUBROUTINE	N=10	N=20	N=40	N=60	N=80
Time Unit (Sec)	.003	.015	.097	.31	.71
TRED1	1	1	1	1	1
TRED2	2	1.8	1.9	2.0	2.0
TRBAK1	1	1.5	1.6	1.7	1.7
BANDR(Z)	1	1.4	1.9	2.0	2.1
BANDR	1	.78	.91	.95	.95
BQR	5	6	4	4	4
BANDV	-	.38	.33	.31	.30
REDUC	1	1.2	1.1	1.2	1.1
REDUC2	1	1.1	1.1	1.1	1.1
REBAK	1	.72	.77	.80	.79
REBAKB	1	.69	.77	.83	.85
TQL2	4	4.8	4.9	4.7	4.6
TQLRAT	1	.88	.45	.29	.21
BISECT	10	7.0	4.1	2.9	2.1
TINVIT	1	.64	.38	.29	.28

PATHS

RSB (BANDR(Z),TQL2)	5	6.2	6.8	6.8	6.7
RSB (BANDR,TQLRAT)	2	1.7	1.4	1.2	1.2
BANDR,BISECT,BANDV	1+1.4M	.78+.73M	.91+.43M	.95+.36M	.95+.33M
BANDR,BISECT	1+1.0M	.78+.35M	.91+.10M	.95+.05M	.95+.03M
RSG (REDUC,TRED2,TQL2,REBAK)	8	8.4	8.8	8.7	8.5
RSG (REDUC,TRED1,TQLRAT)	4	3.0	2.6	2.4	2.3
REDUC,TRED1,BISECT,TINVIT, TRBAK1,REBAK	2+1.2M	2.2+.49M	2.1+.17M	2.1+.09M	2.1+.06M
REDUC,TRED1,BISECT	2+1.0M	2.2+.35M	2.1+.10M	2.1+.05M	2.1+.03M

TABLE 13

SUMMARY OF EXECUTION TIMES FOR THE
EISPACK SUBROUTINES INCLUDED IN THE PATHS FOR
GENERALIZED REAL MATRIX SYSTEMS AND
SINGULAR VALUE DECOMPOSITION

MACHINE: IBM 370/168 Mod 3, Fortran H Extended, OPT=2
STANFORD UNIVERSITY

		ORDER OF MATRIX OR SYSTEM		
SUBROUTINE	N=10	N=20	N=40	N=60	N=80
Time Unit (Sec)	.002	.013	.10	.34	.83
ELMHES	1	1	1	1	1
QZHES(Z)	7	7.5	7.4	7.2	7.0
QZHES	6	6.5	6.1	5.9	5.8
QZIT(Z)	22	22	18	17	14
QZIT	17	15	9.9	8.8	7.2
QZVAL(Z)	1	.23	.06	.02	.02
QZVAL	1	.21	.06	.02	.02
QZVEC	2	1.9	1.6	1.5	1.4
SVD(U)	11	8.9	7.2	6.6	6.2
SVD(V)	11	9.0	7.2	6.6	6.2
SVD	8	4.7	3.1	2.6	2.3
MINFIT	12	9.2	7.3	6.7	6.3

PATHS

	N=10	N=20	N=40	N=60	N=80
RGG (QZHES(Z),QZIT(Z), QZVAL(Z),QZVEC)	32	32	27	25	23
RGG (QZHES,QZIT,QZVAL)	24	21	16	15	13

TABLE 14

SUMMARY OF EXECUTION TIMES FOR THE
EISPACK SUBROUTINES INCLUDED IN THE PATHS FOR
REAL SYMMETRIC BAND MATRICES AND
GENERALIZED REAL SYMMETRIC MATRIX SYSTEMS

MACHINE: Burroughs 6700, Fortran IV (2.6)
UNIVERSITY OF CALIFORNIA, SAN DIEGO

	ORDER OF MATRIX OR SYSTEM			
SUBROUTINE	N=10	N=20	N=40	N=60
Time Unit (Sec)	.078	.53	4.1	14
TRED1	1	1	1	1
TRED2	1.8	2.0	2.2	2.1
TRBAK1	1.3	1.5	1.7	1.7
BANDR(Z)	1.1	2.0	2.5	2.5
BANDR	.43	.67	.81	.79
BQR	5	5	4	4
BANDV	.40	.36	.36	.36
REDUC	1.1	1.1	1.2	1.1
REDUC2	1.1	1.2	1.2	1.2
REBAK	.76	.82	.85	.85
REBAKB	.72	.77	.85	.93
TQL2	4.5	4.9	4.8	4.7
TQLRAT	.75	.36	.17	.11
BISECT	4.2	2.2	1.1	.76
TINVIT	.81	.45	.25	.19

PATHS

	N=10	N=20	N=40	N=60
RSB (BANDR(Z),TQL2)	5.7	6.9	7.3	7.3
RSB (BANDR,TQLRAT)	1.2	1.0	.98	.90
BANDR,BISECT,BANDV	.43+.82M	.67+.47M	.81+.39M	.79+.37M
BANDR,BISECT	.43+.42M	.67+.11M	.81+.03M	.79+.01M
RSG (REDUC,TRED2,TQL2,REBAK)	8.2	8.9	9.0	8.8
RSG (REDUC,TRED1,TQLRAT)	2.9	2.5	2.3	2.3
REDUC,TRED1,BISECT,TINVIT, TRBAK1,REBAK	2.1+.70M	2.1+.25M	2.1+.10M	2.1+.06M
REDUC,TRED1,BISECT	2.1+.42M	2.1+.11M	2.1+.03M	2.1+.01M

TABLE 15

SUMMARY OF EXECUTION TIMES FOR THE
EISPACK SUBROUTINES INCLUDED IN THE PATHS FOR
GENERALIZED REAL MATRIX SYSTEMS AND
SINGULAR VALUE DECOMPOSITION

MACHINE: Burroughs 6700, Fortran IV (2.6)
UNIVERSITY OF CALIFORNIA, SAN DIEGO

SUBROUTINE	ORDER OF MATRIX OR SYSTEM			
	N=10	N=20	N=40	N=60
Time Unit (Sec)	.087	.75	6.5	20
ELMHES	1	1	1	1
QZHES(Z)	6.6	6.1	6.2	6.2
QZHES	5.6	5.2	5.0	5.2
QZIT(Z)	16	14	11	11
QZIT	11	8.5	5.5	5.7
QZVAL(Z)	.20	.06	.01	.01
QZVAL	.20	.05	.01	.01
QZVEC	1.5	1.2	1.0	.99
SVD(U)	6.5	5.3	4.8	4.7
SVD(V)	6.4	5.3	4.7	4.7
SVD	3.2	2.2	1.7	1.7
MINFIT	6.4	5.4	4.8	4.5
PATHS				
RGG (QZHES(Z),QZIT(Z), QZVAL(Z),QZVEC)	24	22	19	18
RGG (QZHES,QZIT,QZVAL)	16	14	11	11

TABLE 16

SUMMARY OF EXECUTION TIMES FOR THE
EISPACK SUBROUTINES INCLUDED IN THE PATHS FOR
REAL SYMMETRIC BAND MATRICES AND
GENERALIZED REAL SYMMETRIC MATRIX SYSTEMS

MACHINE: CDC 6600, FTN Extended Version 4 Compiler
KIRTLAND AIR FORCE BASE

	ORDER OF MATRIX OR SYSTEM				
SUBROUTINE	N=10	N=20	N=40	N=60	N=80
Time Unit (Sec)	.007	.033	.20	.62	1.4
TRED1	1	1	1	1	1
TRED2	1.5	1.9	2.0	2.1	2.2
TRBAK1	1.1	1.4	1.7	1.7	1.7
BANDR(Z)	.81	1.3	1.7	1.8	1.8
BANDR	.60	.75	.75	.81	.79
BQR	6	6	5	6	5
BANDV	.60	.49	.43	.40	.39
REDUC	1.4	1.3	1.3	1.3	1.3
REDUC2	1.2	1.3	1.3	1.3	1.3
REBAK	.78	.86	.96	.94	.98
REBAKB	.77	.81	.85	.87	.89
TQL2	3.0	3.6	3.7	3.8	3.8
TQLRAT	.99	.64	.34	.24	.18
BISECT	12	9.0	5.6	4.0	3.1
TINVIT	.97	.70	.43	.34	.41

PATHS

RSB (BANDR(Z),TQL2)	3.8	4.9	5.4	5.6	5.6
RSB (BANDR,TQLRAT)	1.6	1.4	1.1	1.1	.97
BANDR,BISECT,BANDV	.60+1.8M	.75+.94M	.75+.57M	.81+.47M	.79+.43M
BANDR,BISECT	.60+1.2M	.75+.45M	.75+.14M	.81+.07M	.79+.04M
RSG (REDUC,TRED2,TQL2,REBAK)	6.7	7.6	8.0	8.1	8.2
RSG (REDUC,TRED1,TQLRAT)	3.3	2.9	2.7	2.5	2.4
REDUC,TRED1,BISECT,TINVIT, TRBAK1,REBAK	2.4+1.5M	2.3+.60M	2.3+.22M	2.3+.12M	2.3+.08M
REDUC,TRED1,BISECT	2.4+1.2M	2.3+.45M	2.3+.14M	2.3+.07M	2.3+.04M

TABLE 17

SUMMARY OF EXECUTION TIMES FOR THE
EISPACK SUBROUTINES INCLUDED IN THE PATHS FOR
GENERALIZED REAL MATRIX SYSTEMS AND
SINGULAR VALUE DECOMPOSITION

MACHINE: CDC 6600, FTN Extended Version 4 Compiler
KIRTLAND AIR FORCE BASE

| SUBROUTINE | ORDER OF MATRIX OR SYSTEM | | | | |
	N=10	N=20	N=40	N=60	N=80
Time Unit (Sec)	.006	.037	.27	.85	2.0
ELMHES	1	1	1	1	1
QZHES(Z)	5.6	6.2	6.2	6.5	6.3
QZHES	5.3	5.3	5.2	5.4	5.2
QZIT(Z)	14	14	11	11	10
QZIT	9.9	8.7	6.0	5.6	4.7
QZVAL(Z)	.48	.13	.03	.01	.01
QZVAL	.55	.14	.04	.02	.01
QZVEC	1.9	1.5	1.1	1.1	1.0
SVD(U)	6.7	5.6	5.0	4.7	4.6
SVD(V)	6.7	5.5	4.9	4.8	4.5
SVD	4.3	3.0	2.2	2.0	1.9
MINFIT	7.0	5.8	5.0	4.9	4.6
PATHS					
RGG (QZHES(Z),QZIT(Z), QZVAL(Z),QZVEC)	22	22	19	19	17
RGG (QZHES,QZIT,QZVAL)	16	14	11	11	9.9

TABLE 18

SUMMARY OF EXECUTION TIMES FOR THE
EISPACK SUBROUTINES INCLUDED IN THE PATHS FOR
REAL SYMMETRIC BAND MATRICES AND
GENERALIZED REAL SYMMETRIC MATRIX SYSTEMS

MACHINE: CDC CYBER 175, FTN 4.6+420 Compiler, OPT=2
NASA LANGLEY RESEARCH CENTER

SUBROUTINE	ORDER OF MATRIX OR SYSTEM				
	N=10	N=20	N=40	N=60	N=80
Time Unit (Sec)	.002	.008	.051	.16	.37
TRED1	1	1	1	1	1
TRED2	2	2.0	2.1	2.1	2.2
TRBAK1	1	1.3	1.6	1.6	1.7
BANDR(Z)	1	1.6	1.9	1.9	2.0
BANDR	1	.92	.84	.77	.76
BQR	6	6	4	5	4
BANDV	1	.55	.54	.51	.56
REDUC	1	1.4	1.3	1.2	1.2
REDUC2	1	1.4	1.3	1.2	1.2
REBAK	1	.83	.86	.85	.87
REBAKB	1	.82	.84	.85	.85
TQL2	4	5.1	5.3	5.0	5.1
TQLRAT	1	.53	.27	.18	.12
BISECT	13	9.7	5.5	3.8	2.9
TINVIT	1	.66	.43	.31	.36

PATHS

	N=10	N=20	N=40	N=60	N=80
RSB (BANDR(Z),TQL2)	5	6.7	7.2	6.9	7.1
RSB (BANDR,TQLRAT)	2	1.5	1.1	.95	.88
BANDR,BISECT,BANDV	1+2.0M	.92+1.0M	.84+.68M	.77+.57M	.76+.60M
BANDR,BISECT	1+1.3M	.92+.49M	.84+.14M	.77+.06M	.76+.04M
RSG (REDUC,TRED2,TQL2,REBAK)	7	9.3	9.5	9.2	9.4
RSG (REDUC,TRED1,TQLRAT)	3	2.9	2.6	2.4	2.3
REDUC,TRED1,BISECT,TINVIT, TRBAK1,REBAK	2+1.6M	2.4+.63M	2.3+.21M	2.2+.11M	2.2+.07M
REDUC,TRED1,BISECT	2+1.3M	2.4+.49M	2.3+.14M	2.2+.06M	2.2+.04M

TABLE 19

SUMMARY OF EXECUTION TIMES FOR THE
EISPACK SUBROUTINES INCLUDED IN THE PATHS FOR
GENERALIZED REAL MATRIX SYSTEMS AND
SINGULAR VALUE DECOMPOSITION

MACHINE: CDC CYBER 175, FTN 4.6+420 Compiler, OPT=2
NASA LANGLEY RESEARCH CENTER

	ORDER OF MATRIX OR SYSTEM				
SUBROUTINE	N=10	N=20	N=40	N=60	N=80
Time Unit (Sec)	.001	.010	.076	.25	.57
ELMHES	1	1	1	1	1
QZHES(Z)	8	6.4	6.4	6.3	6.4
QZHES	6	5.3	5.2	5.1	5.1
QZIT(Z)	22	18	15	14	13
QZIT	16	11	8.0	7.1	6.5
QZVAL(Z)	-	.12	.04	.02	.01
QZVAL	-	.10	.04	.02	.01
QZVEC	2	1.4	1.1	.98	.91
SVD(U)	9	5.6	4.7	4.3	4.2
SVD(V)	9	5.6	4.7	4.3	4.2
SVD	6	3.1	2.3	1.9	1.8
MINFIT	9	5.6	4.8	4.4	4.2
PATHS					
RGG (QZHES(Z),QZIT(Z), QZVAL(Z),QZVEC)	32	26	22	21	20
RGG (QZHES,QZIT,QZVAL)	23	17	13	12	12

TABLE 20

SUMMARY OF EXECUTION TIMES FOR THE
EISPACK SUBROUTINES INCLUDED IN THE PATHS FOR
REAL SYMMETRIC BAND MATRICES AND
GENERALIZED REAL SYMMETRIC MATRIX SYSTEMS

MACHINE: CDC 7600, Local Compiler
NATIONAL CENTER FOR ATMOSPHERIC RESEARCH

SUBROUTINE	ORDER OF MATRIX OR SYSTEM				
	N=10	N=20	N=40	N=60	N=80
Time Unit (Sec)	.001	.007	.041	.13	.28
TRED1	1	1	1	1	1
TRED2	2	1.8	1.9	2.0	2.0
TRBAK1	2	1.3	1.5	1.5	1.6
BANDR(Z)	1	1.5	2.1	2.3	2.4
BANDR	1	.88	1.1	1.2	1.3
BQR	9	7	6	6	7
BANDV	1	.60	.89	.94	1.0
REDUC	2	1.2	1.2	1.1	1.1
REDUC2	2	1.2	1.2	1.2	1.2
REBAK	1	.84	.87	.87	.87
REBAKB	1	.74	.77	.77	.77
TQL2	4	3.4	3.6	3.5	3.5
TQLRAT	2	.71	.43	.29	.21
BISECT	22	11	7.0	5.0	3.9
TINVIT	1	.68	.39	.32	.31

PATHS

	N=10	N=20	N=40	N=60	N=80
RSB (BANDR(Z),TQL2)	5	5.0	5.7	5.8	5.9
RSB (BANDR,TQLRAT)	2	1.6	1.6	1.5	1.5
BANDR,BISECT,BANDV	1+3.0M	.88+1.2M	1.1+1.1M	1.2+1.0M	1.3+1.1M
BANDR,BISECT	1+2.2M	.88+.56M	1.1+.17M	1.2+.08M	1.3+.05M
RSG (REDUC,TRED2,TQL2,REBAK)	9	7.2	7.5	7.5	7.5
RSG (REDUC,TRED1,TQLRAT)	5	2.9	2.6	2.4	2.3
REDUC,TRED1,BISECT,TINVIT, TRBAK1,REBAK	3+2.5M	2.2+.70M	2.1+.24M	2.1+.13M	2.1+.08M
REDUC,TRED1,BISECT	3+2.2M	2.2+.56M	2.1+.17M	2.1+.08M	2.1+.05M

TABLE 21

SUMMARY OF EXECUTION TIMES FOR THE
EISPACK SUBROUTINES INCLUDED IN THE PATHS FOR
GENERALIZED REAL MATRIX SYSTEMS AND
SINGULAR VALUE DECOMPOSITION

MACHINE: CDC 7600, Local Compiler
NATIONAL CENTER FOR ATMOSPHERIC RESEARCH

SUBROUTINE	ORDER OF MATRIX OR SYSTEM				
	N=10	N=20	N=40	N=60	N=80
Time Unit (Sec)	.001	.007	.050	.16	.38
ELMHES	1	1	1	1	1
QZHES(Z)	6	6.5	6.5	6.5	6.4
QZHES	6	5.5	5.4	5.4	5.3
QZIT(Z)	17	16	13	13	11
QZIT	13	11	7.3	6.6	5.5
QZVAL(Z)	-	.12	.03	.01	.01
QZVAL	-	.12	.04	.01	.01
QZVEC	2	1.5	1.2	1.1	1.1
SVD(U)	8	5.8	4.8	4.5	4.3
SVD(V)	7	5.6	4.8	4.4	4.2
SVD	5	3.4	2.4	2.1	1.9
MINFIT	8	5.8	4.8	4.5	4.2

PATHS

RGG (QZHES(Z),QZIT(Z), QZVAL(Z),QZVEC)	26	24	21	20	19
RGG (QZHES,QZIT,QZVAL)	19	16	13	12	11

TABLE 22

SUMMARY OF EXECUTION TIMES FOR THE
EISPACK SUBROUTINES INCLUDED IN THE PATHS FOR
REAL SYMMETRIC BAND MATRICES AND
GENERALIZED REAL SYMMETRIC MATRIX SYSTEMS

MACHINE: CDC 7600, CHAT Compiler, Optimized
LAWRENCE LIVERMORE LABORATORY

	ORDER OF MATRIX OR SYSTEM				
SUBROUTINE	N=10	N=20	N=40	N=60	N=80
Time Unit (Sec)	.002	.011	.074	.24	.54
TRED1	1	1	1	1	1
TRED2	1.5	1.5	1.5	1.5	1.5
TRBAK1	.95	1.0	1.0	1.0	1.0
BANDR(Z)	.72	1.1	1.2	1.3	1.3
BANDR	.40	.59	.66	.67	.68
BQR	5	5	4	5	5
BANDV	.56	.50	.47	.47	.47
REDUC	1.2	1.2	1.2	1.2	1.2
REDUC2	1.1	.96	.90	.86	.85
REBAK	.58	.51	.45	.42	.41
REBAKB	.61	.58	.54	.52	.52
TQL2	2.9	3.4	4.8	4.9	5.1
TQLRAT	.77	.42	.21	.13	.10
BISECT	12	7.5	4.1	2.8	2.1
TINVIT	.83	.50	.28	.21	.21

PATHS

	N=10	N=20	N=40	N=60	N=80
RSB (BANDR(Z),TQL2)	3.6	4.4	6.0	6.1	6.4
RSB (BANDR,TQLRAT)	1.2	1.0	.87	.80	.78
BANDR,BISECT,BANDV	.40+1.8M	.59+.87M	.66+.57M	.67+.52M	.68+.50M
BANDR,BISECT	.40+1.2M	.59+.37M	.66+.10M	.67+.05M	.68+.03M
RSG (REDUC,TRED2,TQL2,REBAK)	6.1	6.6	8.0	8.0	8.3
RSG (REDUC,TRED1,TQLRAT)	3.0	2.6	2.4	2.4	2.3
REDUC,TRED1,BISECT,TINVIT, TRBAK1,REBAK	2.2+1.5M	2.2+.48M	2.2+.15M	2.2+.07M	2.2+.05M
REDUC,TRED1,BISECT	2.2+1.2M	2.2+.37M	2.2+.10M	2.2+.05M	2.2+.03M

TABLE 23

SUMMARY OF EXECUTION TIMES FOR THE
EISPACK SUBROUTINES INCLUDED IN THE PATHS FOR
GENERALIZED REAL MATRIX SYSTEMS AND
SINGULAR VALUE DECOMPOSITION

MACHINE: CDC 7600, CHAT Compiler, Optimized
LAWRENCE LIVERMORE LABORATORY

	ORDER OF MATRIX OR SYSTEM				
SUBROUTINE	N=10	N=20	N=40	N=60	N=80
Time Unit (Sec)	.001	.010	.077	.26	.61
ELMHES	1	1	1	1	1
QZHES(Z)	5.8	5.6	5.6	5.5	5.5
QZHES	5.0	4.7	4.6	4.5	4.5
QZIT(Z)	17	16	13	12	11
QZIT	12	10	7.6	6.5	5.7
QZVAL(Z)	.28	.08	.02	.01	.01
QZVAL	.26	.08	.02	.01	.01
QZVEC	1.7	1.2	.98	.89	.85
SVD(U)	6.7	5.2	5.2	5.4	5.3
SVD(V)	6.6	5.2	4.4	5.4	5.3
SVD	4.1	2.8	2.1	2.0	1.9
MINFIT	6.7	5.1	5.0	5.4	5.3
PATHS					
RGG (QZHES(Z),QZIT(Z), QZVAL(Z),QZVEC)	24	23	20	18	18
RGG (QZHES,QZIT,QZVAL)	17	15	12	11	10

TABLE 24

SUMMARY OF EXECUTION TIMES FOR THE
EISPACK SUBROUTINES INCLUDED IN THE PATHS FOR
REAL SYMMETRIC BAND MATRICES AND
GENERALIZED REAL SYMMETRIC MATRIX SYSTEMS

MACHINE: CDC 6400, FTN 3.0 Compiler, OPT=2
NORTHWESTERN UNIVERSITY

SUBROUTINE	ORDER OF MATRIX OR SYSTEM				
	N=10	N=20	N=40	N=60	N=80
Time Unit (Sec)	.017	.10	.68	2.1	4.9
TRED1	1	1	1	1	1
TRED2	1.9	1.8	1.9	2.0	2.0
TRBAK1	1.2	1.3	1.5	1.5	1.5
BANDR(Z)	1.2	1.6	2.0	2.2	2.3
BANDR	.65	.97	1.1	1.2	1.2
BQR	8	6	6	3	7
BANDV	.65	.39	.37	.36	.36
REDUC	1.5	1.2	1.2	1.1	1.1
REDUC2	1.4	1.3	1.2	1.2	1.1
REBAK	1.0	.83	.82	.81	.81
REBAKB	.94	.84	.82	.81	.81
TQL2	4.1	4.3	4.6	4.6	4.7
TQLRAT	1.4	.73	.36	.25	.17
BISECT	11	6.2	3.5	2.5	1.9
TINVIT	1.2	.64	.36	.29	.30

PATHS

RSB (BANDR(Z),TQL2)	5.3	5.9	6.6	6.7	6.9
RSB (BANDR,TQLRAT)	2.1	1.7	1.5	1.4	1.4
BANDR,BISECT,BANDV	.65+1.8M	.97+.70M	1.1+.46M	1.2+.40M	1.2+.38M
BANDR,BISECT	.65+1.1M	.97+.31M	1.1+.09M	1.2+.04M	1.2+.02M
RSG (REDUC,TRED2,TQL2,REBAK)	8.5	8.2	8.5	8.5	8.6
RSG (REDUC,TRED1,TQLRAT)	3.9	2.9	2.5	2.4	2.3
REDUC,TRED1,BISECT,TINVIT, TRBAK1,REBAK	2.5+1.5M	2.2+.45M	2.2+.15M	2.1+.08M	2.1+.06M
REDUC,TRED1,BISECT	2.5+1.1M	2.2+.31M	2.2+.09M	2.1+.04M	2.1+.02M

TABLE 25

SUMMARY OF EXECUTION TIMES FOR THE
EISPACK SUBROUTINES INCLUDED IN THE PATHS FOR
GENERALIZED REAL MATRIX SYSTEMS AND
SINGULAR VALUE DECOMPOSITION

MACHINE: CDC 6400, FTN 3.0 Compiler, OPT=2
NORTHWESTERN UNIVERSITY

	ORDER OF MATRIX OR SYSTEM				
SUBROUTINE	N=10	N=20	N=40	N=60	N=80
Time Unit (Sec)	.015	.11	.80	2.7	6.3
ELMHES	1	1	1	1	1
QZHES(Z)	7.3	7.0	7.2	7.0	7.0
QZHES	6.9	6.0	6.1	5.9	5.8
QZIT(Z)	24	16	18	15	14
QZIT	17	9.6	9.7	7.7	6.9
QZVAL(Z)	.53	.12	.05	.02	.01
QZVAL	.47	.13	.05	.02	.01
QZVEC	2.3	1.6	1.5	1.3	1.2
SVD(U)	9.5	7.0	6.5	5.8	5.7
SVD(V)	9.3	6.9	6.4	5.8	5.6
SVD	5.4	3.3	2.5	2.1	2.0
MINFIT	10	7.4	7.1	6.3	6.2
PATHS					
RGG (QZHES(Z),QZIT(Z), QZVAL(Z),QZVEC)	34	24	26	23	22
RGG (QZHES,QZIT,QZVAL)	25	16	16	14	13

TABLE 26

SUMMARY OF EXECUTION TIMES FOR THE
EISPACK SUBROUTINES INCLUDED IN THE PATHS FOR
REAL SYMMETRIC BAND MATRICES AND
GENERALIZED REAL SYMMETRIC MATRIX SYSTEMS

MACHINE: CDC 6400/6500, FUN Compiler
PURDUE UNIVERSITY

	ORDER OF MATRIX OR SYSTEM				
SUBROUTINE	N=10	N=20	N=40	N=60	N=80
Time Unit (Sec)	.024	.13	.83	2.5	5.6
TRED1	1	1	1	1	1
TRED2	1.6	1.8	1.9	2.0	2.0
TRBAK1	1.1	1.3	1.5	1.6	1.6
BANDR(Z)	.96	2.0	2.8	3.2	3.4
BANDR	.60	1.3	1.8	2.0	2.2
BQR	6	6	5	5	5
BANDV	.49	.43	.41	.40	.40
REDUC	1.1	1.1	1.1	1.1	1.1
REDUC2	1.1	1.1	1.1	1.1	1.1
REBAK	.72	.75	.74	.75	.74
REBAKB	.75	.80	.82	.83	.83
TQL2	3.6	4.2	4.5	4.5	4.5
TQLRAT	.87	.53	.29	.20	.15
BISECT	9.1	6.0	3.6	2.6	1.9
TINVIT	.98	.67	.43	.34	.34

PATHS

	N=10	N=20	N=40	N=60	N=80
RSB (BANDR(Z),TQL2)	4.6	6.2	7.4	7.7	7.9
RSB (BANDR,TQLRAT)	1.5	1.8	2.1	2.2	2.3
BANDR,BISECT,BANDV	.60+1.4M	1.3+.73M	1.8+.50M	2.0+.44M	2.2+.42M
BANDR,BISECT	.60+.91M	1.3+.30M	1.8+.09M	2.0+.04M	2.2+.02M
RSG (REDUC,TRED2,TQL2,REBAK)	7.1	7.8	8.3	8.4	8.4
RSG (REDUC,TRED1,TQLRAT)	3.0	2.7	2.4	2.3	2.3
REDUC,TRED1,BISECT,TINVIT, TRBAK1,REBAK	2.1+1.2M	2.1+.43M	2.1+.16M	2.1+.09M	2.1+.06M
REDUC,TRED1,BISECT	2.1+.91M	2.1+.30M	2.1+.09M	2.1+.04M	2.1+.02M

TABLE 27

SUMMARY OF EXECUTION TIMES FOR THE
EISPACK SUBROUTINES INCLUDED IN THE PATHS FOR
GENERALIZED REAL MATRIX SYSTEMS AND
SINGULAR VALUE DECOMPOSITION

MACHINE: CDC 6400/6500, FUN Compiler
PURDUE UNIVERSITY

	ORDER OF MATRIX OR SYSTEM				
SUBROUTINE	N=10	N=20	N=40	N=60	N=80
Time Unit (Sec)	.017	.12	.92	3.0	6.9
ELMHES	1	1	1	1	1
QZHES(Z)	7.5	7.3	7.2	7.3	7.3
QZHES	6.7	6.3	6.1	6.1	6.1
QZIT(Z)	21	20	17	16	15
QZIT	15	12	9.0	8.0	7.2
QZVAL(Z)	.39	.12	.03	.01	.01
QZVAL	.38	.12	.03	.02	.01
QZVEC	2.4	1.8	1.5	1.4	1.4
SVD(U)	9.7	7.7	6.7	6.5	6.4
SVD(V)	9.5	7.7	6.7	6.5	6.4
SVD	5.4	3.4	2.5	2.2	2.1
MINFIT	9.7	7.4	6.3	6.1	6.0

PATHS

RGG (QZHES(Z),QZIT(Z), QZVAL(Z),QZVEC)	31	29	26	25	23
RGG (QZHES,QZIT,QZVAL)	22	19	15	14	13

TABLE 28

SUMMARY OF EXECUTION TIMES FOR THE
EISPACK SUBROUTINES INCLUDED IN THE PATHS FOR
REAL SYMMETRIC BAND MATRICES AND
GENERALIZED REAL SYMMETRIC MATRIX SYSTEMS

MACHINE: CDC 6600/6400, RUN Compiler
THE UNIVERSITY OF TEXAS

	ORDER OF MATRIX OR SYSTEM				
SUBROUTINE	N=10	N=20	N=40	N=60	N=80
Time Unit (Sec)	.016	.048	.22	.65	1.4
TRED1	1	1	1	1	1
TRED2	1.1	1.7	2.0	2.1	2.1
TRBAK1	1.1	1.4	1.7	1.8	1.9
BANDR(Z)	1.1	2.0	3.6	4.3	4.7
BANDR	1.1	1.4	2.4	2.8	3.0
BQR	4	6	6	8	7
BANDV	1.0	.66	.58	.57	.56
REDUC	1.1	1.3	1.3	1.3	1.3
REDUC2	1.0	1.1	1.1	1.0	1.0
REBAK	1.1	.70	.72	.66	.65
REBAKB	1.0	.98	1.0	1.0	1.0
TQL2	2.1	3.1	4.1	4.1	4.2
TQLRAT	1.0	.70	.44	.30	.22
BISECT	7.2	8.2	6.4	4.8	3.8
TINVIT	1.0	1.0	.66	.49	.47

PATHS

	N=10	N=20	N=40	N=60	N=80
RSB (BANDR(Z),TQL2)	3.1	5.1	7.7	8.3	8.9
RSB (BANDR,TQLRAT)	2.1	2.1	2.8	3.1	3.3
BANDR,BISECT,BANDV	1.1+1.7M	1.4+1.1M	2.4+.74M	2.8+.65M	3.0+.61M
BANDR,BISECT	1.1+.72M	1.4+.41M	2.4+.16M	2.8+.08M	3.0+.05M
RSG (REDUC,TRED2,TQL2,REBAK)	5.4	6.8	8.1	8.1	8.3
RSG (REDUC,TRED1,TQLRAT)	3.1	3.0	2.7	2.6	2.5
REDUC,TRED1,BISECT,TINVIT, TRBAK1,REBAK	2.1+1.0M	2.3+.56M	2.3+.24M	2.3+.13M	2.3+.09M
REDUC,TRED1,BISECT	2.1+.72M	2.3+.41M	2.3+.16M	2.3+.08M	2.3+.05M

TABLE 29

SUMMARY OF EXECUTION TIMES FOR THE
EISPACK SUBROUTINES INCLUDED IN THE PATHS FOR
GENERALIZED REAL MATRIX SYSTEMS AND
SINGULAR VALUE DECOMPOSITION

MACHINE: CDC 6600/6400, RUN Compiler
THE UNIVERSITY OF TEXAS

			ORDER OF MATRIX OR SYSTEM		
SUBROUTINE	N=10	N=20	N=40	N=60	N=80
Time Unit (Sec)	.016	.048	.25	.78	1.8
ELMHES	1	1	1	1	1
QZHES(Z)	2.9	5.5	7.3	7.5	7.6
QZHES	2.8	4.8	6.1	6.2	6.2
QZIT(Z)	7.2	15	16	16	15
QZIT	5.5	9.7	9.2	8.4	7.6
QZVAL(Z)	.99	.33	.06	.02	.02
QZVAL	.99	.34	.07	.03	.02
QZVEC	.97	1.7	1.8	1.7	1.6
SVD(U)	3.9	6.4	7.5	7.4	7.3
SVD(V)	3.9	6.3	7.4	7.3	7.3
SVD	2.2	3.1	2.8	2.6	2.4
MINFIT	3.8	5.7	6.3	6.1	6.0
PATHS					
RGG (QZHES(Z),QZIT(Z), QZVAL(Z),QZVEC)	12	22	26	25	24
RGG (QZHES,QZIT,QZVAL)	9.3	15	15	15	14

TABLE 30

SUMMARY OF EXECUTION TIMES FOR THE
EISPACK SUBROUTINES INCLUDED IN THE PATHS FOR
REAL SYMMETRIC BAND MATRICES AND
GENERALIZED REAL SYMMETRIC MATRIX SYSTEMS

MACHINE: Honeywell 6070 Fortran-Y(SR-H) Optimized
BELL LABORATORIES

SUBROUTINE	ORDER OF MATRIX OR SYSTEM				
	N=10	N=20	N=40	N=60	N=80
Time Unit (Sec)	.012	.072	.49	1.6	3.6
TRED1	1	1	1	1	1
TRED2	1.6	1.8	1.9	2.0	2.0
TRBAK1	.94	1.2	1.3	1.4	1.4
BANDR(Z)	.97	1.8	2.3	2.5	2.6
BANDR	.53	.84	1.0	1.1	1.1
BQR	6	5	4	5	4
BANDV	.51	.45	.42	.42	.42
REDUC	1.1	1.1	1.1	1.1	1.1
REDUC2	1.1	1.0	1.0	1.1	1.1
REBAK	.81	.84	.85	.86	.87
REBAKB	.69	.72	.75	.76	.78
TQL2	4.1	4.4	4.4	4.2	4.2
TQLRAT	1.1	.62	.32	.21	.15
BISECT	5.3	3.1	1.6	1.1	.81
TINVIT	1.1	.71	.40	.30	.29

PATHS

	N=10	N=20	N=40	N=60	N=80
RSB (BANDR(Z),TQL2)	5.0	6.2	6.7	6.7	6.8
RSB (BANDR,TQLRAT)	1.7	1.5	1.3	1.3	1.3
BANDR,BISECT,BANDV	.53+1.0M	.84+.60M	1.0+.46M	1.1+.44M	1.1+.43M
BANDR,BISECT	.53+.53M	.84+.15M	1.0+.04M	1.1+.02M	1.1+.01M
RSG (REDUC,TRED2,TQL2,REBAK)	7.5	8.1	8.3	8.1	8.2
RSG (REDUC,TRED1,TQLRAT)	3.2	2.7	2.4	2.3	2.3
REDUC,TRED1,BISECT,TINVIT, TRBAK1,REBAK	2.1+.82M	2.1+.29M	2.1+.10M	2.1+.06M	2.1+.04M
REDUC,TRED1,BISECT	2.1+.53M	2.1+.15M	2.1+.04M	2.1+.02M	2.1+.01M

TABLE 31

SUMMARY OF EXECUTION TIMES FOR THE
EISPACK SUBROUTINES INCLUDED IN THE PATHS FOR
GENERALIZED REAL MATRIX SYSTEMS AND
SINGULAR VALUE DECOMPOSITION

MACHINE: Honeywell 6070 Fortran-Y(SR-H) Optimized
BELL LABORATORIES

SUBROUTINE	ORDER OF MATRIX OR SYSTEM				
	N=10	N=20	N=40	N=60	N=80
Time Unit (Sec)	.009	.069	.54	1.8	4.2
ELMHES	1	1	1	1	1
QZHES(Z)	7.4	7.2	7.1	7.0	7.0
QZHES	6.4	6.1	5.8	5.7	5.7
QZIT(Z)	17	16	11	11	9.9
QZIT	13	10	6.4	5.6	4.9
QZVAL(Z)	.56	.16	.04	.02	.01
QZVAL	.56	.16	.04	.02	.01
QZVEC	2.1	1.7	1.4	1.3	1.3
SVD(U)	9.1	7.5	6.2	5.9	5.7
SVD(V)	9.0	7.4	6.2	5.9	5.6
SVD	5.4	3.5	2.5	2.2	2.0
MINFIT	9.4	7.6	6.2	5.9	5.7
PATHS					
RGG (QZHES(Z),QZIT(Z), QZVAL(Z),QZVEC)	27	25	20	19	18
RGG (QZHES,QZIT,QZVAL)	20	17	12	11	11

TABLE 32

SUMMARY OF EXECUTION TIMES FOR THE
EISPACK SUBROUTINES INCLUDED IN THE PATHS FOR
REAL SYMMETRIC BAND MATRICES AND
GENERALIZED REAL SYMMETRIC MATRIX SYSTEMS

MACHINE: Univac 1110, Fortran V(9) Compiler
THE UNIVERSITY OF WISCONSIN

	ORDER OF MATRIX OR SYSTEM				
SUBROUTINE	N=10	N=20	N=40	N=60	N=80
Time Unit (Sec)	.012	.065	.40	1.2	2.8
TRED1	1	1	1	1	1
TRED2	1.6	1.7	1.8	1.9	2.0
TRBAK1	.82	1.1	1.3	1.4	1.5
BANDR(Z)	.96	1.9	2.6	2.9	3.1
BANDR	.57	1.1	1.4	1.5	1.6
BQR	9	10	9	8	10
BANDV	.76	.73	.74	.76	.77
REDUC	1.2	1.1	1.1	1.1	1.1
REDUC2	1.2	1.2	1.1	1.1	1.1
REBAK	.82	.84	.84	.85	.85
REBAKB	.72	.76	.79	.81	.81
TQL2	3.3	3.8	4.1	4.0	4.2
TQLRAT	1.0	.66	.38	.26	.20
BISECT	6.4	3.9	2.2	1.5	1.2
TINVIT	1.2	.82	.51	.39	.37

PATHS

	N=10	N=20	N=40	N=60	N=80
RSB (BANDR(Z),TQL2)	4.2	5.7	6.7	6.9	7.2
RSB (BANDR,TQLRAT)	1.6	1.7	1.8	1.8	1.8
BANDR,BISECT,BANDV	.57+1.4M	1.1+.93M	1.4+.80M	1.5+.79M	1.6+.78M
BANDR,BISECT	.57+.64M	1.1+.20M	1.4+.06M	1.5+.03M	1.6+.01M
RSG (REDUC,TRED2,TQL2,REBAK)	6.8	7.4	7.9	7.9	8.1
RSG (REDUC,TRED1,TQLRAT)	3.2	2.8	2.5	2.4	2.3
REDUC,TRED1,BISECT,TINVIT, TRBAK1,REBAK	2.2+.92M	2.1+.33M	2.1+.12M	2.1+.07M	2.1+.05M
REDUC,TRED1,BISECT	2.2+.64M	2.1+.20M	2.1+.06M	2.1+.03M	2.1+.01M

TABLE 33

SUMMARY OF EXECUTION TIMES FOR THE
EISPACK SUBROUTINES INCLUDED IN THE PATHS FOR
GENERALIZED REAL MATRIX SYSTEMS AND
SINGULAR VALUE DECOMPOSITION

MACHINE: Univac 1110, Fortran V(9) Compiler
THE UNIVERSITY OF WISCONSIN

	ORDER OF MATRIX OR SYSTEM				
SUBROUTINE	N=10	N=20	N=40	N=60	N=80
Time Unit (Sec)	.009	.062	.45	1.5	3.4
ELMHES	1	1	1	1	1
QZHES(Z)	6.6	7.0	7.3	7.4	7.5
QZHES	5.8	5.9	6.0	6.1	6.1
QZIT(Z)	17	16	12	12	11
QZIT	13	11	7.0	6.5	5.5
QZVAL(Z)	.38	.12	.04	.02	.01
QZVAL	.39	.12	.04	.02	.01
QZVEC	1.9	1.5	1.3	1.2	1.2
SVD(U)	7.8	6.6	5.8	5.7	5.6
SVD(V)	7.8	6.6	5.8	5.7	5.6
SVD	4.7	3.2	2.4	2.1	2.0
MINFIT	8.0	6.7	5.9	5.8	5.6
PATHS					
RGG (QZHES(Z),QZIT(Z), QZVAL(Z),QZVEC)	26	25	21	21	20
RGG (QZHES,QZIT,QZVAL)	19	17	13	13	12

TABLE 34

SUMMARY OF EXECUTION TIMES FOR THE
EISPACK SUBROUTINES INCLUDED IN THE PATHS FOR
REAL SYMMETRIC BAND MATRICES AND
GENERALIZED REAL SYMMETRIC MATRIX SYSTEMS

MACHINE: DEC KA-PDP-10, F40 Compiler
YALE UNIVERSITY

SUBROUTINE	ORDER OF MATRIX OR SYSTEM			
	N=10	N=20	N=30	N=40
Time Unit (Sec)	.092	.62	1.9	4.4
TRED1	1	1	1	1
TRED2	1.8	2.0	2.0	2.1
TRBAK1	1.3	1.5	1.6	1.7
BANDR(Z)	1.2	2.0	2.4	2.5
BANDR	.47	.75	.85	.90
BQR	5	4	3	4
BANDV	.53	.42	.40	.38
REDUC	1.2	1.2	1.2	1.2
REDUC2	1.1	1.2	1.2	1.2
REBAK	.80	.86	.89	.91
REBAKB	.76	.82	.86	.87
TQL2	3.6	3.8	3.8	3.7
TQLRAT	.80	.42	.28	.21
BISECT	4.1	2.1	1.4	1.0
TINVIT	1.2	.69	.50	.40

PATHS

RSB (BANDR(Z),TQL2)	4.8	5.8	6.1	6.2
RSB (BANDR,TQLRAT)	1.3	1.2	1.1	1.1
BANDR,BISECT,BANDV	.47+.94M	.75+.52M	.85+.45M	.90+.41M
BANDR,BISECT	.47+.41M	.75+.10M	.85+.05M	.90+.03M
RSG (REDUC,TRED2,TQL2,REBAK)	7.4	7.8	7.9	7.9
RSG (REDUC,TRED1,TQLRAT)	3.0	2.6	2.5	2.4
REDUC,TRED1,BISECT,TINVIT, TRBAK1,REBAK	2.2+.74M	2.2+.26M	2.2+.15M	2.2+.10M
REDUC,TRED1,BISECT	2.2+.41M	2.2+.10M	2.2+.05M	2.2+.03M

TABLE 35

SUMMARY OF EXECUTION TIMES FOR THE
EISPACK SUBROUTINES INCLUDED IN THE PATHS FOR
GENERALIZED REAL MATRIX SYSTEMS AND
SINGULAR VALUE DECOMPOSITION

MACHINE: DEC KA-PDP-10, F40 Compiler
YALE UNIVERSITY

SUBROUTINE	ORDER OF MATRIX OR SYSTEM			
	N=10	N=20	N=30	N=40
Time Unit (Sec)	.089	.77	2.5	6.0
ELMHES	1	1	1	1
QZHES(Z)	7.0	6.5	6.7	6.7
QZHES	6.0	5.4	5.5	5.6
QZIT(Z)	15	14	12	11
QZIT	11	8.2	6.7	6.0
QZVAL(Z)	.25	.06	.03	.02
QZVAL	.27	.06	.02	.01
QZVEC	1.7	1.3	1.2	1.2
SVD(U)	6.6	5.3	5.0	4.9
SVD(V)	6.6	5.3	5.1	4.9
SVD	3.2	2.2	1.9	1.8
MINFIT	6.7	5.3	5.0	4.9
PATHS				
RGG (QZHES(Z),QZIT(Z), QZVAL(Z),QZVEC)	24	22	20	19
RGG (QZHES,QZIT,QZVAL)	17	14	12	12

TABLE 36

SUMMARY OF EXECUTION TIMES FOR THE
EISPACK SUBROUTINES INCLUDED IN THE PATHS FOR
REAL SYMMETRIC BAND MATRICES AND
GENERALIZED REAL SYMMETRIC MATRIX SYSTEMS

MACHINE: Amdahl 470V/6, Fortran H, OPT=2
UNIVERSITY OF MICHIGAN

SUBROUTINE	ORDER OF MATRIX OR SYSTEM				
	N=10	N=20	N=40	N=60	N=80
Time Unit (Sec)	.002	.014	.092	.30	.71
TRED1	1	1	1	1	1
TRED2	1.6	1.8	2.0	2.0	2.0
TRBAK1	1.2	1.4	1.6	1.6	1.6
BANDR(Z)	.88	1.5	1.9	2.0	2.0
BANDR	.52	.74	.83	.84	.83
BQR	6	5	4	4	4
BANDV	.43	.35	.33	.32	.32
REDUC	1.1	1.0	1.0	1.0	1.1
REDUC2	.98	.98	.98	.99	.98
REBAK	.61	.67	.70	.72	.70
REBAKB	.55	.63	.70	.74	.74
TQL2	4.8	5.2	5.2	4.9	4.6
TQLRAT	1.5	.85	.42	.27	.19
BISECT	11	6.9	3.8	2.6	1.9
TINVIT	1.1	.68	.39	.29	.29

PATHS

	N=10	N=20	N=40	N=60	N=80
RSB (BANDR(Z),TQL2)	5.7	6.7	7.1	6.9	6.6
RSB (BANDR,TQLRAT)	2.0	1.6	1.3	1.1	1.0
BANDR,BISECT,BANDV	.52+1.5M	.74+.69M	.83+.42M	.84+.36M	.83+.34M
BANDR,BISECT	.52+1.1M	.74+.34M	.83+.09M	.84+.04M	.83+.02M
RSG (REDUC,TRED2,TQL2,REBAK)	8.1	8.7	8.9	8.7	8.4
RSG (REDUC,TRED1,TQLRAT)	3.5	2.9	2.5	2.3	2.2
REDUC,TRED1,BISECT,TINVIT, TRBAK1,REBAK	2.1+1.4M	2.0+.48M	2.0+.16M	2.0+.09M	2.0+.06M
REDUC,TRED1,BISECT	2.1+1.1M	2.0+.34M	2.0+.09M	2.0+.04M	2.0+.02M

TABLE 37

SUMMARY OF EXECUTION TIMES FOR THE
EISPACK SUBROUTINES INCLUDED IN THE PATHS FOR
GENERALIZED REAL MATRIX SYSTEMS AND
SINGULAR VALUE DECOMPOSITION

MACHINE: Amdahl 470V/6, Fortran H, OPT=2
UNIVERSITY OF MICHIGAN

SUBROUTINE	ORDER OF MATRIX OR SYSTEM				
	N=10	N=20	N=40	N=60	N=80
Time Unit (Sec)	.002	.014	.12	.40	.99
ELMHES	1	1	1	1	1
QZHES(Z)	7.7	7.1	6.8	6.4	6.1
QZHES	6.8	6.1	5.7	5.4	5.1
QZIT(Z)	24	21	16	15	13
QZIT	18	13	9.0	7.7	6.3
QZVAL(Z)	.58	.17	.04	.02	.01
QZVAL	.57	.16	.04	.02	.01
QZVEC	2.2	1.6	1.3	1.2	1.1
SVD(U)	11	8.3	6.6	5.9	5.5
SVD(V)	11	8.2	6.6	5.8	5.4
SVD	6.7	3.9	2.5	2.0	1.8
MINFIT	12	8.5	6.7	6.0	5.6
PATHS					
RGG (QZHES(Z),QZIT(Z), QZVAL(Z),QZVEC)	34	30	25	23	20
RGG (QZHES,QZIT,QZVAL)	25	20	15	13	11

TABLE 38

EXECUTION TIMES FOR SELECTED EISPACK DRIVER SUBROUTINES, SVD AND MINFIT
OVER VARIOUS COMPUTER SYSTEMS MEASURED ON PROBLEMS OF ORDER 40
BOTH WITH EIGENVECTORS COMPUTED (1) AND WITHOUT (0)

MACHINE	RSB(1)	RSB(0)	RSG(1)	RSG(0)	RGG(1)	RGG(0)	SVD	MINFIT
Time Unit (Sec)	.22	.061	.30	.11	1.0	.63	.14	.28
IBM 370/195 (ARGONNE NATIONAL LABORATORY)	1	1	1	1	1	1	1	1
IBM 360/75 (UNIVERSITY OF ILLINOIS)	15	9.2	14	11	13	13	9.7	13
IBM 360/65 (AMES LABORATORY)	27	17	24	18	24	22	17	22
IBM 370/165 (THE UNIVERSITY OF TORONTO)	3.9	2.7	3.4	2.9	3.5	3.2	2.6	3.4
IBM 370/168 Mod 3 (STANFORD UNIVERSITY)	3.0	2.2	2.8	2.4	2.7	2.6	2.3	2.7
BURROUGHS 6700 (UNIVERSITY OF CALIFORNIA, SAN DIEGO)	138	67	123	91	119	108	82	110
CDC 6600 (KIRTLAND AIR FORCE BASE)	5.0	3.6	5.4	5.1	4.9	4.8	4.4	4.8
CDC CYBER 175 (NASA LANGLEY RESEARCH CENTER)	1.7	.94	1.6	1.2	1.7	1.6	1.2	1.3
CDC 7600 (NATIONAL CENTER FOR ATMOSPHERIC RESEARCH)	1.1	1.0	1.0	1.0	1.0	1.0	.87	.86
CDC 7600 (LAWRENCE LIVERMORE LABORATORY)	2.1	1.1	2.0	1.7	1.5	1.5	1.2	1.4
CDC 6400 (NORTHWESTERN UNIVERSITY)	21	17	19	16	21	20	15	20
CDC 6400/6500 (PURDUE UNIVERSITY)	28	29	23	19	23	22	17	21

TABLE 38 (Cont'd)

EXECUTION TIMES FOR SELECTED EISPACK DRIVER SUBROUTINES, SVD AND MINFIT
OVER VARIOUS COMPUTER SYSTEMS MEASURED ON PROBLEMS OF ORDER 40
BOTH WITH EIGENVECTORS COMPUTED (1) AND WITHOUT (0)

MACHINE	RSB(1)	RSB(0)	RSG(1)	RSG(0)	RGG(1)	RGG(0)	SVD	MINFIT
Time Unit (Sec)	.22	.061	.30	.11	1.0	.63	.14	.28
IBM 370/195 (ARGONNE NATIONAL LABORATORY)	1	1	1	1	1	1	1	1
CDC 6600/6400 (THE UNIVERSITY OF TEXAS)	7.9	10	6.0	5.8	6.3	6.1	5.2	5.7
HONEYWELL 6070 (BELL LABORATORIES)	15	11	13	11	11	10	9.6	12
UNIVAC 1110 (THE UNIVERSITY OF WISCONSIN)	12	12	11	9.5	9.3	9.3	7.7	9.5
DEC KA-PDP-10 (YALE UNIVERSITY)	126	92	109	125	114	109	79	104
AMDAHL 470V/6 (UNIVERSITY OF MICHIGAN)	3.0	1.9	2.7	2.2	2.8	2.7	2.1	2.8

TABLE 39

SUMMARY OF EXECUTION TIMES FOR SELECTED PROBLEMS
USING THE EISPAC CONTROL PROGRAM

MACHINE: IBM 370/195, Fortran H, OPT=2
ARGONNE NATIONAL LABORATORY

Time Unit: 1 second

PROBLEM CLASS	EIGEN-VALUES	EIGEN-VECTORS	GUIDE SECTION	ORDER OF MATRIX OR SYSTEM				
				N=10	N=20	N=40	N=60	N=80
RSB	All	All	2.1.1	.012	.041	.23	.70	1.6
RSB	All	None	2.1.2	.008	.016	.066	.18	.39
RSB	Some(M=N)	Some(M=N)	2.1.3	.031	.13	1.0	4.1	12
RSB	Some(M=N)	None	2.1.4	.023	.068	.26	.61	1.1
RSG	All	All	2.1.5	.019	.058	.31	.93	2.0
RSG	All	None	2.1.6	.014	.028	.11	.31	.68
RSG	Some(M=N)	Some(M=N)	2.1.7	.034	.10	.43	1.1	2.2
RSG	Some(M=N)	None	2.1.8	.029	.080	.31	.75	1.4
RGG	All	All	2.1.9	.031	.16	1.1	3.1	6.8
RGG	All	None	2.1.10	.024	.11	.66	1.9	4.0

Section 4.2

REPEATABILITY AND RELIABILITY OF THE MEASURED EXECUTION TIMES

In the multi-program environment of modern computers, it is often very difficult to reliably measure the execution time of a program. Significant variations can occur depending on the load on the machine and the amount of I/O interference. For the EISPACK subroutines in particular, allowance has to be made also for the dependence of execution times upon the matrix or matrix system (see Section 4.3).

Towards improving the usefulness of the timing information for the various machines, each subroutine was run a number of times on different matrices and the average time reported. Also, the timing programs were structured to perform no output until all the timings had been collected. For the most part, the timing routines used to measure execution time factor out external interrupts which may occur. The reported times, therefore, although not to be interpreted as absolute bounds, should be useful in giving a feeling for the execution time required by the individual subroutines or paths.

Section 4.3

DEPENDENCE OF THE EXECUTION TIMES UPON THE MATRIX OR MATRIX SYSTEM

To characterize the dependence of the execution times of the EISPACK
subroutines upon the matrix or matrix system, it is helpful to divide the
subroutines into two main categories: first, the non-iterative reduction
and back transformation subroutines; and second, the iterative reduced-form
eigenvalue-eigenvector subroutines.

For the first category of subroutines, the execution times for all non-
sparse matrices and matrix systems of a given order are approximately constant,
close to those given in the tables of Section 4.1. For sparse matrices, some
of the reduction transformations may be skipped and the arithmetic unit may
consume less time to manipulate the many zero operands; however, except for
special sparse matrices, the decrease in execution time of these subroutines
is marginal.

For the second category of subroutines, their execution times depend
greatly upon the structure of the input matrix or matrices (e.g., diagonally
dominant, blocked, sparse), the closeness of the eigenvalues, and the defec-
tiveness of the matrix or system. Based upon our experiments on the IBM
370/195, random matrices tend to produce slower execution of category two
subroutines, and therefore the execution times given in the tables of
Section 4.1 appear to be near the maximum for these subroutines.

Subroutines SVD and MINFIT, each of which is completely self-contained,
have components in both categories distinguished above; the reduction step
to bi-diagonal form is non-iterative, while the determination of the singular
values from the bi-diagonal form is iterative. On the other hand, subroutines BISECT, TINVIT, and BANDV, although seemingly second category candidates

by their roles, are better placed into the first category -- BISECT because
it employs a fixed number of bisections, and TINVIT and BANDV because, although formally iterative, they almost always converge on the first iteration.

Section 4.4

EXTRAPOLATION OF TIMING RESULTS TO OTHER MACHINES AND COMPILERS

The extrapolation of timing results to other machines and compilers may appear straightforward but can be grossly inaccurate if characteristics of the particular machines and compilers are not carefully considered. To illustrate this point, we make two comparisons: first, the execution times of EISPACK on an IBM 360/75 and 370/195, and second, the execution times of EISPACK compiled with the CDC 6600 Fortran RUN and FTN compilers.

The eigensystems of several random matrices of order 80 were determined using identical object modules on the IBM 360/75 and 370/195. The ratios of the IBM 360/75 times to the 370/195 times show large variations from subroutine to subroutine (compare Tables 4-5 with Tables 6-7). Many of the ratios are between 11 and 14, but at opposite extremes the ratios for BISECT and BANDV are 6.7 and 7.8, respectively, whereas for TQL2, 19.4.

These large variations in the ratios of execution times among the subroutines are attributable to the special architecture of the IBM 370/195; namely, the buffered or two-level memory, the pipe line or parallel arithmetic units, and the instruction stack. Some of the EISPACK subroutines are able to take advantage of these special features of the 370/195 better than others.

The compiler can also affect the relative efficiencies of EISPACK subroutines. On two comparable CDC 6600 computers, one employing the RUN compiler and the other the FTN compiler, the ratios of the execution times for the EISPACK subroutines were determined (compare Tables 16-17 with Tables 28-29). Many of the ratios are close to 1, but extremes as large as 1.4 for BANDV, 2.6 for BANDR with accumulation, and 3.8 for BANDR without accumulation of transformations obtain for real symmetric band matrices of order 80.

It is clear from these examples that the relative efficiency of an algorithm can be very machine and compiler dependent, and hence that the extrapolation of our timing results to other systems must necessarily include these considerations.

Section 4.5

TIMING CONSIDERATIONS FOR BAND PROBLEMS AND SINGULAR VALUE DECOMPOSITION

The tables of Section 4.1 limit themselves, in the timings for real symmetric band problems and singular value decomposition, to a single matrix shape each -- for band problems the (half) band width (MB) is always chosen to be 3/10 of the order (N), while for singular value decomposition the coefficient matrix is always chosen to be square (M = N) with one constant vector (IP = 1) transmitted to MINFIT. The following information may be useful towards attempting to estimate the corresponding times in other problem situations.

Let two symmetric band matrices be described as *similar* if the ratio of (half) band width to order is the same for each. Analogously, two rectangular matrices will be described as *similar* if the ratio of row dimension to column dimension is the same for each. Thus, all band matrices used in the timings of Section 4.1 are similar with common ratio 3/10, and all rectangular matrices used in the timings of SVD and MINFIT are similar with common ratio 1. Then, the ratios of execution times for the EISPACK subroutines on a pair of similar band matrices are approximately the same as the corresponding ratios for another pair of similar band matrices of the same orders. And, analogously, the ratios of execution times for SVD or MINFIT on a pair of similar rectangular matrices are approximately the same as the corresponding ratios for another pair of similar rectangular matrices with the same larger dimensions.

The following charts report the IBM 370/195 timings for BANDR, BQR, and BANDV on band matrices of order 80 with differing (half) band widths, and for SVD and MINFIT on several rectangular matrices with larger dimension 80. The times are in seconds. These charts, in combination with the tables of Section 4.1, should be useful in estimating execution times for band matrices and rectangular matrices of different dimensions on a specific machine.

SUBROUTINE	(N,MB)= (80,4)	(N,MB)= (80,8)	(N,MB)= (80,12)	(N,MB)= (80,16)	(N,MB)= (80,20)	(N,MB)= (80,24)
BANDR(Z)	.27	.39	.47	.52	.57	.61
BANDR	.066	.14	.20	.25	.29	.33
BQR	.15	.35	.68	1.1	1.6	1.7
BANDV	.009	.024	.046	.072	.10	.13

SUBROUTINE	(M,N)=(80,20)	(M,N)=(80,40)	(M,N)=(40,80)	(M,N)=(80,80)
SVD(U)	.16	.58	.50	1.9
SVD(V)	.10	.42	.82	1.9
SVD	.08	.26	.27	.78
MINFIT	.10	.42	.79	1.9

For example, to estimate the execution time $T(60,12)$ on the IBM 370/195 for BANDR(Z) on a band matrix of order 60 and (half) band width 12, proceed from the proportion $T(60,12)/T(80,16) = T(60,18)/T(80,24)$ and substitute, using the chart above and Table 4, to obtain $T(60,12)/.52 = .25/.61$, from which $T(60,12)$ is estimated as .21 seconds. To convert this estimate to one for a different machine, multiply by the ratio of speeds of the two machines for this subroutine, which can be estimated from corresponding entries in the tables of Section 4.1.

The entries for MINFIT in the tables of Section 4.1 and in the chart above are obtained from problems where the constant matrix is a single (column) vector (IP = 1). The additional time required when the constant matrix has more columns is generally small and varies approximately linearly with the number of columns.

The following chart reports the IBM 370/195 timings (in seconds) for MINFIT when it is called successively with no constant matrix (IP = 0), one column vector (IP = 1), and two column vectors (IP = 2).

SUBROUTINE	(M,N)=(80,20)	(M,N)=(80,40)	(M,N)=(40,80)	(M,N)=(80,80)
MINFIT(IP = 0)	.09	.41	.78	1.9
MINFIT(IP = 1)	.10	.42	.79	1.9
MINFIT(IP = 2)	.10	.43	.80	2.0

Section 4.6

THE SAMPLE MATRICES FOR THE TIMING RESULTS

In this section, Fortran listings of the program segments which generate the sample matrices for the timing results are provided. The matrix elements are pseudo-random integers sampled from a uniform distribution on the interval $(-2^{15}, +2^{15})$. A listing of the auxiliary subroutine RANDOM which generates the random integers is also provided.

```
C       REAL GENERAL MATRIX
C
        DO 20 I = 1,N
          DO 10 J = 1,N
            CALL RANDOM (INIT, A(I,J))
   10     CONTINUE
   20   CONTINUE


C       REAL SYMMETRIC BAND MATRIX
C
        MB = (3*N) / 10
        DO 20 I = 1,N
          DO 10 J = 1,MB
            CALL RANDOM (INIT, A(I,J))
   10     CONTINUE
   20   CONTINUE


C       GENERALIZED REAL SYMMETRIC MATRIX SYSTEM
C
        DO 30 I = 1,N
          SUM = 0.0
          DO 10 J = I,N
            CALL RANDOM (INIT, A(I,J))
            A(J,I) = A(I,J)
            CALL RANDOM (INIT, B(I,J))
            B(J,I) = B(I,J)
   10     CONTINUE
          DO 20 J = 1,N
            SUM = SUM + ABS(B(I,J))
   20     CONTINUE
          B(I,I) = SUM
   30   CONTINUE
```

```
C       GENERALIZED REAL MATRIX SYSTEM
C
        DO 20 I = 1,N
          DO 10 J = 1,N
              CALL RANDOM (INIT, A(I,J))
              CALL RANDOM (INIT, B(I,J))
   10     CONTINUE
   20   CONTINUE
```

Subroutine RANDOM:

```
        SUBROUTINE RANDOM (INIT,X)
        REAL X
        INIT = MOD(3125*INIT, 65536)
        X = INIT - 32768
        RETURN
        END
```

Subroutine RANDOM produces pseudo-random integer elements X between -2^{15} and 2^{15} from a starting integer INIT. It was designed so that it could be implemented in Fortran and would produce the same set of pseudo-random numbers on different machines. As a result it has some shortcomings as a random number generator, including a rather short period of 2^{14} numbers.

Section 5

CERTIFICATION AND AVAILABILITY OF EISPACK

Under the auspices of the NATS Project, the subroutines constituting
Release 2 of EISPACK have been tested on and are certified for the following computer systems and working precisions (test site names are indicated
in parentheses):

MACHINE	OPERATING SYSTEM	COMPILER	WORKING PRECISION
IBM 370/195	OS/360 (21.7) FTN IV G,H(21.7),WATFIV (ARGONNE NATIONAL LABORATORY)		LONG
IBM 360/75	OS/360 (21.7) FTN IV H(21.7) (UNIVERSITY OF ILLINOIS AT URBANA-CHAMPAIGN)		LONG
IBM 370/168	MTS FTN IV G,H (UNIVERSITY OF MICHIGAN)		LONG
IBM 360/75	OS/360 (21.7) FTN IV H EXTENDED(2.1) (STOCKHOLM DATA CENTER)		LONG
IBM 370/165	OS/360 (21.7) FTN IV H EXTENDED(2.1) (THE UNIVERSITY OF TORONTO)		LONG
BURROUGHS 6700	MCP 2.6 FORTRAN IV(2.6) (UNIVERSITY OF CALIFORNIA, SAN DIEGO)		SINGLE
CDC 6600	SCOPE 3.4.2 FTN(4.2) (KIRTLAND AIR FORCE BASE/AFWL)		SINGLE
CDC 6600	KRONOS 2.1 RUN(2.3) (ICASE/NASA LANGLEY RESEARCH CENTER)		SINGLE
CDC 7600	(LOCAL) (LOCAL) (NATIONAL CENTER FOR ATMOSPHERIC RESEARCH)		SINGLE
CDC 6400	SCOPE 3.3 RUN(2.3),FTN(3.0) (NORTHWESTERN UNIVERSITY)		SINGLE
CDC 6400/6500	(LOCAL) FUN (PURDUE UNIVERSITY)		SINGLE
CDC 6600/6400	UT2D-85 RUN(60.2),MNF,RUNW (THE UNIVERSITY OF TEXAS AT AUSTIN)		SINGLE
HONEYWELL 6070	GECOS SR-F FORTRAN-Y(SR-F) (BELL LABORATORIES AT MURRAY HILL)		SINGLE
UNIVAC 1110	EXEC-8(31.244) FORTRAN V(9) (THE UNIVERSITY OF WISCONSIN)		SINGLE
DEC PDP-10	TOPS-10(506B) FORTRAN F40 (YALE UNIVERSITY)		SINGLE

The control program EISPAC has been tested on and is certified for the IBM systems at Argonne, Illinois, Stockholm, and Toronto listed above. Additional testing of EISPACK was carried out at Stanford University, Harvard University, and on the Amdahl 470V/6 machine at University of Michigan.

Certification implies the full support of the NATS project in the sense that reports of poor or incorrect performance on at least the computer systems listed above will be examined and any necessary corrections made. This support holds only when the software is obtained through the channels indicated below and has not been modified; it will continue to hold throughout the useful life of EISPACK or until, in the estimation of the developers, the package is superseded or incorporated into other supported, widely-available program libraries. The following individual serves as a contact for information about EISPACK, accepting reports from users concerning performance:

Burton S. Garbow
Applied Mathematics Division
Argonne National Laboratory
Argonne, Illinois 60439 U.S.A.
Phone: 312-739-7711 x4342

EISPACK is distributed from the Argonne Code Center. Versions exist for IBM 360-370, CDC 6000-7000, Univac 1110, Honeywell 6070, DEC PDP-10, and Burroughs 6700 machines. Requesters interested in obtaining EISPACK (Fortran source decks, documentation, and testing aids) should write to the following address for complete information on the acquisition procedures:

Argonne Code Center
Building 221
Argonne National Laboratory
Argonne, Illinois 60439 U.S.A.

Section 6

DIFFERENCES BETWEEN THE EISPACK SUBROUTINES AND
THE HANDBOOK ALGOL PROCEDURES

This section describes, subroutine by subroutine, the major differences
between the EISPACK subroutines covered in this volume and their Algol antecedents in the Handbook [1]. These differences fall into four categories:
1) correction of several errors, 2) minor algorithmic improvements, 3) changes
based on consideration of Fortran language efficiency, and finally, 4) changes
to better unify the individual programs into a package.

Specific changes to individual members of EISPACK are as follows.

BANDR - The lower triangle of the matrix is stored rather than the upper
triangle, thus placing, in particular, the main diagonal elements
in the last column. The Algol column range of 0 to M has been
translated to 1 to M by redefining M to include the main diagonal.

- The Givens reduction transformations are formulated in square-root
free form.

BQR - Storage organization, column labeling, and definition of M as for
BANDR.

- The orthogonality threshold parameter TOL has been replaced by the
scaling technique discussed in the "Organisational and Notational
Details" section of the Handbook, Contribution II/2, p. 221.

MINFIT - Separate storage entities are provided for the coefficient and
constant matrices rather than maintaining a single augmented array.

- The parameter TOL has been replaced as in BQR.

          – An error parameter has been introduced that is set in instances of non-convergence.

          – A test has been inserted to avoid a possible divide exception.

REBAK – Instead of back transforming eigenvectors M1 through M2 as is done in the Handbook, REBAK transforms eigenvectors 1 through M.

REBAKB – As for REBAK.

SVD   – The replacement of TOL, the introduction of an error parameter, and the insertion of a test to avoid a possible divide exception are done as in MINFIT.

          – It is not required that the matrix be presented with at least as many rows as columns; it is recommended, however, for greater efficiency.

Section 7

DOCUMENTATION AND SOURCE LISTINGS

This section contains the documentation and source listings for the
EISPACK subroutines covered in this volume and the documentation for the
control program EISPAC. The subroutines appear in alphabetical order in
Section 7.1 with the source listing for each subroutine following its document. Section 7.2 contains the document for EISPAC, but because of its
size and machine dependencies the listing is not included.

Both the subroutine documents and source listings have been systemati-
cally edited for this publication to eliminate duplicate text; they therefore
differ from the material distributed to requesters of EISPACK. The statement
of certification of item 6 has been removed from the individual documents and
appears here in Section 5. The reference to this publication which appears
in item 4 and the brief discussion of testing that appears in items 5.A and
5.C of the distributed documents have been removed; the latter has been
replaced by a pointer to the more extensive discussion of testing here in
Section 3.

Two modifications have been made to the subroutine listings published
here. First, they have been shortened by eliminating comments related to
usage, calling sequence, and error exits which basically duplicate text in
the documents. Second, statements initializing the machine-dependent
variable MACHEP, which in each distributed version of EISPACK are completed
to contain its appropriate numerical value, appear here as

$$MACHEP = ?$$

(The correct value for MACHEP is the smallest positive working precision
floating point number which, when added to 1.0 using the working precision
addition operation on your machine, gives a number larger than 1.0.)

Appropriate values of MACHEP for several machines are summarized in the following table.

MACHINE	MACHEP
Burroughs 6700	2.**(-37)
CDC 6000 and 7000 Series	2.**(-47)
DEC PDP-10	2.**(-26)
Honeywell 6070	2.**(-26)
Univac 1110	2.**(-26)
IBM 360-370	
Double precision	16.D0**(-13)
Single precision	16.**(-5)

Except for the statements initializing MACHEP, the published listings are ANSI Fortran. The double precision version certified for IBM equipment employs non-standard Fortran to the extent of using REAL*8 declarations.

NATS PROJECT

EIGENSYSTEM SUBROUTINE PACKAGE (EISPACK)

F226   BANDR

A Fortran IV Subroutine to Reduce a Real Symmetric Band Matrix
to a Symmetric Tridiagonal Matrix Using and Optionally
Accumulating Orthogonal Transformations.

July, 1975

1. PURPOSE.

The Fortran IV subroutine BANDR reduces a real symmetric
band matrix to a symmetric tridiagonal matrix using and
optionally accumulating orthogonal similarity
transformations. This reduced form is used by other
subroutines to find the eigenvalues and/or eigenvectors of
the original matrix. See section 2C for the specific
routines.

2. USAGE.

A. Calling Sequence.

The SUBROUTINE statement is

SUBROUTINE BANDR(NM,N,MB,A,D,E,E2,MATZ,Z)

The parameters are discussed below and the
interpretation of working precision for various machines
is given in the section discussing certification.

NM   is an integer input variable set equal to
            the row dimension of the two-dimensional
            array A (and Z if MATZ is true) as
            specified in the DIMENSION statement for A
            (and Z) in the calling program.

N   is an integer input variable set equal to
            the order of the matrix A. N must be not
            greater than NM.

MB   is an integer input variable set equal to the (half) band width of the matrix A, defined as the number of adjacent diagonals, including the principal diagonal, required to specify the non-zero portion of the lower triangle of the matrix. MB must be not greater than N.

A   is a working precision real two-dimensional variable with row dimension NM and column dimension at least MB. On input, A contains the lower triangle of the symmetric band matrix of order N and (half) band width MB to be reduced to tridiagonal form. Its lowest subdiagonal is stored in the last N+1-MB positions of the first column, its next subdiagonal in the last N+2-MB positions of the second column, further subdiagonals similarly, and finally its principal diagonal in the N positions of the last column. Contents of storage locations not part of the matrix are arbitrary. For example, when N=5 and MB=3, A should contain

```
(   *          *        A(1,1) )
(   *        A(2,1)     A(2,2) )
( A(3,1)     A(3,2)     A(3,3) )
( A(4,2)     A(4,3)     A(4,4) )
( A(5,3)     A(5,4)     A(5,5) )
```

where the subscripts for each element refer to the row and column of the element in the standard two-dimensional representation, and (*) denotes an arbitrary value. On output, A has been destroyed, except for its last two columns which contain a copy of the tridiagonal matrix.

D   is a working precision real output one-dimensional variable of dimension at least N containing the diagonal elements of the tridiagonal matrix.

E   is a working precision real output one-dimensional variable of dimension at least N containing, in its last N-1 positions, the subdiagonal elements of the tridiagonal matrix. The element E(1) is set to zero.

E2 is a working precision real output one-dimensional variable of dimension at least N containing, in its last N-1 positions, the squares of the subdiagonal elements of the tridiagonal matrix. The element E2(1) is set to zero. E2 need not be distinct from E (non-standard usage acceptable with at least those compilers included in the certification statement), in which case no squares are returned.

MATZ is a logical input variable set true if the transformation matrix is to be accumulated and set false otherwise.

Z is, if MATZ is true, a working precision real output two-dimensional variable with row dimension NM and column dimension at least N. It contains the orthogonal transformation matrix produced in the reduction to the tridiagonal form. If MATZ is false, Z is not referenced and can be a dummy (working precision) variable.

B. Error Conditions and Returns.

None.

C. Applicability and Restrictions.

If all the eigenvalues of the original matrix are desired, this subroutine should be followed by TQL1 (F289), IMTQL1 (F291), or TQLRAT (F235).

If all the eigenvalues and eigenvectors of the original matrix are desired, this subroutine should be followed by TQL2 (F290) or IMTQL2 (F292), identifying the output Z matrix above with the input Z matrix to TQL2 or IMTQL2.

If some of the eigenvalues of the original matrix are desired, this subroutine should be followed by BISECT (F294) or TRIDIB (F237).

If some of the eigenvalues and eigenvectors of the original matrix are desired, this subroutine should be followed by BISECT (F294) or TRIDIB (F237) and then by BANDV (F227). Note, however, that the input matrix A must be saved before BANDR for the later use by BANDV, since BANDR destroys it.

3. DISCUSSION OF METHOD AND ALGORITHM.

The tridiagonal reduction is performed in the following way. Starting with J=1, the elements in the J-th column within the band and below the principal subdiagonal are eliminated successively, starting from the lowermost element, by fast Givens transformations (2). Each such transformation preserves symmetry but introduces a new element outside of the band. To maintain the band form, these elements are eliminated by a sequence of additional transformations with the effect of shifting them downwards and finally beyond the border of the matrix. By accumulating the transformations in Z, full information is saved for later use in the determination of the eigenvectors.

The above steps are repeated on further columns of the transformed A until A is reduced to tridiagonal form; that is, repeated for J = 2,3,...,N-2.

Finally, the elements of the tridiagonal form are copied into D and E and the squares of the subdiagonal elements stored in E2.

This subroutine is a translation of the Algol procedure BANDRD written and discussed in detail by Schwarz (1).

4. REFERENCES.

1) Schwarz, H.R., Tridiagonalization of a Symmetric Band Matrix, Num. Math. 12,231-241 (1968). (Reprinted in Handbook for Automatic Computation, Volume II, Linear Algebra, J. H. Wilkinson - C. Reinsch, Contribution II/8, 273-283, Springer-Verlag, 1971.)

2) Gentleman, W.M., Least Squares Computations by Givens Transformations Without Square Roots, J. Inst. Maths Applic 12,329-336 (1973).

5. CHECKOUT.

A. Test Cases.

See the section discussing testing of the codes for real symmetric band matrices.

B. Accuracy.

The accuracy of BANDR can best be described in terms
of its role in those paths of EISPACK which find
eigenvalues and eigenvectors of real symmetric band
matrices.   In these paths, this subroutine is
numerically stable (1,2).   This stability contributes to
the property of these paths that the computed
eigenvalues are the exact eigenvalues of a matrix close
to the original matrix and the computed eigenvectors are
close (but not necessarily equal) to the eigenvectors of
that matrix.

```
      SUBROUTINE BANDR(NM,N,MB,A,D,E,E2,MATZ,Z)
C
      INTEGER J,K,L,N,R,I1,I2,J1,J2,KR,MB,MR,M1,NM,N2,R1,UGL,MAXL,MAX
      REAL A(NM,MB),D(N),E(N),E2(N),Z(NM,N)
      REAL G,U,B1,B2,C2,F1,F2,S2,DMIN,DMINRT
      REAL SQRT
      INTEGER MAX0,MIN0,MOD
      LOGICAL MATZ
C
      DMIN = 2.0**(-64)
      DMINRT = 2.0**(-32)
C     ********** INITIALIZE DIAGONAL SCALING MATRIX **********
      DO 30 J = 1, N
   30 D(J) = 1.0
C
      IF (.NOT. MATZ) GO TO 60
C
      DO 50 J = 1, N
C
         DO 40 K = 1, N
   40    Z(J,K) = 0.0
C
         Z(J,J) = 1.0
   50 CONTINUE
C
   60 M1 = MB - 1
      IF (M1 - 1) 900, 800, 70
   70 N2 = N - 2
C
      DO 700 K = 1, N2
         MAXR = MIN0(M1,N-K)
C     ********** FOR R=MAXR STEP -1 UNTIL 2 DO -- **********
         DO 600 R1 = 2, MAXR
            R = MAXR + 2 - R1
            KR = K + R
            MR = MB - R
            G = A(KR,MR)
            A(KR-1,1) = A(KR-1,MR+1)
            UGL = K
C
            DO 500 J = KR, N, M1
               J1 = J - 1
               J2 = J1 - 1
               IF (G .EQ. 0.0) GO TO 600
               B1 = A(J1,1) / G
               B2 = B1 * D(J1) / D(J)
               S2 = 1.0 / (1.0 + B1 * B2)
               IF (S2 .GE. 0.5 ) GO TO 450
               B1 = G / A(J1,1)
               B2 = B1 * D(J) / D(J1)
               C2 = 1.0 - S2
               D(J1) = C2 * D(J1)
               D(J) = C2 * D(J)
               F1 = 2.0 * A(J,M1)
```

```
                F2 = B1 * A(J1,MB)
                A(J,M1) = -B2 * (B1 * A(J,M1) - A(J,MB)) - F2 + A(J,M1)
                A(J1,MB) = B2 * (B2 * A(J,MB) + F1) + A(J1,MB)
                A(J,MB) = B1 * (F2 - F1) + A(J,MB)
C
                DO 200 L = UGL, J2
                   I2 = MB - J + L
                   U = A(J1,I2+1) + B2 * A(J,I2)
                   A(J,I2) = -B1 * A(J1,I2+1) + A(J,I2)
                   A(J1,I2+1) = U
  200           CONTINUE
C
                UGL = J
                A(J1,1) = A(J1,1) + B2 * G
                IF (J .EQ. N) GO TO 350
                MAXL = MIN0(M1,N-J1)
C
                DO 300 L = 2, MAXL
                   I1 = J1 + L
                   I2 = MB - L
                   U = A(I1,I2) + B2 * A(I1,I2+1)
                   A(I1,I2+1) = -B1 * A(I1,I2) + A(I1,I2+1)
                   A(I1,I2) = U
  300           CONTINUE
C
                I1 = J + M1
                IF (I1 .GT. N) GO TO 350
                G = B2 * A(I1,1)
  350           IF (.NOT. MATZ) GO TO 500
C
                DO 400 L = 1, N
                   U = Z(L,J1) + B2 * Z(L,J)
                   Z(L,J) = -B1 * Z(L,J1) + Z(L,J)
                   Z(L,J1) = U
  400           CONTINUE
C
                GO TO 500
C
  450           U = D(J1)
                D(J1) = S2 * D(J)
                D(J) = S2 * U
                F1 = 2.0 * A(J,M1)
                F2 = B1 * A(J,MB)
                U = B1 * (F2 - F1) + A(J1,MB)
                A(J,M1) = B2 * (B1 * A(J,M1) - A(J1,MB)) + F2 - A(J,M1)
                A(J1,MB) = B2 * (B2 * A(J1,MB) + F1) + A(J,MB)
                A(J,MB) = U
C
                DO 460 L = UGL, J2
                   I2 = MB - J + L
                   U = B2 * A(J1,I2+1) + A(J,I2)
                   A(J,I2) = -A(J1,I2+1) + B1 * A(J,I2)
                   A(J1,I2+1) = U
  460           CONTINUE
```

```
C
            UGL = J
            A(J1,1) = B2 * A(J1,1) + G
            IF (J .EQ. N) GO TO 480
            MAXL = MINO(M1,N-J1)
C
            DO 470 L = 2, MAXL
               I1 = J1 + L
               I2 = MB - L
               U = B2 * A(I1,I2) + A(I1,I2+1)
               A(I1,I2+1) = -A(I1,I2) + B1 * A(I1,I2+1)
               A(I1,I2) = U
  470       CONTINUE
C
            I1 = J + M1
            IF (I1 .GT. N) GO TO 480
            G = A(I1,1)
            A(I1,1) = B1 * A(I1,1)
  480       IF (.NOT. MATZ) GO TO 500
C
            DO 490 L = 1, N
               U = B2 * Z(L,J1) + Z(L,J)
               Z(L,J) = -Z(L,J1) + B1 * Z(L,J)
               Z(L,J1) = U
  490       CONTINUE
C
  500    CONTINUE
C
  600 CONTINUE
C
      IF (MOD(K,64) .NE. 0) GO TO 700
C    ********** RESCALE TO AVOID UNDERFLOW OR OVERFLOW **********
      DO 650 J = K, N
         IF (D(J) .GE. DMIN) GO TO 650
         MAXL = MAX0(1,MB+1-J)
C
         DO 610 L = MAXL, M1
  610    A(J,L) = DMINRT * A(J,L)
C
         IF (J .EQ. N) GO TO 630
         MAXL = MINO(M1,N-J)
C
         DO 620 L = 1, MAXL
            I1 = J + L
            I2 = MB - L
            A(I1,I2) = DMINRT * A(I1,I2)
  620    CONTINUE
C
  630    IF (.NOT. MATZ) GO TO 645
C
         DO 640 L = 1, N
  640    Z(L,J) = DMINRT * Z(L,J)
```

```
C
  645        A(J,MB) = DMIN * A(J,MB)
             D(J) = D(J) / DMIN
  650     CONTINUE
C
  700 CONTINUE
C     ********** FORM SQUARE ROOT OF SCALING MATRIX **********
  800 DO 810 J = 2, N
  810 E(J) = SQRT(D(J))
C
      IF (.NOT. MATZ) GO TO 840
C
      DO 830 J = 1, N
C
         DO 820 K = 2, N
  820    Z(J,K) = E(K) * Z(J,K)
C
  830 CONTINUE
C
  840 U = 1.0
C
      DO 850 J = 2, N
         A(J,M1) = U * E(J) * A(J,M1)
         U = E(J)
         E2(J) = A(J,M1) ** 2
         A(J,MB) = D(J) * A(J,MB)
         D(J) = A(J,MB)
         E(J) = A(J,M1)
  850 CONTINUE
C
      D(1) = A(1,MB)
      E(1) = 0.0
      E2(1) = 0.0
      GO TO 1001
C
  900 DO 950 J = 1, N
         D(J) = A(J,MB)
         E(J) = 0.0
         E2(J) = 0.0
  950 CONTINUE
C
 1001 RETURN
      END
```

NATS PROJECT

EIGENSYSTEM SUBROUTINE PACKAGE (EISPACK)

F227 BANDV

A Fortran IV Subroutine to Determine Some Eigenvectors of
a Real Symmetric Band Matrix or Solve Band Equations.

July, 1975

1. PURPOSE.

The Fortran IV subroutine BANDV determines those
eigenvectors of a real symmetric band matrix corresponding to
a set of ordered approximate eigenvalues, using inverse
iteration. It can also be used to solve a system of linear
equations with a symmetric or non-symmetric band coefficient
matrix, or a succession of related systems.

2. USAGE.

A. Calling Sequence.

The SUBROUTINE statement is

SUBROUTINE BANDV(NM,N,MBW,A,E21,M,W,Z,
                              IERR,NV,RV,RV6)

The parameters are discussed below and the
interpretation of working precision for various machines
is given in the section discussing certification.

NM   is an integer input variable set equal to
        the row dimension of the two-dimensional
        arrays A and Z as specified in the
        DIMENSION statements for A and Z in the
        calling program.

N   is an integer input variable set equal to
        the order of the matrix A. N must be not
        greater than NM.

MBW   is an integer input variable set equal to
        the number of columns of the array A used
        to store the band matrix. If the matrix is
        symmetric, MBW is its (half) band width,

denoted MB and defined as the number of adjacent diagonals, including the principal diagonal, required to specify the non-zero portion of the lower triangle of the matrix.

If BANDV is being used to solve systems of linear equations and the coefficient matrix is not symmetric, it must have the same number of adjacent diagonals above the main diagonal as below, and so in this case MBW=2*MB-1.

MB must be not greater than N.

A   is a working precision real input two-dimensional variable with row dimension NM and column dimension at least MBW . If the band matrix is symmetric, A contains its lower triangle of order N and (half) band width MB. Its lowest subdiagonal is stored in the last N+1-MB positions of the first column, its next subdiagonal in the last N+2-MB positions of the second column, further subdiagonals similarly, and finally its principal diagonal in the N positions of the last column. Contents of storage locations not part of the matrix are arbitrary. For example, when N=5 and MB=3, A should contain

```
(     *          *       A(1,1) )
(     *        A(2,1)    A(2,2) )
( A(3,1)      A(3,2)    A(3,3) )
( A(4,2)      A(4,3)    A(4,4) )
( A(5,3)      A(5,4)    A(5,5) )
```

where the subscripts for each element refer to the row and column of the element in the standard two-dimensional representation, and (*) denotes an arbitrary value.

If BANDV is being used to solve systems of linear equations and the coefficient matrix is not symmetric, A is N by 2*MB-1 instead with lower triangle as above and with its first superdiagonal stored in the first N-1 positions of column MB+1, its second superdiagonal in the first N-2 positions of column MB+2, further superdiagonals similarly, and finally its highest super-diagonal in the first N+1-MB positions of the last column. In the example above, A would be augmented with two additional columns containing

```
( A(1,2)   A(1,3) )
( A(2,3)   A(2,4) )
( A(3,4)   A(3,5) )
( A(4,5)     *    )
(   *        *    ).
```

E21   is a working precision real input variable specifying the ordering of the eigenvalues. E21 should contain 0.0 if the eigenvalues are in ascending order and 2.0 if the eigenvalues are in descending order.

            If BANDV is being used to solve systems of linear equations, E21 should contain 1.0 if the coefficient matrix is symmetric and -1.0 if not.

M   is an integer input variable set equal to the number of specified eigenvalues for which the corresponding eigenvectors are to be determined.

            If BANDV is being used to solve systems of linear equations, M is equal to the number of systems.

W   is a working precision real input one-dimensional variable of dimension at least M containing the M specified eigenvalues of the symmetric band matrix. The eigenvalues must be in either ascending or descending order in W. The ordering is required to insure the determination of independent orthogonal eigenvectors associated with close eigenvalues.

            If BANDV is being used to solve systems of linear equations, W contains M parameters (commonly zero) which, together with A, define the coefficient matrices $A-W(J)*I$, $J=1,2,...,M$ of the successive systems, where I is the identity matrix.

Z   is a working precision real two-dimensional variable with row dimension NM and column dimension at least M. On output, it contains M orthonormal eigenvectors of the symmetric band matrix corresponding to the M eigenvalues in W.

If BANDV is being used to solve systems of linear equations, then on input, Z contains the M associated constant vectors of the successive systems $(A-W*I)*X=Z$ and on output, Z contains the corresponding solution vectors X.

IERR   is an integer output variable set equal to an error completion code described in section 2B. The normal completion code is zero.

NV   is an integer input variable set equal to the dimension of the array RV as specified in the DIMENSION statement for RV in the calling program. NV must be not less than $N*(2*MB-1)$.

RV   is a working precision real temporary array variable of dimension at least $N*(2*MB-1)$ used to store the upper triangular matrix produced in the inverse iteration process.

RV6   is a working precision real temporary one-dimensional variable of dimension at least N used to hold the approximate eigenvectors or solution vectors in the inverse iteration process.

B. Error Conditions and Returns.

If none of the initial vectors for the inverse iteration process produces an acceptable approximation to an eigenvector, BANDV terminates the computation for that eigenvector and sets IERR to -R where R is the index of the eigenvector. If this failure occurs for more than one eigenvector, the last occurrence is recorded in IERR. The columns of Z corresponding to failures of the above sort are set to zero vectors.

If BANDV is being used to solve systems of linear equations and near singularity of the coefficient matrix is detected, BANDV continues the computation but sets IERR to -R where R is the index of the linear system. If this failure occurs for more than one system, the last occurrence is recorded in IERR.

If the above error condition does not occur, BANDV sets IERR to zero.

C. Applicability and Restrictions.

To determine some of the eigenvalues and eigenvectors of a symmetric band matrix, BANDV should be preceded by BANDR (F226) to provide a suitable symmetric tridiagonal matrix for BISECT (F294) or TRIDIB (F237) which can then be used to determine the eigenvalues.

If MACHEP denotes the relative machine precision, then the computation of the eigenvectors by inverse iteration requires that the precision of the eigenvalues be commensurate with small relative perturbations of the order of MACHEP in the matrix elements. For most symmetric band matrices, it is enough that the absolute error in the eigenvalues for which eigenvectors are desired be approximately MACHEP times a norm of the matrix. But some matrices require a smaller absolute error, perhaps as small as MACHEP times the eigenvalue of smallest magnitude.

3. DISCUSSION OF METHOD AND ALGORITHM.

The eigenvectors of the matrix are computed by inverse iteration. First, the LU decomposition of the matrix with an approximate eigenvalue subtracted from its diagonal elements is achieved by Gaussian elimination using partial pivoting. The upper triangular matrix is stored in the temporary array RV. An approximate vector, stored in RV6, is computed starting from an initial vector, and the norm of the approximate vector is compared with a norm of the matrix to determine whether the growth is sufficient to accept it as an eigenvector. If this vector is accepted, its Euclidean norm is made 1. At most N orthogonal initial vectors are tried to obtain the required growth. If no vector is accepted, the parameter IERR is set to indicate this failure and BANDV proceeds to compute the next eigenvector.

Eigenvectors computed in the above way corresponding to well separated eigenvalues of the matrix will be orthogonal. However, eigenvectors corresponding to close eigenvalues of the matrix may not be satisfactorily orthogonal. Hence, to insure orthogonal eigenvectors, each approximate vector is made orthogonal to those previously computed eigenvectors whose eigenvalues are close to the current eigenvalue. The growth test is made after the orthogonalization process.

Identical eigenvalues are perturbed slightly in an attempt to obtain independent eigenvectors. These perturbations are not recorded in the eigenvalue array W.

If BANDV is being used to solve systems of linear equations, the procedure described above is followed (omitting the growth test and orthogonalization process), choosing as initial vector the appropriate constant vector. Upon return from BANDV, the determinant (up to sign) of A-W(M)*I can be computed, if desired, by forming the product of the first N elements of RV.

This subroutine is patterned after the eigenvector determination portion of the Fortran subroutine TSTURM (F293), with initial vectors chosen as in INVIT (F288). These latter subroutines are translations of the Algol procedures TRISTURM and INVIT, respectively, written and discussed in detail by Peters and Wilkinson (1).

4. REFERENCES.

1) Peters, G. and Wilkinson, J.H., The Calculation of Specified Eigenvectors by Inverse Iteration, Handbook for Automatic Computation, Volume II, Linear Algebra, J. H. Wilkinson - C. Reinsch, Contribution II/18, 418-439, Springer-Verlag, 1971.

5. CHECKOUT.

A. Test Cases.

See the section discussing testing of the codes for real symmetric band matrices.

B. Accuracy.

The accuracy of BANDV can best be described in terms of its role in those paths of EISPACK which find eigenvalues and eigenvectors of real symmetric band matrices. In these paths, this subroutine is numerically stable (1). This stability contributes to the property of these paths that the computed eigenvalues are the exact eigenvalues of a matrix close to the original matrix and the computed eigenvectors are close (but not necessarily equal) to the eigenvectors of that matrix.

```
      SUBROUTINE BANDV(NM,N,MBW,A,E21,M,W,Z,IERR,NV,RV,RV6)
C
      INTEGER I,J,K,M,N,R,II,IJ,JJ,KJ,MB,M1,NM,NV,IJ1,ITS,KJ1,MBW,M2
     X        IERR,MAXJ,MAXK,GROUP
      REAL A(NM,MBW),W(M),Z(NM,M),RV(NV),RV6(N)
      REAL U,V,UK,XU,X0,X1,E21,EPS2,EPS3,EPS4,NORM,ORDER,MACHEP
      REAL SQRT,ABS,FLOAT,SIGN
      INTEGER MIN0
C
C     ********** MACHEP IS A MACHINE DEPENDENT PARAMETER SPECIFYING
C                THE RELATIVE PRECISION OF FLOATING POINT ARITHMETIC
C
C                **********
      MACHEP = ?
C
      IERR = 0
      IF (M .EQ. 0) GO TO 1001
      MB = MBW
      IF (E21 .LT. 0.0) MB = (MBW + 1) / 2
      M1 = MB - 1
      M21 = M1 + MB
      ORDER = 1.0 - ABS(E21)
C     ********** FIND VECTORS BY INVERSE ITERATION **********
      DO 920 R = 1, M
         ITS = 1
         X1 = W(R)
         IF (R .NE. 1) GO TO 100
C     ********** COMPUTE NORM OF MATRIX **********
         NORM = 0.0
C
         DO 60 J = 1, MB
            JJ = MB + 1 - J
            KJ = JJ + M1
            IJ = 1
C
            DO 40 I = JJ, N
               NORM = NORM + ABS(A(I,J))
               IF (E21 .GE. 0.0) GO TO 40
               NORM = NORM + ABS(A(IJ,KJ))
               IJ = IJ + 1
   40       CONTINUE
C
   60    CONTINUE
C
         IF (E21 .LT. 0.0) NORM = 0.5 * NORM
C     ********** EPS2 IS THE CRITERION FOR GROUPING,
C                EPS3 REPLACES ZERO PIVOTS AND EQUAL
C                ROOTS ARE MODIFIED BY EPS3,
C                EPS4 IS TAKEN VERY SMALL TO AVOID OVERFLOW ********
         IF (NORM .EQ. 0.0) NORM = 1.0
         EPS2 = 1.0E-3 * NORM * ABS(ORDER)
         EPS3 = MACHEP * NORM
         UK = SQRT(FLOAT(N))
         EPS4 = UK * EPS3
```

```
   80      GROUP = 0
           GO TO 120
C      ********** LOOK FOR CLOSE OR COINCIDENT ROOTS **********
  100      IF (ABS(X1-X0) .GE. EPS2) GO TO 80
           GROUP = GROUP + 1
           IF (ORDER * (X1 - X0) .LE. 0.0) X1 = X0 + ORDER * EPS3
C      ********** EXPAND MATRIX, SUBTRACT EIGENVALUE,
C                 AND INITIALIZE VECTOR **********
  120      DO 200 I = 1, N
              IJ = I + MINO(0,I-M1) * N
              KJ = IJ + MB * N
              IJ1 = KJ + M1 * N
              IF (M1 .EQ. 0) GO TO 180
C
              DO 150 J = 1, M1
                 IF (IJ .GT. M1) GO TO 125
                 IF (IJ .GT. 0) GO TO 130
                 RV(IJ1) = 0.0
                 IJ1 = IJ1 + N
                 GO TO 130
  125            RV(IJ) = A(I,J)
  130            IJ = IJ + N
                 II = I + J
                 IF (II .GT. N) GO TO 150
                 JJ = MB - J
                 IF (E21 .GE. 0.0) GO TO 140
                 II = I
                 JJ = MB + J
  140            RV(KJ) = A(II,JJ)
                 KJ = KJ + N
  150         CONTINUE
C
  180         RV(IJ) = A(I,MB) - X1
              RV6(I) = EPS4
              IF (ORDER .EQ. 0.0) RV6(I) = Z(I,R)
  200      CONTINUE
C
           IF (M1 .EQ. 0) GO TO 600
C      ********** ELIMINATION WITH INTERCHANGES **********
           DO 580 I = 1, N
              II = I + 1
              MAXK = MINO(I+M1-1,N)
              MAXJ = MINO(N-I,M21-2) * N
C
              DO 360 K = I, MAXK
                 KJ1 = K
                 J = KJ1 + N
                 JJ = J + MAXJ
C
                 DO 340 KJ = J, JJ, N
                    RV(KJ1) = RV(KJ)
                    KJ1 = KJ
  340            CONTINUE
```

```
C
                RV(KJ1) = 0.0
   360          CONTINUE
C
                IF (I .EQ. N) GO TO 580
                U = 0.0
                MAXK = MINO(I+M1,N)
                MAXJ = MINO(N-II,M21-2) * N
C
                DO 450 J = I, MAXK
                   IF (ABS(RV(J)) .LT. ABS(U)) GO TO 450
                   U = RV(J)
                   K = J
   450          CONTINUE
C
                J = I + N
                JJ = J + MAXJ
                IF (K .EQ. I) GO TO 520
                KJ = K
C
                DO 500 IJ = I, JJ, N
                   V = RV(IJ)
                   RV(IJ) = RV(KJ)
                   RV(KJ) = V
                   KJ = KJ + N
   500          CONTINUE
C
                IF (ORDER .NE. 0.0) GO TO 520
                V = RV6(I)
                RV6(I) = RV6(K)
                RV6(K) = V
   520          IF (U .EQ. 0.0) GO TO 580
C
                DO 560 K = II, MAXK
                   V = RV(K) / U
                   KJ = K
C
                   DO 540 IJ = J, JJ, N
                      KJ = KJ + N
                      RV(KJ) = RV(KJ) - V * RV(IJ)
   540             CONTINUE
C
                   IF (ORDER .EQ. 0.0) RV6(K) = RV6(K) - V * RV6(I)
   560          CONTINUE
C
   580       CONTINUE
C     ********* BACK SUBSTITUTION
C                   FOR I=N STEP -1 UNTIL 1 DO -- *********
   600       DO 630 II = 1, N
                I = N + 1 - II
                MAXJ = MINO(II,M21)
                IF (MAXJ .EQ. 1) GO TO 620
                IJ1 = I
                J = IJ1 + N
```

```
                JJ = J + (MAXJ - 2) * N
C
                DO 610 IJ = J, JJ, N
                   IJ1 = IJ1 + 1
                   RV6(I) = RV6(I) - RV(IJ) * RV6(IJ1)
  610           CONTINUE
C
  620           V = RV(I)
                IF (ABS(V) .GE. EPS3) GO TO 625
C     ********** SET ERROR -- NEARLY SINGULAR LINEAR SYSTEM **********
                IF (ORDER .EQ. 0.0) IERR = -R
                V = SIGN(EPS3,V)
  625           RV6(I) = RV6(I) / V
  630        CONTINUE
C
             XU = 1.0
             IF (ORDER .EQ. 0.0) GO TO 870
C     ********** ORTHOGONALIZE WITH RESPECT TO PREVIOUS
C                     MEMBERS OF GROUP **********
             IF (GROUP .EQ. 0) GO TO 700
C
             DO 680 JJ = 1, GROUP
                J = R - GROUP - 1 + JJ
                XU = 0.0
C
                DO 640 I = 1, N
  640           XU = XU + RV6(I) * Z(I,J)
C
                DO 660 I = 1, N
  660           RV6(I) = RV6(I) - XU * Z(I,J)
C
  680        CONTINUE
C
  700        NORM = 0.0
C
             DO 720 I = 1, N
  720        NORM = NORM + ABS(RV6(I))
C
             IF (NORM .GE. 1.0E-1) GO TO 840
C     ********** IN-LINE PROCEDURE FOR CHOOSING
C                     A NEW STARTING VECTOR **********
             IF (ITS .GE. N) GO TO 830
             ITS = ITS + 1
             XU = EPS4 / (UK + 1.0)
             RV6(1) = EPS4
C
             DO 760 I = 2, N
  760        RV6(I) = XU
C
             RV6(ITS) = RV6(ITS) - EPS4 * UK
             GO TO 600
```

```
C      ********** SET ERROR -- NON-CONVERGED EIGENVECTOR **********
  830     IERR = -R
          XU = 0.0
          GO TO 870
C      ********** NORMALIZE SO THAT SUM OF SQUARES IS
C                   1 AND EXPAND TO FULL ORDER **********
  840     U = 0.0
C
          DO 860 I = 1, N
  860     U = U + RV6(I)**2
C
          XU = 1.0 / SQRT(U)
C
  870     DO 900 I = 1, N
  900     Z(I,R) = RV6(I) * XU
C
          X0 = X1
  920 CONTINUE
C
 1001 RETURN
      END
```

NATS PROJECT

EIGENSYSTEM SUBROUTINE PACKAGE (EISPACK)

F294-2   BISECT

A Fortran IV Subroutine to Determine Some Eigenvalues
of a Symmetric Tridiagonal Matrix.

May, 1972
February, 1977

1. PURPOSE.

The Fortran IV subroutine BISECT   determines those
eigenvalues of a symmetric tridiagonal matrix in a specified
interval using Sturm sequencing.

2. USAGE.

A. Calling Sequence.

The SUBROUTINE statement is

SUBROUTINE BISECT(N,EPS1,D,E,E2,LB,UB,
                   MM,M,W,IND,IERR,RV4,RV5)

The parameters are discussed below and the
interpretation of working precision for various machines
is given in the section discussing certification.

N   is an integer input variable set equal to
         the order of the matrix.

EPS1   is a working precision real variable. On
         input, it specifies an absolute error
         tolerance for the computed eigenvalues. If
         the input EPS1 is non-positive, it is
         reset to a default value described in
         section 2C.

D   is a working precision real input one-
         dimensional variable of dimension at least
         N containing the diagonal elements of the
         symmetric tridiagonal matrix.

E   is a working precision real input one-
         dimensional variable of dimension at least
         N containing, in its last N-1 positions,
         the subdiagonal elements of the symmetric
         tridiagonal matrix. E(1) is arbitrary.

E2   is a working precision real one-dimensional variable of dimension at least N. On input, the last N-1 positions in this array contain the squares of the subdiagonal elements of the symmetric tridiagonal matrix. E2(1) is arbitrary. On output, E2(1) is set to zero. If any of the elements in E are regarded as negligible, the corresponding elements of E2 are set to zero, and so the matrix splits into a direct sum of submatrices.

LB,UB are working precision real input variables specifying the lower and upper endpoints, respectively, of the interval to be searched for the eigenvalues. If LB is not less than UB, BISECT computes no eigenvalues. See section 2C for further details.

MM   is an integer input variable set equal to an upper bound for the number of eigenvalues in the interval (LB,UB).

M   is an integer output variable set equal to the number of eigenvalues determined to lie in the interval (LB,UB).

W   is a working precision real output one-dimensional variable of dimension at least MM containing the M eigenvalues of the symmetric tridiagonal matrix in the interval (LB,UB). The eigenvalues are in ascending order in W.

IND   is an integer output one-dimensional variable of dimension at least MM containing the submatrix indices associated with the corresponding M eigenvalues in W. Eigenvalues belonging to the first submatrix have index 1, those belonging to the second submatrix have index 2, etc.

IERR   is an integer output variable set equal to an error completion code described in section 2B. The normal completion code is zero.

RV4,RV5 are working precision real temporary one-dimensional variables of dimension at least N used to hold the lower and upper bounds for the eigenvalues in the bisection process.

B. Error Conditions and Returns.

If M exceeds MM, BISECT terminates with no eigenvalues computed, and IERR is set to 3*N+1. Upon this error exit, M contains the number of eigenvalues determined to lie in (LB,UB).

If M does not exceed MM, IERR is set to zero.

C. Applicability and Restrictions.

To determine some of the eigenvalues of a full symmetric matrix, BISECT should be preceded by TRED1 (F277) to provide a suitable symmetric tridiagonal matrix for BISECT.

To determine some of the eigenvalues of a complex Hermitian matrix, BISECT should be preceded by HTRIDI (F284) to provide a suitable real symmetric tridiagonal matrix for BISECT.

Some of the eigenvalues of certain non-symmetric tridiagonal matrices can be computed using the combination of FIGI (F280) and BISECT. See F280 for the description of this special class of matrices. For these matrices, BISECT should be preceded by FIGI to provide a suitable symmetric matrix for BISECT.

To determine eigenvectors associated with the computed eigenvalues, BISECT should be followed by TINVIT (F223) and the appropriate back transformation subroutine -- TRBAK1 (F279) after TRED1, HTRIBK (F285) after HTRIDI, or BAKVEC (F281) after FIGI.

The subroutines TQL1 (F289) and IMTQL1 (F291) determine all the eigenvalues of a symmetric tridiagonal matrix faster than BISECT determines 25 percent of them. Hence, if more than 25 percent of them are desired, it is recommended that TQL1 or IMTQL1 be used.

The interval (LB,UB) is formally half-open, not including the upper endpoint UB. However, because of rounding errors, the true eigenvalues very close to the endpoints of the interval may be erroneously counted or missed.

The input interval (LB,UB) may be refined internally to a smaller interval known to contain all the eigenvalues in (LB,UB). This insures that BISECT will not perform unnecessary bisection steps to determine the eigenvalues in (LB,UB).

The precision of the computed eigenvalues is controlled through the parameter EPS1. To obtain eigenvalues accurate to within a certain absolute error, EPS1 should be set to that error. In particular, if MACHEP denotes the relative machine precision, then to obtain the eigenvalues to an accuracy commensurate with small relative perturbations of the order of MACHEP in the matrix elements, it is enough for most tridiagonal matrices that EPS1 be approximately MACHEP times a norm of the matrix. But some matrices require a smaller EPS1 for this accuracy, perhaps as small as MACHEP times the eigenvalue of smallest magnitude in (LB,UB). Note, however, that if EPS1 is smaller than required, BISECT will perform unnecessary bisection steps to determine the eigenvalues. For further discussion of EPS1, see reference (1).

If the input EPS1 is non-positive, BISECT resets it, for each submatrix, to -MACHEP times the 1-norm of the submatrix and uses its magnitude. This value is tentatively considered adequate for computing the eigenvalues to an accuracy commensurate with small relative perturbations of the order of MACHEP in the matrix elements.

3. DISCUSSION OF METHOD AND ALGORITHM.

The eigenvalues are determined by the method of bisection applied to the Sturm sequence.

The calculations proceed as follows. First, the subdiagonal elements are tested for negligibility. If an element is considered negligible, its square is set to zero, and so the matrix splits into a direct sum of submatrices. Then, the Sturm sequence for the entire matrix is evaluated at UB and LB giving the number of eigenvalues of the matrix less than UB and LB respectively. The difference is the number of eigenvalues in (LB,UB).

Next, a submatrix is examined for its eigenvalues in the interval (LB,UB). The Gerschgorin interval, known to contain all the eigenvalues, is determined and used to refine the input interval (LB,UB). If the input EPS1 is non-positive, it is reset to the default value described in section 2C. Then, subintervals, each enclosing an eigenvalue in (LB,UB), are shrunk using a bisection process until the endpoints of each subinterval are close enough to be accepted as an eigenvalue of the submatrix. Here the endpoints of each subinterval are close enough when they differ by less than MACHEP times twice the sum of the magnitudes of the endpoints plus the absolute error tolerance EPS1.

The submatrix eigenvalues are then merged with previously found eigenvalues into an ordered set.

The above steps are repeated on each submatrix until all the eigenvalues in the interval (LB,UB) are computed.

This subroutine is a subset (except for the section merging eigenvalues of submatrices) of the Fortran subroutine TSTURM (F293), which is a translation of the Algol procedure TRISTURM written and discussed in detail by Peters and Wilkinson (2). A similar Algol procedure BISECT is discussed in detail by Barth, Martin, and Wilkinson (1).

4. REFERENCES.

1) Barth, W., Martin, R.S., and Wilkinson, J.H., Calculation of the Eigenvalues of a Symmetric Tridiagonal Matrix by the Method of Bisection, Num. Math. 9,386-393 (1967).

2) Peters, G. and Wilkinson, J.H., The Calculation of Specified Eigenvectors by Inverse Iteration, Handbook for Automatic Computation, Volume II, Linear Algebra, J. H. Wilkinson - C. Reinsch, Contribution II/18, 418-439, Springer-Verlag, 1971.

5. CHECKOUT.

A. Test Cases.

See the section discussing testing of the codes for complex Hermitian, real symmetric, real symmetric tridiagonal, and certain real non-symmetric tridiagonal matrices.

B. Accuracy.

The subroutine BISECT is numerically stable (1,2); that is, the computed eigenvalues are close to those of the original matrix. In addition, they are the exact eigenvalues of a matrix close to the original real symmetric tridiagonal matrix.

```
      SUBROUTINE BISECT(N,EPS1,D,E,E2,LB,UB,MM,M,W,IND,IERR,RV4,RV5)
C
      INTEGER I,J,K,L,M,N,P,Q,R,S,II,MM,M1,M2,TAG,IERR,ISTURM
      REAL D(N),E(N),E2(N),W(MM),RV4(N),RV5(N)
      REAL U,V,LB,T1,T2,UB,XU,X0,X1,EPS1,MACHEP
      REAL ABS,AMAX1,AMIN1,FLOAT
      INTEGER IND(MM)
C
C     ********** MACHEP IS A MACHINE DEPENDENT PARAMETER SPECIFYING
C                THE RELATIVE PRECISION OF FLOATING POINT ARITHMETIC.
C
C                **********
      MACHEP = ?
C
      IERR = 0
      TAG = 0
      T1 = LB
      T2 = UB
C     ********** LOOK FOR SMALL SUB-DIAGONAL ENTRIES **********
      DO 40 I = 1, N
         IF (I .EQ. 1) GO TO 20
         IF (ABS(E(I)) .GT. MACHEP * (ABS(D(I)) + ABS(D(I-1))))
     X        GO TO 40
   20    E2(I) = 0.0
   40 CONTINUE
C     ********** DETERMINE THE NUMBER OF EIGENVALUES
C                IN THE INTERVAL **********
      P = 1
      Q = N
      X1 = UB
      ISTURM = 1
      GO TO 320
   60 M = S
      X1 = LB
      ISTURM = 2
      GO TO 320
   80 M = M - S
      IF (M .GT. MM) GO TO 980
      Q = 0
      R = 0
C     ********** ESTABLISH AND PROCESS NEXT SUBMATRIX, REFINING
C                INTERVAL BY THE GERSCHGORIN BOUNDS **********
  100 IF (R .EQ. M) GO TO 1001
      TAG = TAG + 1
      P = Q + 1
      XU = D(P)
      X0 = D(P)
      U = 0.0
```

```
C
      DO 120 Q = P, N
         X1 = U
         U = 0.0
         V = 0.0
         IF (Q .EQ. N) GO TO 110
         U = ABS(E(Q+1))
         V = E2(Q+1)
  110    XU = AMIN1(D(Q)-(X1+U),XU)
         XO = AMAX1(D(Q)+(X1+U),XO)
         IF (V .EQ. 0.0) GO TO 140
  120 CONTINUE
C
  140 X1 = AMAX1(ABS(XU),ABS(XO)) * MACHEP
      IF (EPS1 .LE. 0.0) EPS1 = -X1
      IF (P .NE. Q) GO TO 180
C     ********* CHECK FOR ISOLATED ROOT WITHIN INTERVAL *********
      IF (T1 .GT. D(P) .OR. D(P) .GE. T2) GO TO 940
      M1 = P
      M2 = P
      RV5(P) = D(P)
      GO TO 900
  180 X1 = X1 * FLOAT(Q-P+1)
      LB = AMAX1(T1,XU-X1)
      UB = AMIN1(T2,XO+X1)
      X1 = LB
      ISTURM = 3
      GO TO 320
  200 M1 = S + 1
      X1 = UB
      ISTURM = 4
      GO TO 320
  220 M2 = S
      IF (M1 .GT. M2) GO TO 940
C     ********* FIND ROOTS BY BISECTION *********
      XO = UB
      ISTURM = 5
C
      DO 240 I = M1, M2
         RV5(I) = UB
         RV4(I) = LB
  240 CONTINUE
C     ********* LOOP FOR K-TH EIGENVALUE
C               FOR K=M2 STEP -1 UNTIL M1 DO --
C               (-DO- NOT USED TO LEGALIZE -COMPUTED GO TO-) *********
      K = M2
  250    XU = LB
C     ********* FOR I=K STEP -1 UNTIL M1 DO -- *********
         DO 260 II = M1, K
            I = M1 + K - II
            IF (XU .GE. RV4(I)) GO TO 260
            XU = RV4(I)
            GO TO 280
  260    CONTINUE
```

```
C
  280     IF (XO .GT. RV5(K)) XO = RV5(K)
C     ********** NEXT BISECTION STEP **********
  300     X1 = (XU + XO) * 0.5
          IF ((XO - XU) .LE. (2.0 * MACHEP *
   X        (ABS(XU) + ABS(XO)) + ABS(EPS1))) GO TO 420
C     ********** IN-LINE PROCEDURE FOR STURM SEQUENCE **********
  320     S = P - 1
          U = 1.0
C
          DO 340 I = P, Q
            IF (U .NE. 0.0) GO TO 325
            V = ABS(E(I)) / MACHEP
            IF (E2(I) .EQ. 0.0) V = 0.0
            GO TO 330
  325       V = E2(I) / U
  330       U = D(I) - X1 - V
            IF (U .LT. 0.0) S = S + 1
  340     CONTINUE
C
          GO TO (60,80,200,220,360), ISTURM
C     ********** REFINE INTERVALS **********
  360     IF (S .GE. K) GO TO 400
          XU = X1
          IF (S .GE. M1) GO TO 380
          RV4(M1) = X1
          GO TO 300
  380     RV4(S+1) = X1
          IF (RV5(S) .GT. X1) RV5(S) = X1
          GO TO 300
  400     XO = X1
          GO TO 300
C     ********** K-TH EIGENVALUE FOUND **********
  420     RV5(K) = X1
          K = K - 1
          IF (K .GE. M1) GO TO 250
C     ********** ORDER EIGENVALUES TAGGED WITH THEIR
C               SUBMATRIX ASSOCIATIONS **********
  900 S = R
          R = R + M2 - M1 + 1
          J = 1
          K = M1
C
          DO 920 L = 1, R
            IF (J .GT. S) GO TO 910
            IF (K .GT. M2) GO TO 940
            IF (RV5(K) .GE. W(L)) GO TO 915
C
            DO 905 II = J, S
              I = L + S - II
              W(I+1) = W(I)
              IND(I+1) = IND(I)
  905       CONTINUE
```

```
C
  910     W(L) = RV5(K)
          IND(L) = TAG
          K = K + 1
          GO TO 920
  915     J = J + 1
  920 CONTINUE
C
  940 IF (Q .LT. N) GO TO 100
      GO TO 1001
C    ********** SET ERROR -- UNDERESTIMATE OF NUMBER OF
C                EIGENVALUES IN INTERVAL **********
  980 IERR = 3 * N + 1
 1001 LB = T1
      UB = T2
      RETURN
      END
```

NATS PROJECT

EIGENSYSTEM SUBROUTINE PACKAGE (EISPACK)

F236 BQR

A Fortran IV Subroutine to Determine Some Eigenvalues
of a Real Symmetric Band Matrix.

July, 1975

1. PURPOSE.

The Fortran IV subroutine BQR determines some of the
eigenvalues of a real symmetric band matrix using the QR
algorithm with shifts of origin. It determines one
eigenvalue for each call, deflating the matrix before
returning. The subroutine could be used to determine all of
the eigenvalues; however, more efficient routines exist in
this case (see section 2C).

2. USAGE.

A. Calling Sequence.

The SUBROUTINE statement is

SUBROUTINE BQR(NM,N,MB,A,T,R,IERR,NV,RV)

The parameters are discussed below and the
interpretation of working precision for various machines
is given in the section discussing certification.

NM   is an integer input variable set equal to
        the row dimension of the two-dimensional
        array A as specified in the DIMENSION
        statement for A in the calling program.

N   is an integer input variable set equal to
        the order of the matrix A. N must be not
        greater than NM.

MB   is an integer input variable set equal to
        the (half) band width of the matrix A,
        defined as the number of adjacent diagonals,
        including the principal diagonal, required
        to specify the non-zero portion of the lower
        triangle of the matrix. MB must be not
        greater than N for the first call of BQR
        (see section 2C).

A   is a working precision real two-dimensional variable with row dimension NM and column dimension at least MB. On input, A contains the lower triangle of the symmetric band matrix of order N and (half) band width MB which with the shift parameter T defines the matrix whose eigenvalues are sought. Its lowest subdiagonal is stored in the last N+1-MB positions of the first column, its next subdiagonal in the last N+2-MB positions of the second column, further subdiagonals similarly, and finally its principal diagonal in the N positions of the last column. Contents of storage locations not part of the matrix are arbitrary. For example, when N=5 and MB=3, A should contain

```
(    *         *       A(1,1) )
(    *       A(2,1)    A(2,2) )
( A(3,1)    A(3,2)    A(3,3) )
( A(4,2)    A(4,3)    A(4,4) )
( A(5,3)    A(5,4)    A(5,5) )
```

where the subscripts for each element refer to the row and column of the element in the standard two-dimensional representation, and (*) denotes an arbitrary value. On output, A has the same form as on input, except having been deflated (by a zeroed last row) to next lower order. It is thus suitable as an input parameter for a further call of BQR if an additional eigenvalue is sought.

T   is a working precision real variable. On input, T specifies the shift applied to the diagonal elements of A; the matrix whose eigenvalue is to be determined is thus A+TI where I is the identity matrix. The output value of T is simultaneously an eigenvalue of A+TI (generally that one nearest to the input T) and the shift applied to the diagonal elements of the output A matrix. It is thus suitable as an input parameter (along with A) for a further call of BQR if an additional eigenvalue is sought.

R   is a working precision real variable used to determine when the last row (and column) of the current transformed band matrix in A can be regarded as negligible. It should be set to zero for the first call of BQR and will be reset by the subroutine at each call to a value suitable as input for the subsequent call (see section 3).

IERR is an integer output variable set equal to an error completion code described in section 2B. The normal completion code is zero.

NV   is an integer input variable set equal to the dimension of the array RV as specified in the DIMENSION statement for RV in the calling program. NV must be not less than 2*MB**2+4*MB-3.

RV   is a working precision real temporary array variable of dimension at least 2*MB**2+4*MB-3. The first 3*MB-2 locations are used for auxiliary storage, thereby permitting the transformed elements of A to be stored back into A. The next 2*MB-1 locations are used to store the scalar (half) lengths of the vectors that define the elementary Hermitians at each stage of the unitary reduction process. The final MB*(2*MB-1) locations are used to store these vectors themselves.

B. Error Conditions and Returns.

If more than 30 iterations are required to determine the eigenvalue, BQR terminates with IERR set to N.

If the eigenvalue is determined within 30 iterations, IERR is set to zero.

C. Applicability and Restrictions.

To determine some of the eigenvalues of a band symmetric matrix, BQR should be called successively for each eigenvalue, transmitting the output parameters from the previous call except for replacement of N by N-1. Note that MB should not be altered even when it exceeds the current N. The eigenvalues determined will usually be those nearest to the input value of T.

To determine all the eigenvalues of a band symmetric
matrix, subroutine BANDR (F226) should be used
instead, followed by TQL1 (F289), IMTQL1 (F291), or
TQLRAT (F235).

To determine eigenvectors associated with the computed
eigenvalues, BQR should be followed by BANDV (F227).
Note, however, that the matrix A+TI defined by the
original A and T parameters must be saved before
BQR for its later use by BANDV.

If the matrix has elements of widely varying magnitudes,
the larger ones should be in the top left-hand corner.

3. DISCUSSION OF METHOD AND ALGORITHM.

The aim of the algorithm is to obtain the eigenvalue of A
of smallest magnitude; i.e., the eigenvalue of A+TI nearest
to T. The eigenvalue is determined by the QR method. The
essence of this method is a process whereby a sequence of
symmetric band matrices, unitarily similar to the original
symmetric band matrix with shifted origin is formed which
converges to a matrix with a zero last row (and column). The
sum of the origin shifts is then taken as an eigenvalue of
A, and this number added to the input T is returned as the
desired eigenvalue of A+TI.

Shifting is deferred until the off-diagonal elements of the
last row of the transformed A become small enough that
their summed magnitudes does not exceed 1/4 of the
tolerance quantity R. Shifting sooner than this could lose
sight of the desired eigenvalue, while shifting too late
would appreciably slow the algorithm. R is reset at each
call to the maximum of its current value and the summed
magnitudes of the off-diagonal elements of the current last
row of A. The shifting criterion adopted is effective as
long as the rows of A are not rapidly increasing from top
to bottom.

When an origin shift finally takes place, it is chosen as the
eigenvalue of the lowest 2x2 principal minor closer to the
second diagonal element of this minor. When the last row
(and column) of the matrix become negligible, then the sum of
the origin shifts added to the input T is returned in T
as the eigenvalue of A+TI and the matrix is deflated by
deleting (zeroing) its last row (and column).

This subroutine is a translation of the Algol procedure BQR
written and discussed in detail by Martin, Reinsch, and
Wilkinson (1).

4. REFERENCES.

1) Martin, R.S., Reinsch, C., and Wilkinson, J.H., The QR
   Algorithm for Band Symmetric Matrices,
   Num. Math. 16,85-92 (1970). (Reprinted in Handbook for
   Automatic Computation, Volume II, Linear Algebra,
   J. H. Wilkinson - C. Reinsch, Contribution II/7, 266-272,
   Springer-Verlag, 1971.)

5. CHECKOUT.

A. Test Cases.

See the section discussing testing of the codes for
real symmetric band matrices.

B. Accuracy.

The subroutine BQR is numerically stable (1); that is,
the computed eigenvalues are close to those of the
original matrix. In addition, they are the exact
eigenvalues of a matrix close to the original real
symmetric band matrix.

```
      SUBROUTINE BQR(NM,N,MB,A,T,R,IERR,NV,RV)
C
      INTEGER I,J,K,L,M,N,II,IK,JK,JM,KJ,KK,KM,LL,MB,MK,MN,MZ,
     X         M1,M2,M3,M4,NI,NM,NV,ITS,KJ1,M21,M31,IERR,IMULT
      REAL A(NM,MB),RV(NV)
      REAL F,G,Q,R,S,T,SCALE
      REAL SQRT,ABS,SIGN
      INTEGER MAX0,MIN0
C
      IERR = 0
      M1 = MIN0(MB,N)
      M = M1 - 1
      M2 = M + M
      M21 = M2 + 1
      M3 = M21 + M
      M31 = M3 + 1
      M4 = M31 + M2
      MN = M + N
      MZ = MB - M1
      ITS = 0
C     ********** TEST FOR CONVERGENCE **********
   40 G = A(N,MB)
      IF (M .EQ. 0) GO TO 360
      F = 0.0
C
      DO 50 K = 1, M
         MK = K + MZ
         F = F + ABS(A(N,MK))
   50 CONTINUE
C
      IF (ITS .EQ. 0 .AND. F .GT. R) R = F
      IF (R + F .LE. R) GO TO 360
      IF (ITS .EQ. 30) GO TO 1000
      ITS = ITS + 1
C     ********** FORM SHIFT FROM BOTTOM 2 BY 2 MINOR **********
      IF (F .GT. 0.25 * R .AND. ITS .LT. 5) GO TO 90
      F = A(N,MB-1)
      IF (F .EQ. 0.0) GO TO 70
      Q = (A(N-1,MB) - G) / (2.0 * F)
      S = SQRT(Q*Q+1.0)
      G = G - F / (Q + SIGN(S,Q))
   70 T = T + G
C
      DO 80 I = 1, N
   80 A(I,MB) = A(I,MB) - G
C
   90 DO 100 K = M31, M4
  100 RV(K) = 0.0
C
      DO 350 II = 1, MN
         I = II - M
         NI = N - II
         IF (NI .LT. 0) GO TO 230
```

```
C     ********** FORM COLUMN OF SHIFTED MATRIX A-G*I **********
      L = MAXO(1,2-I)
C
      DO 110 K = 1, M3
  110 RV(K) = 0.0
C
      DO 120 K = L, M1
         KM = K + M
         MK = K + MZ
         RV(KM) = A(II,MK)
  120 CONTINUE
C
      LL = MINO(M,NI)
      IF (LL .EQ. 0) GO TO 135
C
      DO 130 K = 1, LL
         KM = K + M21
         IK = II + K
         MK = MB - K
         RV(KM) = A(IK,MK)
  130 CONTINUE
C     ********** PRE-MULTIPLY WITH HOUSEHOLDER REFLECTIONS **********
  135 LL = M2
      IMULT = 0
C     ********** MULTIPLICATION PROCEDURE **********
  140 KJ = M4 - M1
C
      DO 170 J = 1, LL
         KJ = KJ + M1
         JM = J + M3
         IF (RV(JM) .EQ. 0.0) GO TO 170
         F = 0.0
C
         DO 150 K = 1, M1
            KJ = KJ + 1
            JK = J + K - 1
            F = F + RV(KJ) * RV(JK)
  150    CONTINUE
C
         F = F / RV(JM)
         KJ = KJ - M1
C
         DO 160 K = 1, M1
            KJ = KJ + 1
            JK = J + K - 1
            RV(JK) = RV(JK) - RV(KJ) * F
  160    CONTINUE
C
         KJ = KJ - M1
  170 CONTINUE
C
      IF (IMULT .NE. 0) GO TO 280
```

```
C         ********** HOUSEHOLDER REFLECTION **********
          F = RV(M21)
          S = 0.0
          RV(M4) = 0.0
          SCALE = 0.0
C
          DO 180 K = M21, M3
  180     SCALE = SCALE + ABS(RV(K))
C
          IF (SCALE .EQ. 0.0) GO TO 210
C
          DO 190 K = M21, M3
  190     S = S + (RV(K)/SCALE)**2
C
          S = SCALE * SCALE * S
          G = -SIGN(SQRT(S),F)
          RV(M21) = G
          RV(M4) = S - F * G
          KJ = M4 + M2 * M1 + 1
          RV(KJ) = F - G
C
          DO 200 K = 2, M1
             KJ = KJ + 1
             KM = K + M2
             RV(KJ) = RV(KM)
  200     CONTINUE
C         ********** SAVE COLUMN OF TRIANGULAR FACTOR R **********
  210     DO 220 K = L, M1
             KM = K + M
             MK = K + MZ
             A(II,MK) = RV(KM)
  220     CONTINUE
C
  230     L = MAX0(1,M1+1-I)
          IF (I .LE. 0) GO TO 300
C         ********** PERFORM ADDITIONAL STEPS **********
          DO 240 K = 1, M21
  240     RV(K) = 0.0
C
          LL = MIN0(M1,NI+M1)
C         ********** GET ROW OF TRIANGULAR FACTOR R **********
          DO 250 KK = 1, LL
             K = KK - 1
             KM = K + M1
             IK = I + K
             MK = MB - K
             RV(KM) = A(IK,MK)
  250     CONTINUE
C         ********** POST-MULTIPLY WITH HOUSEHOLDER REFLECTIONS **********
          LL = M1
          IMULT = 1
          GO TO 140
```

```
C     ********** STORE COLUMN OF NEW A MATRIX **********
  280     DO 290 K = L, M1
              MK = K + MZ
              A(I,MK) = RV(K)
  290     CONTINUE
C     ********** UPDATE HOUSEHOLDER REFLECTIONS **********
  300     IF (L .GT. 1) L = L - 1
          KJ1 = M4 + L * M1
C
          DO 320 J = L, M2
              JM = J + M3
              RV(JM) = RV(JM+1)
C
              DO 320 K = 1, M1
                  KJ1 = KJ1 + 1
                  KJ = KJ1 - M1
                  RV(KJ) = RV(KJ1)
  320     CONTINUE
C
  350 CONTINUE
C
      GO TO 40
C     ********** CONVERGENCE **********
  360 T = T + G
C
      DO 380 I = 1, N
  380 A(I,MB) = A(I,MB) - G
C
      DO 400 K = 1, M1
          MK = K + MZ
          A(N,MK) = 0.0
  400 CONTINUE
C
      GO TO 1001
C     ********** SET ERROR -- NO CONVERGENCE TO
C                EIGENVALUE AFTER 30 ITERATIONS **********
 1000 IERR = N
 1001 RETURN
      END
```

NATS PROJECT

EIGENSYSTEM SUBROUTINE PACKAGE (EISPACK)

F233 MINFIT

A Fortran IV Subroutine to Compute the Singular Value
Decomposition of an Arbitrary Real Rectangular Matrix
and the Solution of a Related Linear Least Squares Problem.

July, 1975

1. PURPOSE.

The Fortran IV subroutine MINFIT computes the singular
values and complete orthogonal decomposition of the real
rectangular coefficient matrix A of the linear system
AX = B. A is decomposed into

$$U * DIAG(S) * V^T$$

with $U^T U = V^T V = I$. $U^T B$ is formed rather than U
itself, enabling a determination of the solution X of
minimal norm (see section 2C). The diagonal elements of S
are the singular values of A, equal to the non-negative
square roots of the eigenvalues of $A^T A$.

2. USAGE.

A. Calling Sequence.

The SUBROUTINE statement is

SUBROUTINE MINFIT(NM,M,N,A,W,IP,B,IERR,RV1)

The parameters are discussed below and the
interpretation of working precision for various machines
is given in the section discussing certification.

NM   is an integer input variable set equal to
          the row dimension of the two-dimensional
          arrays A and B as specified in the
          DIMENSION statements for A and B in the
          calling program. Note that A and B are

overwritten by N-rowed arrays V and
$U^{T}B$; hence, NM must be at least as large
as the maximum of M and N.

M   is an integer input variable set equal to
the number of rows of rectangular matrices
A and B. M must be not greater than NM.

N   is an integer input variable set equal to
the number of columns of A and the order
of the square matrix V which overwrites
A. N must be not greater than NM.

A   is a working precision real two-dimensional
variable with row dimension NM and column
dimension at least N. On input, A
contains the rectangular (coefficient)
matrix to be decomposed. On output, A has
been overwritten by the orthogonal V
matrix in the decomposition.

W   is a working precision real output one-
dimensional variable of dimension at least
N containing the singular values of A.

IP   is an integer input variable set equal to
the number of columns of B. IP can be
zero.

B   is a working precision real two-dimensional
variable with row dimension NM and column
dimension at least IP. If IP is not
zero, then on input, B contains the
constant matrix of the system. On output,
B has been overwritten by $U^{T}B$. If IP
is zero, then B is not referenced and can
be a dummy (working precision) variable.

IERR   is an integer output variable set equal to
an error completion code described in
section 2B. The normal completion code is
zero.

RV1   is a working precision real temporary one-
dimensional variable of dimension at least
N used to hold the off-diagonal elements of
the bidiagonal form.

B. Error Conditions and Returns.

If more than 30 iterations are required to determine a
singular value, this subroutine terminates with IERR
set to the index of the singular value for which the
failure occurs. The singular values in the W array
should be correct for indices IERR+1,IERR+2,...,N, as
well as the corresponding columns of V (in A) and rows
of $U^T B$ (in B).

If all the singular values are determined within 30
iterations, IERR is set to zero.

C. Applicability and Restrictions.

The minimal norm solution of AX = B can be obtained
from the decomposition in MINFIT by forming

$$V * DIAG(S^+) * U^T B$$

where each element of S^+ is the reciprocal of the
corresponding element of S where non-zero and zero
where S is zero. Some zero threshold would have to be
employed (for example, the product of the square root of
the machine precision and a norm of the matrix). Sample
coding to perform this computation might be:

```
      DO 100 I = 1, N
      DO 100 J = 1, IP
100   X(I,J) = 0.0D0
      DO 300 K = 1, N
      IF (W(K) .LT. THRESH) GO TO 300
      DO 200 I = 1, N
      DO 200 J = 1, IP
200   X(I,J) = X(I,J)+A(I,K)*B(K,J)/W(K)
300   CONTINUE
C     THE COLUMNS OF X ARE THE MINIMAL NORM SOLUTIONS.
```

Solutions of a system of homogeneous linear equations
with coefficient matrix A can be obtained as those
columns of V (or linear combinations of them) which
correspond to zero elements of S.

3. DISCUSSION OF METHOD AND ALGORITHM.

The singular value decomposition $A = U * DIAG(S) * V^T$ is accomplished in two steps. A is first reduced to the bidiagonal form J by two sequences of Householder transformations, those on the left reducing columns of A and B, and those on the right reducing rows of A. Because the transformations are orthogonal, J has the same singular values as A, that is $J = G * DIAG(S) * H^T$. Further, if the product of the left transformations is denoted P and the product of the right transformations Q, so that $J = P^T * A * Q$, then $U = PG$ and $V = QH$.

The bidiagonal form J is then decomposed by a variant of the QR method applied to the symmetric tridiagonal matrix $J^T J$. (The singular values of J are the non-negative square roots of the eigenvalues of $J^T J$.) The essence of this method is a process whereby a sequence of symmetric tridiagonal matrices, unitarily similar to $J^T J$, is formed which converges to a diagonal matrix. The rate of convergence of this sequence is improved by shifting the origin at each iteration. Before the iterations for each eigenvalue, the symmetric tridiagonal matrix is checked for a possible splitting into submatrices. If a splitting occurs, only the lowermost submatrix participates in the next iteration. The left (transposed) and right transformations used in each iteration are accumulated in the $U^T B$ (in B) and V (in A) arrays.

The origin shift at each iteration is an eigenvalue of the current lowermost 2x2 principal minor. Whenever the lowermost 1x1 principal submatrix finally splits from the rest of the matrix, its element is taken to be an eigenvalue of the original matrix and the algorithm proceeds with the remaining submatrix. This process is continued until the matrix has split completely into submatrices of order 1. The tolerances in the splitting tests are proportional to the relative machine precision.

This subroutine is a translation of the Algol procedure MINFIT written and discussed in detail by Golub and Reinsch (1).

4. REFERENCES.

1) Golub, G.H. and Reinsch, C., Singular Value
   Decomposition and Least Squares Solutions,
   Num. Math. 14,403-420 (1970). (Reprinted in Handbook for
   Automatic Computation, Volume II, Linear Algebra,
   J. H. Wilkinson - C. Reinsch, Contribution I/10, 134-151,
   Springer-Verlag, 1971.)

5. CHECKOUT.

   A. Test Cases.

      See the section discussing testing of the codes for
      singular value decomposition.

   B. Accuracy.

      The subroutine MINFIT is numerically stable (1); that
      is each computed singular value is exact for a matrix
      close to the original real rectangular matrix.

```
      SUBROUTINE MINFIT(NM,M,N,A,W,IP,B,IERR,RV1)
C
      INTEGER I,J,K,L,M,N,II,IP,I1,KK,K1,LL,L1,M1,NM,ITS,IERR
      REAL A(NM,N),W(N),B(NM,IP),RV1(N)
      REAL C,F,G,H,S,X,Y,Z,EPS,SCALE,MACHEP
      REAL SQRT,AMAX1,ABS,SIGN
C
C     ********** MACHEP IS A MACHINE DEPENDENT PARAMETER SPECIFYING
C                THE RELATIVE PRECISION OF FLOATING POINT ARITHMETIC.
C
C                **********
      MACHEP = ?
C
      IERR = 0
C     ********** HOUSEHOLDER REDUCTION TO BIDIAGONAL FORM **********
      G = 0.0
      SCALE = 0.0
      X = 0.0
C
      DO 300 I = 1, N
         L = I + 1
         RV1(I) = SCALE * G
         G = 0.0
         S = 0.0
         SCALE = 0.0
         IF (I .GT. M) GO TO 210
C
         DO 120 K = I, M
  120    SCALE = SCALE + ABS(A(K,I))
C
         IF (SCALE .EQ. 0.0) GO TO 210
C
         DO 130 K = I, M
            A(K,I) = A(K,I) / SCALE
            S = S + A(K,I)**2
  130    CONTINUE
C
         F = A(I,I)
         G = -SIGN(SQRT(S),F)
         H = F * G - S
         A(I,I) = F - G
         IF (I .EQ. N) GO TO 160
C
         DO 150 J = L, N
            S = 0.0
C
            DO 140 K = I, M
  140       S = S + A(K,I) * A(K,J)
C
            F = S / H
C
            DO 150 K = I, M
               A(K,J) = A(K,J) + F * A(K,I)
  150    CONTINUE
```

```
C
  160     IF (IP .EQ. 0) GO TO 190
C
          DO 180 J = 1, IP
            S = 0.0
C
            DO 170 K = I, M
  170       S = S + A(K,I) * B(K,J)
C
            F = S / H
C
            DO 180 K = I, M
              B(K,J) = B(K,J) + F * A(K,I)
  180     CONTINUE
C
  190     DO 200 K = I, M
  200     A(K,I) = SCALE * A(K,I)
C
  210     W(I) = SCALE * G
          G = 0.0
          S = 0.0
          SCALE = 0.0
          IF (I .GT. M .OR. I .EQ. N) GO TO 290
C
          DO 220 K = L, N
  220     SCALE = SCALE + ABS(A(I,K))
C
          IF (SCALE .EQ. 0.0) GO TO 290
C
          DO 230 K = L, N
            A(I,K) = A(I,K) / SCALE
            S = S + A(I,K)**2
  230     CONTINUE
C
          F = A(I,L)
          G = -SIGN(SQRT(S),F)
          H = F * G - S
          A(I,L) = F - G
C
          DO 240 K = L, N
  240     RV1(K) = A(I,K) / H
C
          IF (I .EQ. M) GO TO 270
C
          DO 260 J = L, M
            S = 0.0
C
            DO 250 K = L, N
  250       S = S + A(J,K) * A(I,K)
C
            DO 260 K = L, N
              A(J,K) = A(J,K) + S * RV1(K)
  260     CONTINUE
```

```
C
  270     DO 280 K = L, N
  280     A(I,K) = SCALE * A(I,K)
C
  290     X = AMAX1(X,ABS(W(I))+ABS(RV1(I)))
  300 CONTINUE
C     ********** ACCUMULATION OF RIGHT-HAND TRANSFORMATIONS.
C                   FOR I=N STEP -1 UNTIL 1 DO -- **********
      DO 400 II = 1, N
         I = N + 1 - II
         IF (I .EQ. N) GO TO 390
         IF (G .EQ. 0.0) GO TO 360
C
         DO 320 J = L, N
C     ********** DOUBLE DIVISION AVOIDS POSSIBLE UNDERFLOW **********
  320     A(J,I) = (A(I,J) / A(I,L)) / G
C
         DO 350 J = L, N
            S = 0.0
C
            DO 340 K = L, N
  340       S = S + A(I,K) * A(K,J)
C
            DO 350 K = L, N
               A(K,J) = A(K,J) + S * A(K,I)
  350     CONTINUE
C
  360     DO 380 J = L, N
            A(I,J) = 0.0
            A(J,I) = 0.0
  380     CONTINUE
C
  390     A(I,I) = 1.0
         G = RV1(I)
         L = I
  400 CONTINUE
C
      IF (M .GE. N .OR. IP .EQ. 0) GO TO 510
      M1 = M + 1
C
      DO 500 I = M1, N
C
         DO 500 J = 1, IP
            B(I,J) = 0.0
  500 CONTINUE
C     ********** DIAGONALIZATION OF THE BIDIAGONAL FORM **********
  510 EPS = MACHEP * X
C     ********** FOR K=N STEP -1 UNTIL 1 DO -- **********
      DO 700 KK = 1, N
         K1 = N - KK
         K = K1 + 1
         ITS = 0
```

```
C         ********** TEST FOR SPLITTING.
C                     FOR L=K STEP -1 UNTIL 1 DO -- **********
  520     DO 530 LL = 1, K
             L1 = K - LL
             L = L1 + 1
             IF (ABS(RV1(L)) .LE. EPS) GO TO 565
C         ********** RV1(1) IS ALWAYS ZERO, SO THERE IS NO EXIT
C                     THROUGH THE BOTTOM OF THE LOOP **********
             IF (ABS(W(L1)) .LE. EPS) GO TO 540
  530     CONTINUE
C         ********** CANCELLATION OF RV1(L) IF L GREATER THAN 1 **********
  540     C = 0.0
          S = 1.0
C
          DO 560 I = L, K
             F = S * RV1(I)
             RV1(I) = C * RV1(I)
             IF (ABS(F) .LE. EPS) GO TO 565
             G = W(I)
             H = SQRT(F*F+G*G)
             W(I) = H
             C = G / H
             S = -F / H
             IF (IP .EQ. 0) GO TO 560
C
             DO 550 J = 1, IP
                Y = B(L1,J)
                Z = B(I,J)
                B(L1,J) = Y * C + Z * S
                B(I,J) = -Y * S + Z * C
  550        CONTINUE
C
  560     CONTINUE
C         ********** TEST FOR CONVERGENCE **********
  565     Z = W(K)
          IF (L .EQ. K) GO TO 650
C         ********** SHIFT FROM BOTTOM 2 BY 2 MINOR **********
          IF (ITS .EQ. 30) GO TO 1000
          ITS = ITS + 1
          X = W(L)
          Y = W(K1)
          G = RV1(K1)
          H = RV1(K)
          F = ((Y - Z) * (Y + Z) + (G - H) * (G + H)) / (2.0 * H * Y)
          G = SQRT(F*F+1.0)
          F = ((X - Z) * (X + Z) + H * (Y / (F + SIGN(G,F)) - H)) / X
C         ********** NEXT QR TRANSFORMATION **********
          C = 1.0
          S = 1.0
```

```
C
          DO 600 I1 = L, K1
          I = I1 + 1
          G = RV1(I)
          Y = W(I)
          H = S * G
          G = C * G
          Z = SQRT(F*F+H*H)
          RV1(I1) = Z
          C = F / Z
          S = H / Z
          F = X * C + G * S
          G = -X * S + G * C
          H = Y * S
          Y = Y * C
C
          DO 570 J = 1, N
             X = A(J,I1)
             Z = A(J,I)
             A(J,I1) = X * C + Z * S
             A(J,I) = -X * S + Z * C
  570     CONTINUE
C
          Z = SQRT(F*F+H*H)
          W(I1) = Z
C     ********* ROTATION CAN BE ARBITRARY IF Z IS ZERO **********
          IF (Z .EQ. 0.0) GO TO 580
          C = F / Z
          S = H / Z
  580     F = C * G + S * Y
          X = -S * G + C * Y
          IF (IP .EQ. 0) GO TO 600
C
          DO 590 J = 1, IP
             Y = B(I1,J)
             Z = B(I,J)
             B(I1,J) = Y * C + Z * S
             B(I,J) = -Y * S + Z * C
  590     CONTINUE
C
  600     CONTINUE
C
          RV1(L) = 0.0
          RV1(K) = F
          W(K) = X
          GO TO 520
C     ********* CONVERGENCE **********
  650     IF (Z .GE. 0.0) GO TO 700
C     ********* W(K) IS MADE NON-NEGATIVE **********
          W(K) = -Z
C
          DO 690 J = 1, N
  690     A(J,K) = -A(J,K)
```

```
C
  700 CONTINUE
C
      GO TO 1001
C     ********** SET ERROR -- NO CONVERGENCE TO A
C                SINGULAR VALUE AFTER 30 ITERATIONS **********
 1000 IERR = K
 1001 RETURN
      END
```

NATS PROJECT

EIGENSYSTEM SUBROUTINE PACKAGE (EISPACK)

F238   QZHES

A Fortran IV Subroutine to Simultaneously Reduce One of a
Pair of Real General Matrices to Upper Hessenberg Form
and the Other to Upper Triangular Form Using and
Optionally Accumulating Orthogonal Transformations.

July, 1975

1. PURPOSE.

The Fortran IV subroutine QZHES reduces the generalized
real eigenproblem AX = (LAMBDA)BX to an equivalent problem
with A in upper Hessenberg form and B in upper triangular
form, using and optionally accumulating orthogonal
transformations. These reduced forms are used by other
subroutines to find the generalized eigenvalues and/or
eigenvectors of the original matrix system. See section 2C
for the specific routines.

2. USAGE.

A. Calling Sequence.

The SUBROUTINE statement is

SUBROUTINE   QZHES(NM,N,A,B,MATZ,Z)

The parameters are discussed below and the
interpretation of working precision for various machines
is given in the section discussing certification.

NM   is an integer input variable set equal to
          the row dimension of the two-dimensional
          arrays A and B (and Z if MATZ is
          true) as specified in the DIMENSION
          statements for A and B (and Z) in the
          calling program.

N   is an integer input variable set equal to
          the order of the matrices A and B. N
          must be not greater than NM.

A   is a working precision real two-dimensional
             variable with row dimension   NM   and column
             dimension at least   N.   On input,   A
             contains one of the real general matrices of
             order   N   that define the eigenproblem
             AX = (LAMBDA)BX.   On output,   A   contains an
             upper Hessenberg matrix; elements below the
             subdiagonal are set to zero.   See section 3
             for the details.

B   is a working precision real two-dimensional
             variable with row dimension   NM   and column
             dimension at least   N.   On input,   B
             contains the other real general matrix of
             order   N   in the system.   On output,   B
             contains an upper triangular matrix;
             elements below the diagonal are set to zero.
             See section 3 for the details.

MATZ   is a logical input variable set true if the
             (column) transformation matrix is to be
             accumulated and set false otherwise.

Z   is, if   MATZ   is true, a working precision
             real output two-dimensional variable with
             row dimension   NM   and column dimension at
             least   N.   It contains the orthogonal
             (column) transformation matrix produced in
             the reductions to the Hessenberg and
             triangular forms of   A   and   B.   If MATZ
             is false,   Z   is not referenced and can be a
             dummy (working precision) variable.

B. Error Conditions and Returns.

    None.

C. Applicability and Restrictions.

    If all the eigenvalues of the original matrix system are
    desired, this subroutine should be followed by   QZIT
    (F239)   and   QZVAL (F240).

    If all the eigenvalues and eigenvectors of the original
    matrix system are desired, this subroutine should be
    followed by   QZIT (F239),   QZVAL (F240), and   QZVEC
    (F241).

3. DISCUSSION OF METHOD AND ALGORITHM.

B is first reduced to upper triangular form, one column at a time, by Householder row transformations. These transformations are simultaneously applied to A.

A is then reduced to upper Hessenberg form by row rotations while maintaining the triangular form of B. This is possible if the elements of A are annihilated in a precise order, columnwise from the bottom, as for example when N=5:

$$
\begin{pmatrix}
X & X & X & X & X \\
X & X & X & X & X \\
(3) & X & X & X & X \\
(2) & (5) & X & X & X \\
(1) & (4) & (6) & X & X
\end{pmatrix}.
$$

Each rotation annihilating an element of A introduces one nonzero element on the subdiagonal of B. This element is then annihilated by a column rotation which when applied to A does not disturb any of the newly introduced zeros. By accumulating these column rotations in Z, full information is saved for later use in back transforming the eigenvectors of the reduced system into those of the original system.

This subroutine is an implementation of the first step of the QZ algorithm written and discussed in detail by Moler and Stewart (1).

4. REFERENCES.

1) Moler, C.B. and Stewart, G.W., An Algorithm for Generalized Matrix Eigenvalue Problems, SIAM J. Numer. Anal. 10,241-256 (1973).

5. CHECKOUT.

A. Test Cases.

See the section discussing testing of the codes for real generalized matrix systems.

B. Accuracy.

The accuracy of QZHES can best be described in terms of its role in those paths of EISPACK which find eigenvalues and eigenvectors of real generalized matrix systems. In these paths, this subroutine is numerically stable (1). This stability contributes to the property of these paths that each computed eigenvalue and its corresponding eigenvector are exact for a system close to the original system.

```
      SUBROUTINE QZHES(NM,N,A,B,MATZ,Z)
C
      INTEGER I,J,K,L,N,LB,L1,NM,NK1,NM1,NM2
      REAL A(NM,N),B(NM,N),Z(NM,N)
      REAL R,S,T,U1,U2,V1,V2,RHO
      REAL SQRT,ABS,SIGN
      LOGICAL MATZ
C
      IF (.NOT. MATZ) GO TO 10
C
      DO 3 I = 1, N
C
         DO 2 J = 1, N
            Z(I,J) = 0.0
   2     CONTINUE
C
         Z(I,I) = 1.0
   3  CONTINUE
C     ********** REDUCE B TO UPPER TRIANGULAR FORM **********
  10  IF (N .LE. 1) GO TO 170
      NM1 = N - 1
C
      DO 100 L = 1, NM1
         L1 = L + 1
         S = 0.0
C
         DO 20 I = L1, N
            S = S + ABS(B(I,L))
  20     CONTINUE
C
         IF (S .EQ. 0.0) GO TO 100
         S = S + ABS(B(L,L))
         R = 0.0
C
         DO 25 I = L, N
            B(I,L) = B(I,L) / S
            R = R + B(I,L)**2
  25     CONTINUE
C
         R = SIGN(SQRT(R),B(L,L))
         B(L,L) = B(L,L) + R
         RHO = R * B(L,L)
C
         DO 50 J = L1, N
            T = 0.0
C
            DO 30 I = L, N
               T = T + B(I,L) * B(I,J)
  30        CONTINUE
C
            T = -T / RHO
```

```
C
            DO 40 I = L, N
               B(I,J) = B(I,J) + T * B(I,L)
   40       CONTINUE
C
   50    CONTINUE
C
         DO 80 J = 1, N
            T = 0.0
C
            DO 60 I = L, N
               T = T + B(I,L) * A(I,J)
   60       CONTINUE
C
            T = -T / RHO
C
            DO 70 I = L, N
               A(I,J) = A(I,J) + T * B(I,L)
   70       CONTINUE
C
   80    CONTINUE
C
         B(L,L) = -S * R
C
         DO 90 I = L1, N
            B(I,L) = 0.0
   90    CONTINUE
C
  100 CONTINUE
C     ********** REDUCE A TO UPPER HESSENBERG FORM, WHILE
C                KEEPING B TRIANGULAR **********
      IF (N .EQ. 2) GO TO 170
      NM2 = N - 2
C
      DO 160 K = 1, NM2
         NK1 = NM1 - K
C     ********** FOR L=N-1 STEP -1 UNTIL K+1 DO -- **********
         DO 150 LB = 1, NK1
            L = N - LB
            L1 = L + 1
C     ********** ZERO A(L+1,K) **********
            S = ABS(A(L,K)) + ABS(A(L1,K))
            IF (S .EQ. 0.0) GO TO 150
            U1 = A(L,K) / S
            U2 = A(L1,K) / S
            R = SIGN(SQRT(U1*U1+U2*U2),U1)
            V1 =   -(U1 + R) / R
            V2 = -U2 / R
            U2 = V2 / V1
```

```
C
            DO 110 J = K, N
            T = A(L,J) + U2 * A(L1,J)
            A(L,J) = A(L,J) + T * V1
            A(L1,J) = A(L1,J) + T * V2
  110       CONTINUE
C
            A(L1,K) = 0.0
C
            DO 120 J = L, N
            T = B(L,J) + U2 * B(L1,J)
            B(L,J) = B(L,J) + T * V1
            B(L1,J) = B(L1,J) + T * V2
  120       CONTINUE
C     ********** ZERO B(L+1,L) **********
            S = ABS(B(L1,L1)) + ABS(B(L1,L))
            IF (S .EQ. 0.0) GO TO 150
            U1 = B(L1,L1) / S
            U2 = B(L1,L) / S
            R = SIGN(SQRT(U1*U1+U2*U2),U1)
            V1 =  -(U1 + R) / R
            V2 = -U2 / R
            U2 = V2 / V1
C
            DO 130 I = 1, L1
            T = B(I,L1) + U2 * B(I,L)
            B(I,L1) = B(I,L1) + T * V1
            B(I,L) = B(I,L) + T * V2
  130       CONTINUE
C
            B(L1,L) = 0.0
C
            DO 140 I = 1, N
            T = A(I,L1) + U2 * A(I,L)
            A(I,L1) = A(I,L1) + T * V1
            A(I,L) = A(I,L) + T * V2
  140       CONTINUE
C
            IF (.NOT. MATZ) GO TO 150
C
            DO 145 I = 1, N
            T = Z(I,L1) + U2 * Z(I,L)
            Z(I,L1) = Z(I,L1) + T * V1
            Z(I,L) = Z(I,L) + T * V2
  145       CONTINUE
C
  150     CONTINUE
C
  160 CONTINUE
C
  170 RETURN
      END
```

NATS PROJECT

EIGENSYSTEM SUBROUTINE PACKAGE (EISPACK)

F239-2   QZIT

A Fortran IV Subroutine to Reduce One of a Pair of
Real Matrices from Upper Hessenberg to
Quasi-Upper Triangular Form While Maintaining the
Upper Triangular Form of the Other Using and
Optionally Accumulating Orthogonal Transformations.

July, 1975
January, 1977

1. PURPOSE.

The Fortran IV subroutine QZIT reduces the generalized real
eigenproblem AX = (LAMBDA)BX, where A is in upper
Hessenberg form and B is in upper triangular form, to an
equivalent problem with A now in quasi-upper triangular
form and B still in upper triangular form, using and
optionally accumulating orthogonal transformations. These
reduced forms are used by other subroutines to find the
generalized eigenvalues and/or eigenvectors of this matrix
system or of an original real general matrix system from
which this system was itself reduced. See section 2C for the
specific routines.

2. USAGE.

A. Calling Sequence.

The SUBROUTINE statement is

SUBROUTINE QZIT(NM,N,A,B,EPS1,MATZ,Z,IERR)

The parameters are discussed below and the
interpretation of working precision for various machines
is given in the section discussing certification.

NM   is an integer input variable set equal to
            the row dimension of the two-dimensional
            arrays A and B (and Z if MATZ is
            true) as specified in the DIMENSION
            statements for A and B (and Z) in the
            calling program.

N   is an integer input variable set equal to
             the order of the matrices A and B. N
             must be not greater than NM.

A   is a working precision real two-dimensional
             variable with row dimension NM and column
             dimension at least N. On input, A
             contains a real upper Hessenberg matrix;
             contents of storage locations below the
             subdiagonal are arbitrary. On output, A
             contains a quasi-upper triangular matrix,
             that is, triangular except for possible 2x2
             diagonal blocks. See section 3 for the
             details.

B   is a working precision real two-dimensional
             variable with row dimension NM and column
             dimension at least N. On input, B
             contains an upper triangular matrix;
             contents of storage locations below the
             diagonal are arbitrary. On output, B
             still contains an upper triangular matrix
             although the elements have changed. One
             additional location, B(N,1), is used to
             store the product of EPS1 and the norm of
             B for later use by subroutines that may
             follow QZIT. See section 3 for the
             details.

EPS1   is a working precision real input variable
             defining the tolerance used to determine
             negligible elements of A and B in the
             course of the algorithm. An element of
             either matrix will be considered negligible
             and reset to zero if it is not larger than
             the product of EPS1 and the norm of the
             matrix. If EPS1 is non-positive, then a
             default value equal to the relative machine
             precision will be used instead. A positive
             value of EPS1 may result in faster
             execution, but less accurate results.

MATZ   is a logical input variable set true if the
             (column) transformation matrix is to be
             accumulated and set false otherwise.

Z   is, if MATZ is true, a working precision
             real two-dimensional variable with row
             dimension NM and column dimension at least
             N. If A and B are primary data, then on
             input, Z contains the identity matrix of
             order N. If A and B are reduced from a
             real general matrix system, then on input,

Z contains the transformation matrix produced in the reduction. On output, Z contains the orthogonal (column) transformation matrix produced in the reductions to the quasi-triangular and current triangular forms of A and B. If MATZ is false, Z is not referenced and can be a dummy (working precision) variable.

IERR is an integer output variable set equal to an error completion code described in section 2B. The normal completion code is zero.

B. Error Conditions and Returns.

If more than 50 iterations are required to determine a diagonal 1x1 or 2x2 block of the quasi-triangular form, this subroutine terminates with IERR set to the index of the row for which the failure occurs. The principal minor in rows and columns IERR+1,IERR+2,...,N should be in suitable form for a determination of its eigenvalues with QZVAL (F240), but no eigenvectors can be computed.

If all the diagonal blocks of the quasi-triangular form are determined within 50 iterations, IERR is set to zero.

C. Applicability and Restrictions.

To determine all the eigenvalues of a real general matrix system, QZIT should be preceded by QZHES (F238) to produce suitable upper Hessenberg A and upper triangular B matrices for QZIT. QZIT should always be followed by QZVAL (F240).

To determine all the eigenvalues and eigenvectors of a real general matrix system, QZIT should be preceded by QZHES (F238). QZIT should always be followed by QZVAL (F240) and QZVEC (F241).

3. DISCUSSION OF METHOD AND ALGORITHM.

The QR method is effectively applied to the upper Hessenberg matrix $C = AB^{-1}$ without ever having to explicitly form it; unitary equivalences on A and B are chosen so that at each iteration A remains upper

Hessenberg, B remains upper triangular, and the product AB^{-1}, if formed, would be exactly the matrix derived originally from C by the corresponding iteration of the QR method.

The essence of the QR method is a process whereby a sequence of upper Hessenberg matrices, unitarily similar to the original Hessenberg matrix, is formed which converges to a quasi-triangular matrix, that is, an upper Hessenberg matrix whose eigenvalues are the eigenvalues of 1x1 or 2x2 principal submatrices. The rate of convergence of this sequence is improved by shifting the origin at each iteration. The arithmetic throughout the process is kept real, when converging toward 2x2 submatrices with complex eigenvalues, by combining two iterations into one using a pair of complex conjugate origin shifts. Before each iteration, the last Hessenberg form is checked for a possible splitting into submatrices. If a splitting occurs, only the lower submatrix participates in the next iteration.

The origin shifts at each iteration are the eigenvalues of the lowest 2x2 principal minor if complex, or that one of them closer to the second diagonal element of this minor if real. Whenever a lowest 1x1 or 2x2 principal submatrix finally splits from the rest of the matrix, the algorithm proceeds with the remaining submatrix. This process is continued until the matrix has split completely into submatrices of order 1 or 2. The tolerances in the splitting tests are proportional to EPS1.

The operations defining the equivalences on A and B comprise both row and column Householder transformations. By accumulating the column transformations in Z, full information is saved for later use in back transforming the eigenvectors of the reduced system into those of the original system.

This subroutine is an implementation of the second step of the QZ algorithm written and discussed in detail by Moler and Stewart (1) and extended by Ward (2).

4. REFERENCES.

1) Moler, C.B. and Stewart, G.W., An Algorithm for Generalized Matrix Eigenvalue Problems, SIAM J. Numer. Anal. 10,241-256 (1973).

2) Ward, R.C., An Extension of the QZ Algorithm for Solving the Generalized Matrix Eigenvalue Problem, Technical Note NASA TN D-7305 (1973).

5. CHECKOUT.

    A. Test Cases.

       See the section discussing testing of the codes for
       real generalized matrix systems.

    B. Accuracy.

       The accuracy of QZIT can best be described in terms of
       its role in those paths of EISPACK which find
       eigenvalues and eigenvectors of real generalized matrix
       systems. In these paths, this subroutine is numerically
       stable (1,2). This stability contributes to the
       property of these paths that each computed eigenvalue
       and its corresponding eigenvector are exact for a system
       close to the original system.

```
      SUBROUTINE QZIT(NM,N,A,B,EPS1,MATZ,Z,IERR)
C
      INTEGER I,J,K,L,N,EN,K1,K2,LD,LL,L1,NA,NM,ISH,ITS,KM1,LM1,
     X         ENM2,IERR,LOR1,ENORN
      REAL A(NM,N),B(NM,N),Z(NM,N)
      REAL R,S,T,A1,A2,A3,EP,SH,U1,U2,U3,V1,V2,V3,ANI,A11,A12,
     X         A21,A22,A33,A34,A43,A44,BNI,B11,B12,B22,B33,B34,
     X         B44,EPSA,EPSB,EPS1,ANORM,BNORM
      REAL SQRT,ABS,SIGN
      INTEGER MAX0,MIN0
      LOGICAL MATZ,NOTLAS
C
      IERR = 0
C     ********** COMPUTE EPSA,EPSB **********
      ANORM = 0.0
      BNORM = 0.0
C
      DO 30 I = 1, N
         ANI = 0.0
         IF (I .NE. 1) ANI = ABS(A(I,I-1))
         BNI = 0.0
C
         DO 20 J = I, N
            ANI = ANI + ABS(A(I,J))
            BNI = BNI + ABS(B(I,J))
   20    CONTINUE
C
         IF (ANI .GT. ANORM) ANORM = ANI
         IF (BNI .GT. BNORM) BNORM = BNI
   30 CONTINUE
C
      IF (ANORM .EQ. 0.0) ANORM = 1.0
      IF (BNORM .EQ. 0.0) BNORM = 1.0
      EP = EPS1
      IF (EP .GT. 0.0) GO TO 50
C     ********** COMPUTE ROUNDOFF LEVEL IF EPS1 IS ZERO **********
      EP = 1.0
   40 EP = EP / 2.0
      IF (1.0 + EP .GT. 1.0) GO TO 40
   50 EPSA = EP * ANORM
      EPSB = EP * BNORM
C     ********** REDUCE A TO QUASI-TRIANGULAR FORM, WHILE
C                KEEPING B TRIANGULAR **********
      LOR1 = 1
      ENORN = N
      EN = N
C     ********** BEGIN QZ STEP **********
   60 IF (EN .LE. 2) GO TO 1001
      IF (.NOT. MATZ) ENORN = EN
      ITS = 0
      NA = EN - 1
      ENM2 = NA - 1
   70 ISH = 2
C     ********** CHECK FOR CONVERGENCE OR REDUCIBILITY.
```

```
C                   FOR L=EN STEP -1 UNTIL 1 DO -- **********
      DO 80 LL = 1, EN
         LM1 = EN - LL
         L = LM1 + 1
         IF (L .EQ. 1) GO TO 95
         IF (ABS(A(L,LM1)) .LE. EPSA) GO TO 90
   80 CONTINUE
C
   90 A(L,LM1) = 0.0
      IF (L .LT. NA) GO TO 95
C     ********** 1-BY-1 OR 2-BY-2 BLOCK ISOLATED **********
      EN = LM1
      GO TO 60
C     ********** CHECK FOR SMALL TOP OF B **********
   95 LD = L
  100 L1 = L + 1
      B11 = B(L,L)
      IF (ABS(B11) .GT. EPSB) GO TO 120
      B(L,L) = 0.0
      S = ABS(A(L,L)) + ABS(A(L1,L))
      U1 = A(L,L) / S
      U2 = A(L1,L) / S
      R = SIGN(SQRT(U1*U1+U2*U2),U1)
      V1 = -(U1 + R) / R
      V2 = -U2 / R
      U2 = V2 / V1
C
      DO 110 J = L, ENORN
         T = A(L,J) + U2 * A(L1,J)
         A(L,J) = A(L,J) + T * V1
         A(L1,J) = A(L1,J) + T * V2
         T = B(L,J) + U2 * B(L1,J)
         B(L,J) = B(L,J) + T * V1
         B(L1,J) = B(L1,J) + T * V2
  110 CONTINUE
C
      IF (L .NE. 1) A(L,LM1) = -A(L,LM1)
      LM1 = L
      L = L1
      GO TO 90
  120 A11 = A(L,L) / B11
      A21 = A(L1,L) / B11
      IF (ISH .EQ. 1) GO TO 140
C     ********** ITERATION STRATEGY **********
      IF (ITS .EQ. 50) GO TO 1000
      IF (ITS .EQ. 10) GO TO 155
C     ********** DETERMINE TYPE OF SHIFT **********
      B22 = B(L1,L1)
      IF (ABS(B22) .LT. EPSB) B22 = EPSB
      B33 = B(NA,NA)
      IF (ABS(B33) .LT. EPSB) B33 = EPSB
      B44 = B(EN,EN)
      IF (ABS(B44) .LT. EPSB) B44 = EPSB
      A33 = A(NA,NA) / B33
```

```
      A34 = A(NA,EN) / B44
      A43 = A(EN,NA) / B33
      A44 = A(EN,EN) / B44
      B34 = B(NA,EN) / B44
      T = 0.5 * (A43 * B34 - A33 - A44)
      R = T * T + A34 * A43 - A33 * A44
      IF (R .LT. 0.0) GO TO 150
C     ********** DETERMINE SINGLE SHIFT ZEROTH COLUMN OF A **********
      ISH = 1
      R = SQRT(R)
      SH = -T + R
      S = -T - R
      IF (ABS(S-A44) .LT. ABS(SH-A44)) SH = S
C     ********** LOOK FOR TWO CONSECUTIVE SMALL
C                SUB-DIAGONAL ELEMENTS OF A.
C                FOR L=EN-2 STEP -1 UNTIL LD DO -- **********
      DO 130 LL = LD, ENM2
         L = ENM2 + LD - LL
         IF (L .EQ. LD) GO TO 140
         LM1 = L - 1
         L1 = L + 1
         T = A(L,L)
         IF (ABS(B(L,L)) .GT. EPSB) T = T - SH * B(L,L)
         IF (ABS(A(L,LM1)) .LE. ABS(T/A(L1,L)) * EPSA) GO TO 100
  130 CONTINUE
C
  140 A1 = A11 - SH
      A2 = A21
      IF (L .NE. LD) A(L,LM1) = -A(L,LM1)
      GO TO 160
C     ********** DETERMINE DOUBLE SHIFT ZEROTH COLUMN OF A **********
  150 A12 = A(L,L1) / B22
      A22 = A(L1,L1) / B22
      B12 = B(L,L1) / B22
      A1 = ((A33 - A11) * (A44 - A11) - A34 * A43 + A43 * B34 * A11)
     X      / A21 + A12 - A11 * B12
      A2 = (A22 - A11) - A21 * B12 - (A33 - A11) - (A44 - A11)
     X      + A43 * B34
      A3 = A(L1+1,L1) / B22
      GO TO 160
C     ********** AD HOC SHIFT **********
  155 A1 = 0.0
      A2 = 1.0
      A3 = 1.1605
  160 ITS = ITS + 1
      IF (.NOT. MATZ) LOR1 = LD
C     ********** MAIN LOOP **********
      DO 260 K = L, NA
         NOTLAS = K .NE. NA .AND. ISH .EQ. 2
         K1 = K + 1
         K2 = K + 2
         KM1 = MAX0(K-1,L)
         LL = MIN0(EN,K1+ISH)
         IF (NOTLAS) GO TO 190
```

```
C         ********** ZERO A(K+1,K-1) **********
          IF (K .EQ. L) GO TO 170
          A1 = A(K,KM1)
          A2 = A(K1,KM1)
170       S = ABS(A1) + ABS(A2)
          IF (S .EQ. 0.0) GO TO 70
          U1 = A1 / S
          U2 = A2 / S
          R = SIGN(SQRT(U1*U1+U2*U2),U1)
          V1 = -(U1 + R) / R
          V2 = -U2 / R
          U2 = V2 / V1
C
          DO 180 J = KM1, ENORN
             T = A(K,J) + U2 * A(K1,J)
             A(K,J) = A(K,J) + T * V1
             A(K1,J) = A(K1,J) + T * V2
             T = B(K,J) + U2 * B(K1,J)
             B(K,J) = B(K,J) + T * V1
             B(K1,J) = B(K1,J) + T * V2
180       CONTINUE
C
          IF (K .NE. L) A(K1,KM1) = 0.0
          GO TO 240
C         ********** ZERO A(K+1,K-1) AND A(K+2,K-1) **********
190       IF (K .EQ. L) GO TO 200
          A1 = A(K,KM1)
          A2 = A(K1,KM1)
          A3 = A(K2,KM1)
200       S = ABS(A1) + ABS(A2) + ABS(A3)
          IF (S .EQ. 0.0) GO TO 260
          U1 = A1 / S
          U2 = A2 / S
          U3 = A3 / S
          R = SIGN(SQRT(U1*U1+U2*U2+U3*U3),U1)
          V1 = -(U1 + R) / R
          V2 = -U2 / R
          V3 = -U3 / R
          U2 = V2 / V1
          U3 = V3 / V1
C
          DO 210 J = KM1, ENORN
             T = A(K,J) + U2 * A(K1,J) + U3 * A(K2,J)
             A(K,J) = A(K,J) + T * V1
             A(K1,J) = A(K1,J) + T * V2
             A(K2,J) = A(K2,J) + T * V3
             T = B(K,J) + U2 * B(K1,J) + U3 * B(K2,J)
             B(K,J) = B(K,J) + T * V1
             B(K1,J) = B(K1,J) + T * V2
             B(K2,J) = B(K2,J) + T * V3
210       CONTINUE
```

```
C
            IF (K .EQ. L) GO TO 220
            A(K1,KM1) = 0.0
            A(K2,KM1) = 0.0
C     ********** ZERO B(K+2,K+1) AND B(K+2,K) **********
  220       S = ABS(B(K2,K2)) + ABS(B(K2,K1)) + ABS(B(K2,K))
            IF (S .EQ. 0.0) GO TO 240
            U1 = B(K2,K2) / S
            U2 = B(K2,K1) / S
            U3 = B(K2,K) / S
            R = SIGN(SQRT(U1*U1+U2*U2+U3*U3),U1)
            V1 = -(U1 + R) / R
            V2 = -U2 / R
            V3 = -U3 / R
            U2 = V2 / V1
            U3 = V3 / V1
C
            DO 230 I = LOR1, LL
               T = A(I,K2) + U2 * A(I,K1) + U3 * A(I,K)
               A(I,K2) = A(I,K2) + T * V1
               A(I,K1) = A(I,K1) + T * V2
               A(I,K) = A(I,K) + T * V3
               T = B(I,K2) + U2 * B(I,K1) + U3 * B(I,K)
               B(I,K2) = B(I,K2) + T * V1
               B(I,K1) = B(I,K1) + T * V2
               B(I,K) = B(I,K) + T * V3
  230       CONTINUE
C
            B(K2,K) = 0.0
            B(K2,K1) = 0.0
            IF (.NOT. MATZ) GO TO 240
C
            DO 235 I = 1, N
               T = Z(I,K2) + U2 * Z(I,K1) + U3 * Z(I,K)
               Z(I,K2) = Z(I,K2) + T * V1
               Z(I,K1) = Z(I,K1) + T * V2
               Z(I,K) = Z(I,K) + T * V3
  235       CONTINUE
C     ********** ZERO B(K+1,K) **********
  240       S = ABS(B(K1,K1)) + ABS(B(K1,K))
            IF (S .EQ. 0.0) GO TO 260
            U1 = B(K1,K1) / S
            U2 = B(K1,K) / S
            R = SIGN(SQRT(U1*U1+U2*U2),U1)
            V1 = -(U1 + R) / R
            V2 = -U2 / R
            U2 = V2 / V1
C
            DO 250 I = LOR1, LL
               T = A(I,K1) + U2 * A(I,K)
               A(I,K1) = A(I,K1) + T * V1
               A(I,K) = A(I,K) + T * V2
               T = B(I,K1) + U2 * B(I,K)
               B(I,K1) = B(I,K1) + T * V1
```

```
            B(I,K) = B(I,K) + T * V2
  250      CONTINUE
C
           B(K1,K) = 0.0
           IF (.NOT. MATZ) GO TO 260
C
           DO 255 I = 1, N
              T = Z(I,K1) + U2 * Z(I,K)
              Z(I,K1) = Z(I,K1) + T * V1
              Z(I,K) = Z(I,K) + T * V2
  255      CONTINUE
C
  260 CONTINUE
C     ********** END QZ STEP **********
      GO TO 70
C     ********** SET ERROR -- NEITHER BOTTOM SUBDIAGONAL ELEMENT
C                HAS BECOME NEGLIGIBLE AFTER 50 ITERATIONS **********
 1000 IERR = EN
C     ********** SAVE EPSB FOR USE BY QZVAL AND QZVEC **********
 1001 IF (N .GT. 1) B(N,1) = EPSB
      RETURN
      END
```

NATS PROJECT

EIGENSYSTEM SUBROUTINE PACKAGE (EISPACK)

F240-2   QZVAL

A Fortran IV Subroutine to Extract the Generalized
Eigenvalues of a Real Matrix System With One
Matrix in Quasi-Upper Triangular Form and the
Other in Upper Triangular Form Using and
Optionally Accumulating Orthogonal Transformations.

July, 1975
January, 1977

1. PURPOSE.

The Fortran IV subroutine QZVAL reduces the generalized
real eigenproblem AX = (LAMBDA)BX, where A is in quasi-
upper triangular form and B is in upper triangular form, to
an equivalent problem with A further reduced and B still
in upper triangular form, using and optionally accumulating
orthogonal transformations. The reduced A is upper
triangular except for possible 2x2 diagonal blocks
corresponding to pairs of complex eigenvalues. The
subroutine returns quantities whose ratios give the
generalized eigenvalues. The reduced forms may then be used
to find the generalized eigenvectors of this matrix system or
of an original real general matrix system from which this
system was itself reduced. See section 2C.

2. USAGE.

A. Calling Sequence.

The SUBROUTINE statement is

SUBROUTINE   QZVAL(NM,N,A,B,ALFR,ALFI,BETA,MATZ,Z)

The parameters are discussed below and the
interpretation of working precision for various machines
is given in the section discussing certification.

NM   is an integer input variable set equal to
the row dimension of the two-dimensional
arrays A and B (and Z if MATZ is
true) as specified in the DIMENSION
statements for A and B (and Z) in the
calling program.

N   is an integer input variable set equal to
        the order of the matrices A and B. N
        must be not greater than NM.

A   is a working precision real two-dimensional
        variable with row dimension NM and column
        dimension at least N. On input, A
        contains a quasi-upper triangular matrix,
        that is, triangular except for possible 2x2
        diagonal blocks. Contents of storage
        locations below the subdiagonal are
        arbitrary. On output, A has been reduced
        further so that any remaining 2x2 blocks
        correspond to pairs of complex eigenvalues.
        See section 3 for the details.

B   is a working precision real two-dimensional
        variable with row dimension NM and column
        dimension at least N. On input, B
        contains an upper triangular matrix;
        contents of storage locations below the
        diagonal are arbitrary, except for location
        B(N,1) which should contain a number equal
        to the product of the precision of
        computation and the norm of the matrix; this
        number has been previously stored by QZIT
        (F239), if used. On output, B still
        contains an upper triangular matrix although
        the elements have changed. B(N,1) is
        unchanged. See section 3 for the details.

ALFR,ALFI
        are working precision real output one-
        dimensional variables of dimension at least
        N containing the real and imaginary parts,
        respectively, of the diagonal elements of A
        that would result if it were reduced
        completely to triangular form by unitary
        transformations that left the diagonal of B
        real and non-negative. Non-zero values of
        ALFI occur in pairs, the first member
        positive and the second negative.

BETA   is a working precision real output one-
        dimensional variable of dimension at least
        N containing the real non-negative diagonal
        elements of B that would result if A
        were reduced completely to triangular form.
        The generalized eigenvalues are then given
        by the ratios ((ALFR+I*ALFI)/BETA).

MATZ   is a logical input variable set true if the (column) transformation matrix is to be accumulated and set false otherwise.

Z   is, if MATZ is true, a working precision real two-dimensional variable with row dimension NM and column dimension at least N. If A and B are primary data, then on input, Z contains the identity matrix of order N. If A and B are reduced from a real general matrix system, then on input, Z contains the transformation matrix produced in the reduction. On output, Z contains the orthogonal (column) transformation matrix produced in the reductions to the current quasi-triangular and triangular forms of A and B. If MATZ is false, Z is not referenced and can be a dummy (working precision) variable.

B. Error Conditions and Returns.

None.

C. Applicability and Restrictions.

To determine all the eigenvalues of a real general matrix system, QZVAL should be preceded by QZHES (F238) and QZIT (F239) to produce suitable quasi-upper triangular A and upper triangular B matrices for QZVAL.

To determine all the eigenvalues and eigenvectors of a real general matrix system, QZVAL should be preceded by QZHES (F238) and QZIT (F239). QZVAL should always be followed by QZVEC (F241).

3. DISCUSSION OF METHOD AND ALGORITHM.

For 1x1 problems, the diagonal element of A is transferred to ALFR and the diagonal element of B to BETA, with signs reversed if necessary in order that BETA be non-negative.

For 2x2 problems, the diagonal elements of B are first tested for negligibility. If the first one is negligible, then a row rotation can be chosen to triangularize the 2x2 minor of A, reducing the 2x2 problem to two 1x1 problems; if the second one is negligible, then a column rotation can be chosen.

For non-singular 2x2 minors of B, an approximate
eigenvalue of AB^{-1} is first determined from the
characteristic equation. Column and row rotations can then
be chosen which employ this approximation to triangularize
the minor of A while maintaining the triangularity of B,
in a stable manner.

If the rotations are real, they are actually applied. If the
rotations are complex, they are used to compute the diagonal
elements of A and B that would result, but are not
actually applied. In this case, the imaginary parts of the
diagonal elements of A are stored in ALFI (after these
elements are normalized in order that BETA can store the
magnitude of the resulting diagonal element of B, and
possibly also interchanged so that the element with positive
ALFI appears first); for real eigenvalues, ALFI is set to
zero. By accumulating the column transformations in Z, full
information is saved for later use in back transforming the
eigenvectors of the reduced system into those of the original
system.

This subroutine is an implementation of the third step of the
QZ algorithm written and discussed in detail by Moler and
Stewart (1).

4. REFERENCES.

1) Moler, C.B. and Stewart, G.W., An Algorithm for
Generalized Matrix Eigenvalue Problems,
SIAM J. Numer. Anal. 10,241-256 (1973).

5. CHECKOUT.

A. Test Cases.

See the section discussing testing of the codes for
real generalized matrix systems.

B. Accuracy.

The accuracy of QZVAL can best be described in terms
of its role in those paths of EISPACK which find
eigenvalues and eigenvectors of real generalized matrix
systems. In these paths, this subroutine is numerically
stable (1). This stability contributes to the property
of these paths that each computed eigenvalue and its
corresponding eigenvector are exact for a system close
to the original system.

```
      SUBROUTINE QZVAL(NM,N,A,B,ALFR,ALFI,BETA,MATZ,Z)
C
      INTEGER I,J,N,EN,NA,NM,NN,ISW
      REAL A(NM,N),B(NM,N),ALFR(N),ALFI(N),BETA(N),Z(NM,N)
      REAL C,D,E,R,S,T,AN,A1,A2,BN,CQ,CZ,DI,DR,EI,TI,TR,U1,U2,
     X      V1,V2,A1I,A11,A12,A2I,A21,A22,B11,B12,B22,SQI,SQR,
     X      SSI,SSR,SZI,SZR,A11I,A11R,A12I,A12R,A22I,A22R,EPSB
      REAL SQRT,ABS,SIGN
      LOGICAL MATZ
C
      EPSB = B(N,1)
      ISW = 1
C     ********** FIND EIGENVALUES OF QUASI-TRIANGULAR MATRICES.
C                FOR EN=N STEP -1 UNTIL 1 DO -- **********
      DO 510 NN = 1, N
         EN = N + 1 - NN
         NA = EN - 1
         IF (ISW .EQ. 2) GO TO 505
         IF (EN .EQ. 1) GO TO 410
         IF (A(EN,NA) .NE. 0.0) GO TO 420
C     ********** 1-BY-1 BLOCK, ONE REAL ROOT **********
  410    ALFR(EN) = A(EN,EN)
         IF (B(EN,EN) .LT. 0.0) ALFR(EN) = -ALFR(EN)
         BETA(EN) = ABS(B(EN,EN))
         ALFI(EN) = 0.0
         GO TO 510
C     ********** 2-BY-2 BLOCK **********
  420    IF (ABS(B(NA,NA)) .LE. EPSB) GO TO 455
         IF (ABS(B(EN,EN)) .GT. EPSB) GO TO 430
         A1 = A(EN,EN)
         A2 = A(EN,NA)
         BN = 0.0
         GO TO 435
  430    AN = ABS(A(NA,NA)) + ABS(A(NA,EN)) + ABS(A(EN,NA))
     X      + ABS(A(EN,EN))
         BN = ABS(B(NA,NA)) + ABS(B(NA,EN)) + ABS(B(EN,EN))
         A11 = A(NA,NA) / AN
         A12 = A(NA,EN) / AN
         A21 = A(EN,NA) / AN
         A22 = A(EN,EN) / AN
         B11 = B(NA,NA) / BN
         B12 = B(NA,EN) / BN
         B22 = B(EN,EN) / BN
         E = A11 / B11
         EI = A22 / B22
         S = A21 / (B11 * B22)
         T = (A22 - E * B22) / B22
         IF (ABS(E) .LE. ABS(EI)) GO TO 431
         E = EI
         T = (A11 - E * B11) / B11
  431    C = 0.5 * (T - S * B12)
         D = C * C + S * (A12 - E * B12)
         IF (D .LT. 0.0) GO TO 480
```

```
C          ********** TWO REAL ROOTS.
C                     ZERO BOTH A(EN,NA) AND B(EN,NA) **********
           E = E + (C + SIGN(SQRT(D),C))
           A11 = A11 - E * B11
           A12 = A12 - E * B12
           A22 = A22 - E * B22
           IF (ABS(A11) + ABS(A12) .LT.
     X         ABS(A21) + ABS(A22)) GO TO 432
           A1 = A12
           A2 = A11
           GO TO 435
  432      A1 = A22
           A2 = A21
C          ********** CHOOSE AND APPLY REAL Z **********
  435      S = ABS(A1) + ABS(A2)
           U1 = A1 / S
           U2 = A2 / S
           R = SIGN(SQRT(U1*U1+U2*U2),U1)
           V1 = -(U1 + R) / R
           V2 = -U2 / R
           U2 = V2 / V1
C
           DO 440 I = 1, EN
              T = A(I,EN) + U2 * A(I,NA)
              A(I,EN) = A(I,EN) + T * V1
              A(I,NA) = A(I,NA) + T * V2
              T = B(I,EN) + U2 * B(I,NA)
              B(I,EN) = B(I,EN) + T * V1
              B(I,NA) = B(I,NA) + T * V2
  440      CONTINUE
C
           IF (.NOT. MATZ) GO TO 450
C
           DO 445 I = 1, N
              T = Z(I,EN) + U2 * Z(I,NA)
              Z(I,EN) = Z(I,EN) + T * V1
              Z(I,NA) = Z(I,NA) + T * V2
  445      CONTINUE
C
  450      IF (BN .EQ. 0.0) GO TO 475
           IF (AN .LT. ABS(E) * BN) GO TO 455
           A1 = B(NA,NA)
           A2 = B(EN,NA)
           GO TO 460
  455      A1 = A(NA,NA)
           A2 = A(EN,NA)
C          ********** CHOOSE AND APPLY REAL Q **********
  460      S = ABS(A1) + ABS(A2)
           IF (S .EQ. 0.0) GO TO 475
           U1 = A1 / S
           U2 = A2 / S
           R = SIGN(SQRT(U1*U1+U2*U2),U1)
           V1 = -(U1 + R) / R
           V2 = -U2 / R
           U2 = V2 / V1
```

```
C
         DO 470 J = NA, N
         T = A(NA,J) + U2 * A(EN,J)
         A(NA,J) = A(NA,J) + T * V1
         A(EN,J) = A(EN,J) + T * V2
         T = B(NA,J) + U2 * B(EN,J)
         B(NA,J) = B(NA,J) + T * V1
         B(EN,J) = B(EN,J) + T * V2
  470    CONTINUE
C
  475    A(EN,NA) = 0.0
         B(EN,NA) = 0.0
         ALFR(NA) = A(NA,NA)
         ALFR(EN) = A(EN,EN)
         IF (B(NA,NA) .LT. 0.0) ALFR(NA) = -ALFR(NA)
         IF (B(EN,EN) .LT. 0.0) ALFR(EN) = -ALFR(EN)
         BETA(NA) = ABS(B(NA,NA))
         BETA(EN) = ABS(B(EN,EN))
         ALFI(EN) = 0.0
         ALFI(NA) = 0.0
         GO TO 505
C     ********** TWO COMPLEX ROOTS **********
  480    E = E + C
         EI = SQRT(-D)
         A11R = A11 - E * B11
         A11I = EI * B11
         A12R = A12 - E * B12
         A12I = EI * B12
         A22R = A22 - E * B22
         A22I = EI * B22
         IF (ABS(A11R) + ABS(A11I) + ABS(A12R) + ABS(A12I) .LT
     X       ABS(A21) + ABS(A22R) + ABS(A22I)) GO TO 482
         A1 = A12R
         A1I = A12I
         A2 = -A11R
         A2I = -A11I
         GO TO 485
  482    A1 = A22R
         A1I = A22I
         A2 = -A21
         A2I = 0.0
C     ********** CHOOSE COMPLEX Z **********
  485    CZ = SQRT(A1*A1+A1I*A1I)
         IF (CZ .EQ. 0.0) GO TO 487
         SZR = (A1 * A2 + A1I * A2I) / CZ
         SZI = (A1 * A2I - A1I * A2) / CZ
         R = SQRT(CZ*CZ+SZR*SZR+SZI*SZI)
         CZ = CZ / R
         SZR = SZR / R
         SZI = SZI / R
         GO TO 490
  487    SZR = 1.0
         SZI = 0.0
```

```
  490      IF (AN .LT. (ABS(E) + EI) * BN) GO TO 492
           A1 = CZ * B11 + SZR * B12
           A1I = SZI * B12
           A2 = SZR * B22
           A2I = SZI * B22
           GO TO 495
  492      A1 = CZ * A11 + SZR * A12
           A1I = SZI * A12
           A2 = CZ * A21 + SZR * A22
           A2I = SZI * A22
C     ********** CHOOSE COMPLEX Q **********
  495      CQ = SQRT(A1*A1+A1I*A1I)
           IF (CQ .EQ. 0.0) GO TO 497
           SQR = (A1 * A2 + A1I * A2I) / CQ
           SQI = (A1 * A2I - A1I * A2) / CQ
           R = SQRT(CQ*CQ+SQR*SQR+SQI*SQI)
           CQ = CQ / R
           SQR = SQR / R
           SQI = SQI / R
           GO TO 500
  497      SQR = 1.0
           SQI = 0.0
C     ********** COMPUTE DIAGONAL ELEMENTS THAT WOULD RESULT
C               IF TRANSFORMATIONS WERE APPLIED **********
  500      SSR = SQR * SZR + SQI * SZI
           SSI = SQR * SZI - SQI * SZR
           I = 1
           TR = CQ * CZ * A11 + CQ * SZR * A12 + SQR * CZ * A21
      X       + SSR * A22
           TI = CQ * SZI * A12 - SQI * CZ * A21 + SSI * A22
           DR = CQ * CZ * B11 + CQ * SZR * B12 + SSR * B22
           DI = CQ * SZI * B12 + SSI * B22
           GO TO 503
  502      I = 2
           TR = SSR * A11 - SQR * CZ * A12 - CQ * SZR * A21
      X       + CQ * CZ * A22
           TI = -SSI * A11 - SQI * CZ * A12 + CQ * SZI * A21
           DR = SSR * B11 - SQR * CZ * B12 + CQ * CZ * B22
           DI = -SSI * B11 - SQI * CZ * B12
  503      T = TI * DR - TR * DI
           J = NA
           IF (T .LT. 0.0) J = EN
           R = SQRT(DR*DR+DI*DI)
           BETA(J) = BN * R
           ALFR(J) = AN * (TR * DR + TI * DI) / R
           ALFI(J) = AN * T / R
           IF (I .EQ. 1) GO TO 502
  505      ISW = 3 - ISW
  510 CONTINUE
C
      RETURN
      END
```

NATS PROJECT

EIGENSYSTEM SUBROUTINE PACKAGE (EISPACK)

F241   QZVEC

A Fortran IV Subroutine to Determine the Generalized
Eigenvectors of a Real Matrix System With One Matrix
in Quasi-Upper Triangular Form and the Other in
Upper Triangular Form Using Back Substitution.

July, 1975

1. PURPOSE.

The Fortran IV subroutine QZVEC determines the eigenvectors
corresponding to a set of specified eigenvalues for the
generalized real eigenproblem AX = (LAMBDA)BX, where A is
in quasi-upper triangular form and B is in upper triangular
form, using back substitution. Quasi-triangular, in this
case, means triangular except for possible 2x2 diagonal
blocks corresponding to pairs of complex eigenvalues. The
eigenvectors of a real general matrix system can also be
computed if QZHES (F238), QZIT (F239), and QZVAL (F240)
have been used to reduce the matrices of the system to quasi-
triangular and triangular form and to accumulate the
transformations.

2. USAGE.

A. Calling Sequence.

The SUBROUTINE statement is

SUBROUTINE QZVEC(NM,N,A,B,ALFR,ALFI,BETA,Z)

The parameters are discussed below and the
interpretation of working precision for various machines
is given in the section discussing certification.

NM   is an integer input variable set equal to
          the row dimension of the two-dimensional
          arrays A, B, and Z as specified in the
          DIMENSION statements for A, B, and Z in
          the calling program.

N   is an integer input variable set equal to
          the order of the matrices A and B. N
          must be not greater than NM.

A   is a working precision real two-dimensional
     input variable with row dimension NM and
     column dimension at least N containing a
     quasi-upper triangular matrix, that is,
     triangular except for possible 2x2
     diagonal blocks corresponding to pairs of
     complex eigenvalues. Contents of storage
     locations below the subdiagonal are
     arbitrary.

B   is a working precision real two-dimensional
     variable with row dimension NM and column
     dimension at least N. On input, B
     contains an upper triangular matrix;
     contents of storage locations below the
     diagonal are arbitrary, except for location
     B(N,1) which should contain a number equal
     to the product of the precision of
     computation and the norm of the matrix; this
     number has been previously saved by QZVAL
     (F240). On output, B has been destroyed.

ALFR,ALFI
     are working precision real input one-
     dimensional variables of dimension at least
     N containing the real and imaginary parts,
     respectively, of the numerators of the
     generalized eigenvalues.

BETA   is a working precision real input one-
        dimensional variable of dimension at least
        N containing the denominators of the
        generalized eigenvalues, which are thus
        given by the ratios ((ALFR+I*ALFI)/BETA).

Z   is a working precision real two-dimensional
     variable with row dimension NM and column
     dimension at least N. If A and B are
     primary data, then on input, Z contains
     the identity matrix of order N, and on
     output, contains the real and imaginary
     parts of the eigenvectors of this system.
     If A and B are reduced from a real
     general matrix system, then on input, Z
     contains the transformation matrix produced
     in the reduction, and on output, contains
     the real and imaginary parts of the
     eigenvectors of the real general matrix
     system. If the J-th eigenvalue is real,
     the J-th column of Z contains its
     eigenvector. If the J-th and (J+1)-th
     eigenvalues form a complex pair, the J-th
     and (J+1)-th columns of Z contain the
     real and imaginary parts of the eigenvector

associated with the first eigenvalue of the
pair. The conjugate of this vector is the
eigenvector for the conjugate eigenvalue.
Each eigenvector is normalized so that the
modulus of its largest component is 1.0 .

B. Error Conditions and Returns.

None.

C. Applicability and Restrictions.

To determine all the eigenvalues and eigenvectors of a
real general matrix system, QZVEC should be preceded
by QZHES (F238), QZIT (F239), and QZVAL (F240) to
determine the eigenvalues and accumulate the
transformations.

3. DISCUSSION OF METHOD AND ALGORITHM.

The eigenvectors of the system are determined by a back
substitution process, then transformed to the eigenvectors of
the original matrix system using the information in Z, and
finally normalized.

This subroutine is an implementation of the fourth step of
the QZ algorithm written and discussed in detail by Moler
and Stewart (1).

4. REFERENCES.

1) Moler, C.B. and Stewart, G.W., An Algorithm for
   Generalized Matrix Eigenvalue Problems,
   SIAM J. Numer. Anal. 10,241-256 (1973).

5. CHECKOUT.

A. Test Cases.

See the section discussing testing of the codes for
real generalized matrix systems.

B. Accuracy.

The accuracy of QZVEC can best be described in terms
of its role in those paths of EISPACK which find
eigenvalues and eigenvectors of real generalized matrix
systems. In these paths, this subroutine is numerically
stable (1). This stability contributes to the property
of these paths that each computed eigenvalue and its
corresponding eigenvector are exact for a system close
to the original system.

```
      SUBROUTINE QZVEC(NM,N,A,B,ALFR,ALFI,BETA,Z)
C
      INTEGER I,J,K,M,N,EN,II,JJ,NA,NM,NN,ISW,ENM2
      REAL A(NM,N),B(NM,N),ALFR(N),ALFI(N),BETA(N),Z(NM,N)
      REAL D,Q,R,S,T,W,X,Y,DI,DR,RA,RR,SA,TI,TR,T1,T2,W1,X1,ZZ,Z1,
     X      ALFM,ALMI,ALMR,BETM,EPSB
      REAL SQRT,ABS
C
      EPSB = B(N,1)
      ISW = 1
C     ********** FOR EN=N STEP -1 UNTIL 1 DO -- **********
      DO 800 NN = 1, N
         EN = N + 1 - NN
         NA = EN - 1
         IF (ISW .EQ. 2) GO TO 795
         IF (ALFI(EN) .NE. 0.0) GO TO 710
C     ********** REAL VECTOR **********
         M = EN
         B(EN,EN) = 1.0
         IF (NA .EQ. 0) GO TO 800
         ALFM = ALFR(M)
         BETM = BETA(M)
C     ********** FOR I=EN-1 STEP -1 UNTIL 1 DO -- **********
         DO 700 II = 1, NA
            I = EN - II
            W = BETM * A(I,I) - ALFM * B(I,I)
            R = 0.0
C
            DO 610 J = M, EN
  610       R = R + (BETM * A(I,J) - ALFM * B(I,J)) * B(J,EN)
C
            IF (I .EQ. 1 .OR. ISW .EQ. 2) GO TO 630
            IF (BETM * A(I,I-1) .EQ. 0.0) GO TO 630
            ZZ = W
            S = R
            GO TO 690
  630       M = I
            IF (ISW .EQ. 2) GO TO 640
C     ********** REAL 1-BY-1 BLOCK **********
            T = W
            IF (W .EQ. 0.0) T = EPSB
            B(I,EN) = -R / T
            GO TO 700
C     ********** REAL 2-BY-2 BLOCK **********
  640       X = BETM * A(I,I+1) - ALFM * B(I,I+1)
            Y = BETM * A(I+1,I)
            Q = W * ZZ - X * Y
            T = (X * S - ZZ * R) / Q
            B(I,EN) = T
            IF (ABS(X) .LE. ABS(ZZ)) GO TO 650
            B(I+1,EN) = (-R - W * T) / X
            GO TO 690
  650       B(I+1,EN) = (-S - Y * T) / ZZ
  690       ISW = 3 - ISW
```

```
  700      CONTINUE
C      ********** END REAL VECTOR **********
         GO TO 800
C      ********** COMPLEX VECTOR **********
  710      M = NA
           ALMR = ALFR(M)
           ALMI = ALFI(M)
           BETM = BETA(M)
C      ********** LAST VECTOR COMPONENT CHOSEN IMAGINARY SO THAT
C                 EIGENVECTOR MATRIX IS TRIANGULAR **********
           Y = BETM * A(EN,NA)
           B(NA,NA) = -ALMI * B(EN,EN) / Y
           B(NA,EN) = (ALMR * B(EN,EN) - BETM * A(EN,EN)) / Y
           B(EN,NA) = 0.0
           B(EN,EN) = 1.0
           ENM2 = NA - 1
           IF (ENM2 .EQ. 0) GO TO 795
C      ********** FOR I=EN-2 STEP -1 UNTIL 1 DO -- **********
           DO 790 II = 1, ENM2
              I = NA - II
              W = BETM * A(I,I) - ALMR * B(I,I)
              W1 = -ALMI * B(I,I)
              RA = 0.0
              SA = 0.0
C
              DO 760 J = M, EN
                 X = BETM * A(I,J) - ALMR * B(I,J)
                 X1 = -ALMI * B(I,J)
                 RA = RA + X * B(J,NA) - X1 * B(J,EN)
                 SA = SA + X * B(J,EN) + X1 * B(J,NA)
  760         CONTINUE
C
              IF (I .EQ. 1 .OR. ISW .EQ. 2) GO TO 770
              IF (BETM * A(I,I-1) .EQ. 0.0) GO TO 770
              ZZ = W
              Z1 = W1
              R = RA
              S = SA
              ISW = 2
              GO TO 790
  770         M = I
              IF (ISW .EQ. 2) GO TO 780
C      ********** COMPLEX 1-BY-1 BLOCK **********
              TR = -RA
              TI = -SA
  773         DR = W
              DI = W1
C      ********** COMPLEX DIVIDE (T1,T2) = (TR,TI) / (DR,DI) **********
  775         IF (ABS(DI) .GT. ABS(DR)) GO TO 777
              RR = DI / DR
              D = DR + DI * RR
              T1 = (TR + TI * RR) / D
              T2 = (TI - TR * RR) / D
              GO TO (787,782), ISW
```

```
 777         RR = DR / DI
             D = DR * RR + DI
             T1 = (TR * RR + TI) / D
             T2 = (TI * RR - TR) / D
             GO TO (787,782), ISW
C      ********** COMPLEX 2-BY-2 BLOCK **********
 780         X = BETM * A(I,I+1) - ALMR * B(I,I+1)
             X1 = -ALMI * B(I,I+1)
             Y = BETM * A(I+1,I)
             TR = Y * RA - W * R + W1 * S
             TI = Y * SA - W * S - W1 * R
             DR = W * ZZ - W1 * Z1 - X * Y
             DI = W * Z1 + W1 * ZZ - X1 * Y
             IF (DR .EQ. 0.0 .AND. DI .EQ. 0.0) DR = EPSB
             GO TO 775
 782         B(I+1,NA) = T1
             B(I+1,EN) = T2
             ISW = 1
             IF (ABS(Y) .GT. ABS(W) + ABS(W1)) GO TO 785
             TR = -RA - X * B(I+1,NA) + X1 * B(I+1,EN)
             TI = -SA - X * B(I+1,EN) - X1 * B(I+1,NA)
             GO TO 773
 785         T1 = (-R - ZZ * B(I+1,NA) + Z1 * B(I+1,EN)) / Y
             T2 = (-S - ZZ * B(I+1,EN) - Z1 * B(I+1,NA)) / Y
 787         B(I,NA) = T1
             B(I,EN) = T2
 790     CONTINUE
C      ********** END COMPLEX VECTOR **********
 795     ISW = 3 - ISW
 800 CONTINUE
C      ********** END BACK SUBSTITUTION.
C                 TRANSFORM TO ORIGINAL COORDINATE SYSTEM.
C                 FOR J=N STEP -1 UNTIL 1 DO -- **********
     DO 880 JJ = 1, N
         J = N + 1 - JJ
C
         DO 880 I = 1, N
             ZZ = 0.0
C
             DO 860 K = 1, J
 860             ZZ = ZZ + Z(I,K) * B(K,J)
C
             Z(I,J) = ZZ
 880 CONTINUE
C      ********** NORMALIZE SO THAT MODULUS OF LARGEST
C                 COMPONENT OF EACH VECTOR IS 1.
C                 (ISW IS 1 INITIALLY FROM BEFORE) **********
     DO 950 J = 1, N
         D = 0.0
         IF (ISW .EQ. 2) GO TO 920
         IF (ALFI(J) .NE. 0.0) GO TO 945
```

```
C
      DO 890 I = 1, N
         IF (ABS(Z(I,J)) .GT. D) D = ABS(Z(I,J))
  890    CONTINUE
C
      DO 900 I = 1, N
  900    Z(I,J) = Z(I,J) / D
C
      GO TO 950
C
  920    DO 930 I = 1, N
         R = ABS(Z(I,J-1)) + ABS(Z(I,J))
         IF (R .NE. 0.0) R = R * SQRT((Z(I,J-1)/R)**2
     X                                +(Z(I,J)/R)**2)
         IF (R .GT. D) D = R
  930    CONTINUE
C
      DO 940 I = 1, N
         Z(I,J-1) = Z(I,J-1) / D
         Z(I,J) = Z(I,J) / D
  940    CONTINUE
C
  945    ISW = 3 - ISW
  950 CONTINUE
C
      RETURN
      END
```

NATS PROJECT

EIGENSYSTEM SUBROUTINE PACKAGE (EISPACK)

F225 REBAK

A Fortran IV Subroutine to Back Transform the Eigenvectors of that
Derived Symmetric Matrix Determined by REDUC or REDUC2.

July, 1975

1. PURPOSE.

The Fortran IV subroutine REBAK forms the eigenvectors of a
generalized symmetric eigensystem from the eigenvectors of
that derived symmetric matrix determined by REDUC (F224) or
REDUC2 (F230).

2. USAGE.

A. Calling Sequence.

The SUBROUTINE statement is

SUBROUTINE REBAK(NM,N,B,DL,M,Z)

The parameters are discussed below and the
interpretation of working precision for various machines
is given in the section discussing certification.

NM   is an integer input variable set equal to
the row dimension of the two-dimensional
arrays B and Z as specified in the
DIMENSION statements for B and Z in the
calling program.

N   is an integer input variable set equal to
the order of the matrix system. N must be
not greater than NM.

B   is a working precision real input two-
dimensional variable with row dimension NM
and column dimension at least N. The
strict lower triangle of B contains some
information about the transformation
(Cholesky decomposition) used in the
reduction to the standard form. The
remaining upper part of the matrix is
arbitrary. See section 3 of F224 or of
F230, as appropriate, for the details.

DL is a working precision real input one-dimensional variable of dimension at least N containing the remaining information about the transformation.

M is an integer input variable set equal to the number of columns of Z to be back transformed.

Z is a working precision real two-dimensional variable with row dimension NM and column dimension at least M. On input, the first M columns of Z contain the eigenvectors to be back transformed. On output, these columns of Z contain the transformed eigenvectors.

B. Error Conditions and Returns.

None.

C. Applicability and Restrictions.

This subroutine should be used in conjunction with the subroutine REDUC (F224) or with REDUC2 (F230).

3. DISCUSSION OF METHOD AND ALGORITHM.

Suppose that the generalized symmetric eigensystem GX = (LAMBDA)FX (say) has been reduced to the standard form AZ = (LAMBDA)Z by the transformation $A = L^{-1} G L^{-T}$ or that the system GFX = (LAMBDA)X has been reduced to the standard form by the transformation $A = L^T G L$, where L is a Cholesky factor of F encoded in DL and in the strict lower triangle of B. Then, given an array Z of column vectors, REBAK computes the matrix product $L^{-T} Z$. If the eigenvectors of A are columns of the array Z, then REBAK forms the eigenvectors of the generalized system in their place.

If the input vectors are normalized so that $Z^T Z = 1$, then the output vectors satisfy $X^T FX = 1$.

This subroutine is a translation of the Algol procedure REBAKA written and discussed in detail by Martin and Wilkinson (1).

4. REFERENCES.

1) Martin, R.S. and Wilkinson, J.H., Reduction of the Symmetric Eigenproblem Ax = (Lambda)Bx and Related Problems to Standard Form, Num. Math. 11,99-110 (1968). (Reprinted in Handbook for Automatic Computation, Volume II, Linear Algebra, J. H. Wilkinson - C. Reinsch, Contribution II/10, 303-314, Springer-Verlag, 1971.)

5. CHECKOUT.

A. Test Cases.

See the section discussing testing of the codes for real symmetric generalized matrix systems.

B. Accuracy.

The accuracy of REBAK can best be described in terms of its role in those paths of EISPACK which find eigenvalues and eigenvectors of real symmetric generalized matrix systems. In these paths, this subroutine is numerically stable (1). This stability contributes to the property of these paths that the computed eigenvalues are the exact eigenvalues of a system close to the original system and the computed eigenvectors are close (but not necessarily equal) to the eigenvectors of that system.

```
      SUBROUTINE REBAK(NM,N,B,DL,M,Z)
C
      INTEGER I,J,K,M,N,I1,II,NM
      REAL B(NM,N),DL(N),Z(NM,M)
      REAL X
C
      IF (M .EQ. 0) GO TO 200
C
      DO 100 J = 1, M
C     ********** FOR I=N STEP -1 UNTIL 1 DO -- **********
         DO 100 II = 1, N
            I = N + 1 - II
            I1 = I + 1
            X = Z(I,J)
            IF (I .EQ. N) GO TO 80
C
            DO 60 K = I1, N
   60       X = X - B(K,I) * Z(K,J)
C
   80       Z(I,J) = X / DL(I)
  100 CONTINUE
C
  200 RETURN
      END
```

NATS PROJECT

EIGENSYSTEM SUBROUTINE PACKAGE (EISPACK)

F231 REBAKB

A Fortran IV Subroutine to Back Transform the Eigenvectors
of that Derived Symmetric Matrix Determined by REDUC2.

July, 1975

1. PURPOSE.

The Fortran IV subroutine REBAKB forms the eigenvectors of
a generalized symmetric eigensystem from the eigenvectors of
that derived symmetric matrix determined by REDUC2 (F230).

2. USAGE.

A. Calling Sequence.

The SUBROUTINE statement is

SUBROUTINE REBAKB(NM,N,B,DL,M,Z)

The parameters are discussed below and the
interpretation of working precision for various machines
is given in the section discussing certification.

NM   is an integer input variable set equal to
          the row dimension of the two-dimensional
          arrays B and Z as specified in the
          DIMENSION statements for B and Z in the
          calling program.

N   is an integer input variable set equal to
          the order of the matrix system. N must be
          not greater than NM.

B   is a working precision real input two-
          dimensional variable with row dimension NM
          and column dimension at least N. The
          strict lower triangle of B contains some
          information about the transformation
          (Cholesky decomposition) used in the
          reduction to the standard form. The
          remaining upper part of the matrix is
          arbitrary. See section 3 of F230 for the
          details.

DL   is a working precision real input one-dimensional variable of dimension at least N containing the remaining information about the transformation.

M   is an integer input variable set equal to the number of columns of Z to be back transformed.

Z   is a working precision real two-dimensional variable with row dimension NM and column dimension at least M. On input, the first M columns of Z contain the eigenvectors to be back transformed. On output, these columns of Z contain the transformed eigenvectors.

B. Error Conditions and Returns.

None.

C. Applicability and Restrictions.

This subroutine should be used in conjunction with the subroutine REDUC2 (F230).

3. DISCUSSION OF METHOD AND ALGORITHM.

Suppose that the generalized symmetric eigensystem $FGX = (LAMBDA)X$ (say) has been reduced to the standard form $AZ = (LAMBDA)Z$ by the transformation $A = L^T GL$ where L is a Cholesky factor of F encoded in DL and in the strict lower triangle of B. Then, given an array Z of column vectors, REBAKB computes the matrix product LZ. If the eigenvectors of A are columns of the array Z, then REBAKB forms the eigenvectors of the generalized system in their place.

If the input vectors are normalized so that $Z^T Z = 1$, then the output vectors satisfy $X^T F^{-1} X = 1$.

This subroutine is a translation of the Algol procedure REBAKB written and discussed in detail by Martin and Wilkinson (1).

4. REFERENCES.

1) Martin, R.S. and Wilkinson, J.H., Reduction of the
   Symmetric Eigenproblem Ax = (Lambda)Bx and Related
   Problems to Standard Form, Num. Math. 11,99-110 (1968).
   (Reprinted in Handbook for Automatic Computation,
   Volume II, Linear Algebra, J. H. Wilkinson - C. Reinsch,
   Contribution II/10, 303-314, Springer-Verlag, 1971.)

5. CHECKOUT.

   A. Test Cases.

      See the section discussing testing of the codes for
      real symmetric generalized matrix systems.

   B. Accuracy.

      The accuracy of REBAKB can best be described in terms
      of its role in those paths of EISPACK which find
      eigenvalues and eigenvectors of real symmetric
      generalized matrix systems. In these paths, this
      subroutine is numerically stable (1). This stability
      contributes to the property of these paths that the
      computed eigenvalues are the exact eigenvalues of a
      system close to the original system and the computed
      eigenvectors are close (but not necessarily equal) to
      the eigenvectors of that system.

```
      SUBROUTINE REBAKB(NM,N,B,DL,M,Z)
C
      INTEGER I,J,K,M,N,I1,II,NM
      REAL B(NM,N),DL(N),Z(NM,M)
      REAL X
C
      IF (M .EQ. 0) GO TO 200
C
      DO 100 J = 1, M
C     ********** FOR I=N STEP -1 UNTIL 1 DO -- **********
         DO 100 II = 1, N
            I1 = N - II
            I = I1 + 1
            X = DL(I) * Z(I,J)
            IF (I .EQ. 1) GO TO 80
C
            DO 60 K = 1, I1
   60       X = X + B(I,K) * Z(K,J)
C
   80       Z(I,J) = X
  100 CONTINUE
C
  200 RETURN
      END
```

227

NATS PROJECT

EIGENSYSTEM SUBROUTINE PACKAGE (EISPACK)

F224   REDUC

A Fortran IV Subroutine to Reduce a Certain Generalized
Symmetric Eigenproblem to the Standard Symmetric
Eigenproblem Using Cholesky Decomposition.

July, 1975

1. PURPOSE.

The Fortran IV subroutine REDUC reduces the generalized
symmetric eigenproblem AX = (LAMBDA)BX, where B is
positive definite, to the standard symmetric eigenproblem
using the Cholesky factorization of B.   This reduced form is
used by other subroutines to find the eigenvalues and/or
eigenvectors of the original matrix system.   See section 2C
for the specific routines.

2. USAGE.

A. Calling Sequence.

The SUBROUTINE statement is

SUBROUTINE REDUC(NM,N,A,B,DL,IERR)

The parameters are discussed below and the
interpretation of working precision for various machines
is given in the section discussing certification.

NM   is an integer input variable set equal to
          the row dimension of the two-dimensional
          arrays A and B as specified in the
          DIMENSION statements for A and B in the
          calling program.

N   is an integer input variable set equal to
          the order of the matrices A and B.   If
          the Cholesky factor L of B is already
          available, N should be prefixed with a
          minus sign. ABS(N) must be not greater
          than NM.

A   is a working precision real two-dimensional
variable with row dimension NM and column
dimension at least N. On input, A
contains one of the symmetric matrices of
order N that define the eigenproblem
AX = (LAMBDA)BX. Only the full upper
triangle of the matrix need be supplied. On
output, the full lower triangle of A
contains the full lower triangle of the
symmetric matrix derived from the reduction
to the standard form. The strict upper
triangle of A is unaltered. See section 3
for the details.

B   is a working precision real two-dimensional
variable with row dimension NM and column
dimension at least N. On input, B
contains the positive definite symmetric
matrix of order N in the system. Only the
full upper triangle of the matrix need be
supplied. Alternatively if N is negative,
the strict lower triangle of B contains
the strict lower triangle of its Cholesky
factor L. In this case, the full upper
triangle of the matrix is arbitrary. On
output, the strict lower triangle of B
contains the strict lower triangle of its
Cholesky factor L. The full upper triangle
of B is unaltered. See section 3 for the
details.

DL   is a working precision real one-dimensional
variable of dimension at least N. On
input, if N is negative, DL contains the
diagonal elements of the Cholesky factor L
of B. On output, DL contains the
diagonal elements of the Cholesky factor L
of B.

IERR   is an integer output variable set equal to
an error completion code described in
section 2B. The normal completion code is
zero.

B. Error Conditions and Returns.

If the matrix B is not positive definite, REDUC
terminates with IERR set to 7*N+1. In this case, the
Cholesky factorization of B does not exist.

If B is positive definite, IERR is set to zero.

C. Applicability and Restrictions.

If all the eigenvalues of the original matrix system are desired, this subroutine should be followed by TRED1 (F277), and then by TQL1 (F289), IMTQL1 (F291), or TQLRAT (F235).

If all the eigenvalues and eigenvectors of the original matrix system are desired, this subroutine should be followed by TRED2 (F278), then by TQL2 (F290) or IMTQL2 (F292), and finally by REBAK (F225).

If some of the eigenvalues of the original matrix system are desired, this subroutine should be followed by TRED1 (F277), and then by BISECT (F294) or TRIDIB (F237).

If some of the eigenvalues and eigenvectors of the original matrix system are desired, this subroutine should be followed by TRED1 (F277), then by TSTURM (F293), or by BISECT (F294) and TINVIT (F223), or by TRIDIB (F237) and TINVIT, or by IMTQLV (F234) and TINVIT, then by TRBAK1 (F279), and finally by REBAK (F225).

3. DISCUSSION OF METHOD AND ALGORITHM.

The Cholesky decomposition of B into LL^T where L is lower triangular is first performed. If L is previously known, it may be provided as input (see section 2A) and this step skipped. If B is not positive definite, IERR will be set in the course of this step and an immediate error return made.

Next, the composition $L^{-1}AL^{-T}$ is performed, resulting in a symmetric matrix with the same eigenvalues as the original matrix system and with eigenvectors which can be transformed by subroutine REBAK (F225) into those of the original system.

This subroutine is a translation of the Algol procedure REDUC1 written and discussed in detail by Martin and Wilkinson (1).

4. REFERENCES.

1) Martin, R.S. and Wilkinson, J.H., Reduction of the
   Symmetric Eigenproblem Ax = (Lambda)Bx and Related
   Problems to Standard Form, Num. Math. 11,99-110 (1968).
   (Reprinted in Handbook for Automatic Computation,
   Volume II, Linear Algebra, J. H. Wilkinson - C. Reinsch,
   Contribution II/10, 303-314, Springer-Verlag, 1971.)

5. CHECKOUT.

   A. Test Cases.

      See the section discussing testing of the codes for
      real symmetric generalized matrix systems.

   B. Accuracy.

      The accuracy of REDUC can best be described in terms
      of its role in those paths of EISPACK which find
      eigenvalues and eigenvectors of real symmetric
      generalized matrix systems. In these paths, this
      subroutine is numerically stable (1). This stability
      contributes to the property of these paths that the
      computed eigenvalues are the exact eigenvalues of a
      system close to the original system and the computed
      eigenvectors are close (but not necessarily equal) to
      the eigenvectors of that system.

```
      SUBROUTINE REDUC(NM,N,A,B,DL,IERR)
C
      INTEGER I,J,K,N,I1,J1,NM,NN,IERR
      REAL A(NM,N),B(NM,N),DL(N)
      REAL X,Y
      REAL SQRT
      INTEGER IABS
C
      IERR = 0
      NN = IABS(N)
      IF (N .LT. 0) GO TO 100
C     ********** FORM L IN THE ARRAYS B AND DL **********
      DO 80 I = 1, N
         I1 = I - 1
C
         DO 80 J = I, N
            X = B(I,J)
            IF (I .EQ. 1) GO TO 40
C
            DO 20 K = 1, I1
   20       X = X - B(I,K) * B(J,K)
C
   40       IF (J .NE. I) GO TO 60
            IF (X .LE. 0.0) GO TO 1000
            Y = SQRT(X)
            DL(I) = Y
            GO TO 80
   60       B(J,I) = X / Y
   80 CONTINUE
C     ********** FORM THE TRANSPOSE OF THE UPPER TRIANGLE OF INV(L)*
C                IN THE LOWER TRIANGLE OF THE ARRAY A **********
  100 DO 200 I = 1, NN
         I1 = I - 1
         Y = DL(I)
C
         DO 200 J = I, NN
            X = A(I,J)
            IF (I .EQ. 1) GO TO 180
C
            DO 160 K = 1, I1
  160       X = X - B(I,K) * A(J,K)
C
  180       A(J,I) = X / Y
  200 CONTINUE
C     ********** PRE-MULTIPLY BY INV(L) AND OVERWRITE **********
      DO 300 J = 1, NN
         J1 = J - 1
C
         DO 300 I = J, NN
            X = A(I,J)
            IF (I .EQ. J) GO TO 240
            I1 = I - 1
```

232

```
C
          DO 220 K = J, I1
  220     X = X - A(K,J) * B(I,K)
C
  240     IF (J .EQ. 1) GO TO 280
C
          DO 260 K = 1, J1
  260     X = X - A(J,K) * B(I,K)
C
  280     A(I,J) = X / DL(I)
  300 CONTINUE
C
      GO TO 1001
C     ********** SET ERROR -- B IS NOT POSITIVE DEFINITE **********
 1000 IERR = 7 * N + 1
 1001 RETURN
      END
```

NATS PROJECT

EIGENSYSTEM SUBROUTINE PACKAGE (EISPACK)

F230   REDUC2

A Fortran IV Subroutine to Reduce Certain Generalized
Symmetric Eigenproblems to Standard Symmetric
Eigenproblems Using Cholesky Decomposition.

July, 1975

1. PURPOSE.

The Fortran IV subroutine REDUC2 reduces either of the
generalized symmetric eigenproblems ABX = (LAMBDA)X   or
BAX = (LAMBDA)X, where B is positive definite, to a
standard symmetric eigenproblem using the Cholesky
factorization of B. This reduced form is used by other
subroutines to find the eigenvalues and/or eigenvectors of
the original matrix system. See section 2C for the specific
routines.

2. USAGE.

A. Calling Sequence.

The SUBROUTINE statement is

SUBROUTINE   REDUC2(NM,N,A,B,DL,IERR)

The parameters are discussed below and the
interpretation of working precision for various machines
is given in the section discussing certification.

NM   is an integer input variable set equal to
            the row dimension of the two-dimensional
            arrays A and B as specified in the
            DIMENSION statements for A and B in the
            calling program.

N   is an integer input variable set equal to
            the order of the matrices A and B. If
            the Cholesky factor L of B is already
            available, N should be prefixed with a
            minus sign. ABS(N) must be not greater
            than NM.

A   is a working precision real two-dimensional variable with row dimension NM and column dimension at least N. On input, A contains one of the symmetric matrices of order N that define the generalized eigenproblem. Only the full upper triangle of the matrix need be supplied. On output, the full lower triangle of A contains the full lower triangle of the symmetric matrix derived from the reduction to the standard form. The strict upper triangle of A is unaltered. See section 3 for the details.

B   is a working precision real two-dimensional variable with row dimension NM and column dimension at least N. On input, B contains the positive definite symmetric matrix of order N in the system. Only the full upper triangle of the matrix need be supplied. Alternatively if N is negative, the strict lower triangle of B contains the strict lower triangle of its Cholesky factor L. In this case, the full upper triangle of the matrix is arbitrary. On output, the strict lower triangle of B contains the strict lower triangle of its Cholesky factor L. The full upper triangle of B is unaltered. See section 3 for the details.

DL   is a working precision real one-dimensional variable of dimension at least N. On input, if N is negative, DL contains the diagonal elements of the Cholesky factor L of B. On output, DL contains the diagonal elements of the Cholesky factor L of B.

IERR   is an integer output variable set equal to an error completion code described in section 2B. The normal completion code is zero.

B. Error Conditions and Returns.

If the matrix B is not positive definite, REDUC2 terminates with IERR set to 7*N+1. In this case, the Cholesky factorization of B does not exist.

If B is positive definite, IERR is set to zero.

C. Applicability and Restrictions.

If all the eigenvalues of the original matrix system are desired, this subroutine should be followed by TRED1 (F277), and then by TQL1 (F289), IMTQL1 (F291), or TQLRAT (F235).

If all the eigenvalues and eigenvectors of the original matrix system are desired, this subroutine should be followed by TRED2 (F278), then by TQL2 (F290) or IMTQL2 (F292), and finally by REBAK (F225) for the back transformation of the eigenvectors of ABX = (LAMBDA)X or by REBAKB (F231) for the back transformation of the eigenvectors of BAX = (LAMBDA)X.

If some of the eigenvalues of the original matrix system are desired, this subroutine should be followed by TRED1 (F277), and then by BISECT (F294) or TRIDIB (F237).

If some of the eigenvalues and eigenvectors of the original matrix system are desired, this subroutine should be followed by TRED1 (F277), then by TSTURM (F293), or by BISECT (F294) and TINVIT (F223), or by TRIDIB (F237) and TINVIT, or by IMTQLV (F234) and TINVIT, then by TRBAK1 (F279), and finally by REBAK (F225) for the back transformation of the eigenvectors of ABX = (LAMBDA)X or by REBAKB (F231) for the back transformation of the eigenvectors of BAX = (LAMBDA)X.

Note that left eigenvectors of AB can be obtained by transposing the (right) eigenvectors of BA, and that left eigenvectors of BA can be obtained by transposing the (right) eigenvectors of AB.

3. DISCUSSION OF METHOD AND ALGORITHM.

The Cholesky decomposition of B into LL^T where L is lower triangular is first performed. If L is previously known, it may be provided as input (see section 2A) and this step skipped. If B is not positive definite, IERR will be set in the course of this step and an immediate error return made.

Next, the composition $L^T AL$ is performed, resulting in a symmetric matrix with the same eigenvalues as the original matrix system and with eigenvectors which can be transformed by subroutine REBAK (F225) or REBAKB (F231), as appropriate, into those of the original system.

This subroutine is a translation of the Algol procedure REDUC2 written and discussed in detail by Martin and Wilkinson (1).

4. REFERENCES.

1) Martin, R.S. and Wilkinson, J.H., Reduction of the Symmetric Eigenproblem Ax = (Lambda)Bx and Related Problems to Standard Form, Num. Math. 11,99-110 (1968). (Reprinted in Handbook for Automatic Computation, Volume II, Linear Algebra, J. H. Wilkinson - C. Reinsch, Contribution II/10, 303-314, Springer-Verlag, 1971.)

5. CHECKOUT.

   A. Test Cases.

      See the section discussing testing of the codes for real symmetric generalized matrix systems.

   B. Accuracy.

      The accuracy of REDUC2 can best be described in terms of its role in those paths of EISPACK which find eigenvalues and eigenvectors of real symmetric generalized matrix systems. In these paths, this subroutine is numerically stable (1). This stability contributes to the property of these paths that the computed eigenvalues are the exact eigenvalues of a system close to the original system and the computed eigenvectors are close (but not necessarily equal) to the eigenvectors of that system.

```
      SUBROUTINE REDUC2(NM,N,A,B,DL,IERR)
C
      INTEGER I,J,K,N,I1,J1,NM,NN,IERR
      REAL A(NM,N),B(NM,N),DL(N)
      REAL X,Y
      REAL SQRT
      INTEGER IABS
C
      IERR = 0
      NN = IABS(N)
      IF (N .LT. 0) GO TO 100
C     ********** FORM L IN THE ARRAYS B AND DL **********
      DO 80 I = 1, N
         I1 = I - 1
C
         DO 80 J = I, N
            X = B(I,J)
            IF (I .EQ. 1) GO TO 40
C
            DO 20 K = 1, I1
   20       X = X - B(I,K) * B(J,K)
C
   40       IF (J .NE. I) GO TO 60
            IF (X .LE. 0.0) GO TO 1000
            Y = SQRT(X)
            DL(I) = Y
            GO TO 80
   60       B(J,I) = X / Y
   80 CONTINUE
C     ********** FORM THE LOWER TRIANGLE OF A*L
C                IN THE LOWER TRIANGLE OF THE ARRAY A **********
  100 DO 200 I = 1, NN
         I1 = I + 1
C
         DO 200 J = 1, I
            X = A(J,I) * DL(J)
            IF (J .EQ. I) GO TO 140
            J1 = J + 1
C
            DO 120 K = J1, I
  120       X = X + A(K,I) * B(K,J)
C
  140       IF (I .EQ. NN) GO TO 180
C
            DO 160 K = I1, NN
  160       X = X + A(I,K) * B(K,J)
C
  180       A(I,J) = X
  200 CONTINUE
C     ********** PRE-MULTIPLY BY TRANSPOSE(L) AND OVERWRITE **********
      DO 300 I = 1, NN
         I1 = I + 1
         Y = DL(I)
```

```
C
        DO 300 J = 1, I
           X = Y * A(I,J)
           IF (I .EQ. NN) GO TO 280
C
           DO 260 K = I1, NN
  260      X = X + A(K,J) * B(K,I)
C
  280      A(I,J) = X
  300 CONTINUE
C
      GO TO 1001
C     ********** SET ERROR -- B IS NOT POSITIVE DEFINITE **********
 1000 IERR = 7 * N + 1
 1001 RETURN
      END
```

NATS PROJECT

EIGENSYSTEM SUBROUTINE PACKAGE (EISPACK)

F312   RGG

A Fortran IV Driver Subroutine to Determine the Eigenvalues and
Eigenvectors for the Real General Generalized
Eigenproblem A*X = (LAMBDA)*B*X.

July, 1975

1. PURPOSE.

The Fortran IV subroutine RGG calls the recommended
sequence of subroutines from the eigensystem subroutine
package EISPACK to determine the eigenvalues and
eigenvectors (if desired) for the real general generalized
eigenproblem A*X = (LAMBDA)*B*X.

2. USAGE.

A. Calling Sequence.

The SUBROUTINE statement is

SUBROUTINE RGG(NM,N,A,B,ALFR,ALFI,BETA,MATZ,Z,IERR)

The parameters are discussed below and· the
interpretation of working precision for various machines
is given in the section discussing certification.

NM   is an integer input variable set equal to
       the row dimension of the two-dimensional
       arrays A, B, and Z as specified in the
       DIMENSION statements for A, B, and Z in
       the calling program.

N   is an integer input variable set equal to
       the order of the matrices A and B. N
       must not be greater than NM.

A   is a working precision real two-dimensional
       variable with row dimension NM and column
       dimension at least N. On input, A
       contains one of the real general matrices of
       order N that define the eigenproblem whose
       eigenvalues and eigenvectors are to be
       found. On output, A has been destroyed.

B is a working precision real two-dimensional
variable with row dimension NM and column
dimension at least N. On input, B
contains the other real general matrix of
order N. On output, B has been
destroyed.

ALFR,ALFI
  are working precision real output one-
dimensional variables of dimension at least
N containing the real and imaginary parts,
respectively, of the numerators of the
eigenvalues for the real general generalized
eigenproblem.

BETA is a working precision real output one-
dimensional variable of dimension at least
N containing the denominators of the
eigenvalues which are thus given by the
ratios (ALFR+I*ALFI)/BETA. The eigenvalues
are unordered except that complex conjugate
pairs of eigenvalues appear consecutively
with the eigenvalue having the positive
imaginary part first.

MATZ is an integer input variable set equal to
zero if only eigenvalues are desired;
otherwise it is set to any non-zero integer
for both eigenvalues and eigenvectors.

Z is, if MATZ is non-zero, a working
precision real output two-dimensional
variable with row dimension NM and column
dimension at least N containing the real
and imaginary parts of the eigenvectors. If
the J-th eigenvalue is real, the J-th
column of Z contains its eigenvector. If
the J-th eigenvalue is complex with
positive imaginary part, the J-th and
(J+1)-th columns of Z contain the real
and imaginary parts of its eigenvector. The
conjugate of this vector is the eigenvector
for the conjugate eigenvalue. Each
eigenvector is normalized so that the
modulus of its largest component is 1.0.
If MATZ is zero, Z is not referenced and
can be a dummy variable.

IERR is an integer output variable set equal to
an error completion code described in
section 2B. The normal completion code is
zero.

B. Error Conditions and Returns.

If N is greater than NM, the subroutine terminates with IERR set equal to 10*N.

If more than 50 iterations are required to determine an eigenvalue, the subroutine terminates with IERR set equal to the index of the eigenvalue for which the failure occurs. The eigenvalues in the ALFR, ALFI, and BETA arrays should be correct for indices IERR+1,IERR+2,...,N, but no eigenvectors are computed.

If all the eigenvalues are determined within 50 iterations, IERR is set to zero.

C. Applicability and Restrictions.

This subroutine can be used to find all the eigenvalues and all the eigenvectors (if desired) for the real general generalized eigenproblem A*X = (LAMBDA)*B*X.

3. DISCUSSION OF METHOD AND ALGORITHM.

This subroutine calls the recommended sequence of subroutines from EISPACK to find the eigenvalues and eigenvectors for the real general generalized eigenproblem A*X = (LAMBDA)*B*X.

To find eigenvalues only, the sequence is the following.
    QZHES   - to simultaneously reduce one of a pair of real general matrices to an upper Hessenberg matrix and the other to an upper triangular matrix using orthogonal transformations.
    QZIT   - to reduce one of a pair of real matrices from upper Hessenberg to quasi-triangular form while maintaining the upper triangular form of the other using orthogonal transformations.
    QZVAL   - to extract the eigenvalues for a real general generalized eigenproblem with one matrix in quasi-upper triangular form and the other in upper triangular form using orthogonal transformations.

To find eigenvalues and eigenvectors, the sequence is the following.
    QZHES   - to simultaneously reduce one of a pair of real general matrices to an upper Hessenberg matrix and the other to an upper triangular matrix using and accumulating orthogonal transformations.

QZIT   - to reduce one of a pair of real matrices from
          upper Hessenberg to quasi-triangular form while
          maintaining the upper triangular form of the
          other using and accumulating orthogonal
          transformations.
QZVAL   - to extract the eigenvalues for a real general
          generalized eigenproblem with one matrix in
          quasi-upper triangular form and the other in
          upper triangular form using and accumulating
          orthogonal transformations.
QZVEC   - to determine the corresponding eigenvectors by
          back substitution.

4. REFERENCES.

1) Garbow, B.S. and Dongarra, J.J., EISPACK Path Chart,
    April, 1974.

5. CHECKOUT.

   A. Test Cases.

      See the section discussing testing of the codes for
      real generalized matrix systems.

   B. Accuracy.

      The accuracy of RGG can be best described in terms of
      its role in those paths of EISPACK (1) which find
      eigenvalues and eigenvectors of real generalized matrix
      systems. In these paths, this subroutine is numerically
      stable. This stability contributes to the property of
      these paths that each computed eigenvalue and its
      corresponding eigenvector are exact for a system close
      to the original system.

```
      SUBROUTINE RGG(NM,N,A,B,ALFR,ALFI,BETA,MATZ,Z,IERR)
C
      INTEGER N,NM,IERR,MATZ
      REAL A(NM,N),B(NM,N),ALFR(N),ALFI(N),BETA(N),Z(NM,N)
      LOGICAL TF
C
      IF (N .LE. NM) GO TO 10
      IERR = 10 * N
      GO TO 50
C
   10 IF (MATZ .NE. 0) GO TO 20
C     ********** FIND EIGENVALUES ONLY **********
      TF = .FALSE.
      CALL   QZHES(NM,N,A,B,TF,Z)
      CALL   QZIT(NM,N,A,B,0.0,TF,Z,IERR)
      CALL   QZVAL(NM,N,A,B,ALFR,ALFI,BETA,TF,Z)
      GO TO 50
C     ********** FIND BOTH EIGENVALUES AND EIGENVECTORS **********
   20 TF = .TRUE.
      CALL   QZHES(NM,N,A,B,TF,Z)
      CALL   QZIT(NM,N,A,B,0.0,TF,Z,IERR)
      CALL   QZVAL(NM,N,A,B,ALFR,ALFI,BETA,TF,Z)
      IF (IERR .NE. 0) GO TO 50
      CALL   QZVEC(NM,N,A,B,ALFR,ALFI,BETA,Z)
   50 RETURN
      END
```

NATS PROJECT

EIGENSYSTEM SUBROUTINE PACKAGE (EISPACK)

F308   RSB

A Fortran IV Driver Subroutine to Determine the Eigenvalues and
Eigenvectors of a Real Symmetric Band Matrix.

July, 1975

1. PURPOSE.

   The Fortran IV subroutine RSB calls the recommended
   sequence of subroutines from the eigensystem subroutine
   package EISPACK to determine the eigenvalues and
   eigenvectors (if desired) of a real symmetric band matrix.

2. USAGE.

   A. Calling Sequence.

   The SUBROUTINE statement is

       SUBROUTINE RSB(NM,N,MB,A,W,MATZ,Z,FV1,FV2,IERR)

   The parameters are discussed below and the
   interpretation of working precision for various machines
   is given in the section discussing certification.

   NM   is an integer input variable set equal to
           the row dimension of the two-dimensional
           arrays A and Z as specified in the
           DIMENSION statements for A and Z in the
           calling program.

   N   is an integer input variable set equal to
           the order of the matrix A.   N must not be
           greater than NM.

   MB   is an integer input variable set equal to
           the (half) band width of the matrix A,
           defined as the number of adjacent diagonals,
           including the principal diagonal, required
           to specify the non-zero portion of the lower
           triangle of the matrix. MB must not be
           greater than N.

A   is a working precision real two-dimensional
           variable with row dimension NM and column
           dimension at least MB. On input, A
           contains the lower triangle of the real
           symmetric band matrix of order N and
           (half) band width MB whose eigenvalues and
           eigenvectors are to be found. Its lowest
           subdiagonal is stored in the last N+1-MB
           positions of the first column, its next
           subdiagonal in the last N+2-MB positions
           of the second column, further subdiagonals
           similarly, and finally its principal
           diagonal in the N positions of the last
           column. Contents of storage locations not
           part of the matrix are arbitrary. For
           example, when N=5 and MB=3, A should
           contain

                    (*   *   A(1,1))
                    (*   A(2,1)   A(2,2))
                    (A(3,1)   A(3,2)   A(3,3))
                    (A(4,2)   A(4,3)   A(4,4))
                    (A(5,3)   A(5,4)   A(5,5))

           where the subscripts for each element refer
           to the row and column of the element in the
           standard two-dimensional representation, and
           (*) denotes an arbitrary value. On output,
           A has been destroyed.

W   is a working precision real output one-
           dimensional variable of dimension at least
           N containing the eigenvalues of the real
           symmetric band matrix in ascending order.

MATZ   is an integer input variable set equal to
           zero if only eigenvalues are desired;
           otherwise it is set to any non-zero integer
           for both eigenvalues and eigenvectors.

Z   is, if MATZ is non-zero, a working
           precision real output two-dimensional
           variable with row dimension NM and column
           dimension at least N containing the
           eigenvectors. The eigenvectors are
           orthonormal. If MATZ is zero, Z is not
           referenced and can be a dummy variable.

FV1,FV2   are working precision temporary one-
           dimensional variables of dimension at least
           N.

IERR   is an integer output variable set equal to
an error completion code described in
section 2B. The normal completion code is
zero.

B. Error Conditions and Returns.

If N is greater than NM, the subroutine terminates
with IERR set equal to 10*N.

If MB is either non-positive or greater than N, the
subroutine terminates with IERR set equal to 12*N.

If more than 30 iterations are required to determine
an eigenvalue, the subroutine terminates with IERR set
equal to the index of the eigenvalue for which the
failure occurs. The eigenvalues and eigenvectors in the
W and Z arrays should be correct for indices
1,2,...,IERR-1.

If all the eigenvalues are determined within 30
iterations, IERR is set to zero.

C. Applicability and Restrictions.

This subroutine can be used to find all the eigenvalues
and all the eigenvectors (if desired) of a real
symmetric band matrix.

3. DISCUSSION OF METHOD AND ALGORITHM.

This subroutine calls the recommended sequence of subroutines
from EISPACK to find the eigenvalues and eigenvectors of a
real symmetric band matrix.

To find eigenvalues only, the sequence is the following.
    BANDR - to reduce a real symmetric band matrix to a
             symmetric tridiagonal matrix using orthogonal
             transformations.
    TQLRAT - to determine the eigenvalues of the original
             matrix from the symmetric tridiagonal matrix.

To find eigenvalues and eigenvectors, the sequence is the
following.
    BANDR - to reduce a real symmetric band matrix to a
             symmetric tridiagonal matrix using and
             accumulating orthogonal transformations.
    TQL2   - to determine the eigenvalues and eigenvectors
             of the original matrix from the symmetric
             tridiagonal matrix.

4. REFERENCES.

    1) Garbow, B.S. and Dongarra, J.J., EISPACK Path Chart,
        April, 1974.

5. CHECKOUT.

    A. Test Cases.

        See the section discussing testing of the codes for
        real symmetric band matrices.

    B. Accuracy.

        The accuracy of RSB can best be described in terms of
        its role in those paths of EISPACK (1) which find
        eigenvalues and eigenvectors of real symmetric band
        matrices. In these paths, this subroutine is
        numerically stable. This stability contributes to the
        property of these paths that the computed eigenvalues
        are the exact eigenvalues of a matrix close to the
        original matrix and the computed eigenvectors are close
        (but not necessarily equal) to the eigenvectors of that
        matrix.

```
      SUBROUTINE RSB(NM,N,MB,A,W,MATZ,Z,FV1,FV2,IERR)
C
      INTEGER N,MB,NM,IERR,MATZ
      REAL A(NM,MB),W(N),Z(NM,N),FV1(N),FV2(N)
      LOGICAL TF
C
      IF (N .LE. NM) GO TO 5
      IERR = 10 * N
      GO TO 50
    5 IF (MB .GT. 0) GO TO 10
      IERR = 12 * N
      GO TO 50
   10 IF (MB .LE. N) GO TO 15
      IERR = 12 * N
      GO TO 50
C
   15 IF (MATZ .NE. 0) GO TO 20
C     ********** FIND EIGENVALUES ONLY **********
      TF = .FALSE.
      CALL   BANDR(NM,N,MB,A,W,FV1,FV2,TF,Z)
      CALL   TQLRAT(N,W,FV2,IERR)
      GO TO 50
C     ********** FIND BOTH EIGENVALUES AND EIGENVECTORS **********
   20 TF = .TRUE.
      CALL   BANDR(NM,N,MB,A,W,FV1,FV1,TF,Z)
      CALL   TQL2(NM,N,W,FV1,Z,IERR)
   50 RETURN
      END
```

NATS PROJECT

EIGENSYSTEM SUBROUTINE PACKAGE (EISPACK)

F309 RSG

A Fortran IV Driver Subroutine to Determine the Eigenvalues and
Eigenvectors for the Real Symmetric Generalized
Eigenproblem A*X = (LAMBDA)*B*X.

July, 1975

1. PURPOSE.

The Fortran IV subroutine RSG calls the recommended
sequence of subroutines from the eigensystem subroutine
package EISPACK to determine the eigenvalues and
eigenvectors (if desired) for the real symmetric generalized
eigenproblem A*X = (LAMBDA)*B*X.

2. USAGE.

A. Calling Sequence.

The SUBROUTINE statement is

SUBROUTINE RSG(NM,N,A,B,W,MATZ,Z,FV1,FV2,IERR)

The parameters are discussed below and the
interpretation of working precision for various machines
is given in the section discussing certification.

NM   is an integer input variable set equal to
the row dimension of the two-dimensional
arrays A, B, and Z as specified in the
DIMENSION statements for A, B, and Z in
the calling program.

N   is an integer input variable set equal to
the order of the matrices A and B. N
must not be greater than NM.

A   is a working precision real two-dimensional
variable with row dimension NM and column
dimension at least N. On input, A
contains one of the the real symmetric
matrices of order N that define the

eigenproblem whose eigenvalues and eigenvectors are to be found. Only the full upper triangle of A need be supplied. On output, the strict upper triangle of A is unaltered.

B is a working precision real two-dimensional variable with row dimension NM and column dimension at least N. On input, B contains the other real symmetric matrix of order N. Further, B is required to be positive definite. Only the full upper triangle of B need be supplied. On output, the full upper triangle of B is unaltered.

W is a working precision real output one-dimensional variable of dimension at least N containing the eigenvalues for the real symmetric generalized eigenproblem in ascending order.

MATZ is an integer input variable set equal to zero if only eigenvalues are desired; otherwise it is set to any non-zero integer for both eigenvalues and eigenvectors.

Z is, if MATZ is non-zero, a working precision real output two-dimensional variable with row dimension NM and column dimension at least N containing the eigenvectors. The eigenvectors are normalized so that $Z^T BZ = I$. If MATZ is zero, Z is not referenced and can be a dummy variable.

FV1,FV2 are working precision temporary one-dimensional variables of dimension at least N.

IERR is an integer output variable set equal to an error completion code described in section 2B. The normal completion code is zero.

B. Error Conditions and Returns.

If N is greater than NM, the subroutine terminates with IERR set equal to $10*N$.

If the matrix B is not positive definite, the subroutine terminates with IERR set to $7*N+1$.

251

If more than 30 iterations are required to determine an eigenvalue, the subroutine terminates with IERR set equal to the index of the eigenvalue for which the failure occurs. The eigenvalues in the W array should be correct for indices 1,2,...,IERR-1, but no eigenvectors are computed.

If all the eigenvalues are determined within 30 iterations, IERR is set to zero.

C. Applicability and Restrictions.

This subroutine can be used to find all the eigenvalues and all the eigenvectors (if desired) for the real symmetric generalized eigenproblem A*X = (LAMBDA)*B*X.

3. DISCUSSION OF METHOD AND ALGORITHM.

This subroutine calls the recommended sequence of subroutines from EISPACK to find the eigenvalues and eigenvectors for the real symmetric generalized eigenproblem A*X = (LAMBDA)*B*X.

To find eigenvalues only, the sequence is the following.
REDUC - to reduce the generalized symmetric eigenproblem to the standard symmetric eigenproblem using Cholesky decomposition.
TRED1 - to reduce the real symmetric matrix of the standard problem to a symmetric tridiagonal matrix using orthogonal transformations.
TQLRAT - to determine the eigenvalues for the original problem from the symmetric tridiagonal matrix.

To find eigenvalues and eigenvectors, the sequence is the following.
REDUC - to reduce the generalized symmetric eigenproblem to the standard symmetric eigenproblem using Cholesky decomposition.
TRED2 - to reduce the real symmetric matrix of the standard problem to a symmetric tridiagonal matrix using and accumulating orthogonal transformations.
TQL2   - to determine the eigenvalues and eigenvectors for the standard problem from the symmetric tridiagonal matrix.
REBAK - to backtransform the eigenvectors to those of the original problem.

4. REFERENCES.

1) Garbow, B.S. and Dongarra, J.J., EISPACK Path Chart, April, 1974.

5. CHECKOUT.

   A. Test Cases.

   See the section discussing testing of the codes for real symmetric generalized matrix systems.

   B. Accuracy.

   The accuracy of RSG can best be described in terms of its role in those paths of EISPACK (1) which find eigenvalues and eigenvectors of real symmetric generalized matrix systems. In these paths, this subroutine is numerically stable. This stability contributes to the property of these paths that the computed eigenvalues are the exact eigenvalues of a system close to the original system and the computed eigenvectors are close (but not necessarily equal) to the eigenvectors of that system.

```
      SUBROUTINE RSG(NM,N,A,B,W,MATZ,Z,FV1,FV2,IERR)
C
      INTEGER N,NM,IERR,MATZ
      REAL A(NM,N),B(NM,N),W(N),Z(NM,N),FV1(N),FV2(N)
C
      IF (N .LE. NM) GO TO 10
      IERR = 10 * N
      GO TO 50
C
   10 CALL   REDUC(NM,N,A,B,FV2,IERR)
      IF (IERR .NE. 0) GO TO 50
      IF (MATZ .NE. 0) GO TO 20
C     ********** FIND EIGENVALUES ONLY **********
      CALL   TRED1(NM,N,A,W,FV1,FV2)
      CALL   TQLRAT(N,W,FV2,IERR)
      GO TO 50
C     ********** FIND BOTH EIGENVALUES AND EIGENVECTORS **********
   20 CALL   TRED2(NM,N,A,W,FV1,Z)
      CALL   TQL2(NM,N,W,FV1,Z,IERR)
      IF (IERR .NE. 0) GO TO 50
      CALL   REBAK(NM,N,B,FV2,N,Z)
   50 RETURN
      END
```

NATS PROJECT

EIGENSYSTEM SUBROUTINE PACKAGE (EISPACK)

F310   RSGAB

A Fortran IV Driver Subroutine to Determine the Eigenvalues and
Eigenvectors for the Real Symmetric Generalized
Eigenproblem A*B*X = (LAMBDA)*X.

July, 1975

1. PURPOSE.

   The Fortran IV subroutine RSGAB calls the recommended
   sequence of subroutines from the eigensystem subroutine
   package EISPACK to determine the eigenvalues and
   eigenvectors (if desired) for the real symmetric generalized
   eigenproblem A*B*X = (LAMBDA)*X.

2. USAGE.

   A. Calling Sequence.

      The SUBROUTINE statement is

      SUBROUTINE RSGAB(NM,N,A,B,W,MATZ,Z,FV1,FV2,IERR)

      The parameters are discussed below and the
      interpretation of working precision for various machines
      is given in the section discussing certification.

         NM   is an integer input variable set equal to
                   the row dimension of the two-dimensional
                   arrays A, B, and Z as specified in the
                   DIMENSION statements for A, B, and Z in
                   the calling program.

         N   is an integer input variable set equal to
                   the order of the matrices A and B. N
                   must not be greater than NM.

         A   is a working precision real two-dimensional
                   variable with row dimension NM and column
                   dimension at least N. On input, A
                   contains one of the the real symmetric
                   matrices of order N that define the

eigenproblem whose eigenvalues and
eigenvectors are to be found. Only the full
upper triangle of A need be supplied. On
output, the strict upper triangle of A is
unaltered.

B   is a working precision real two-dimensional
variable with row dimension NM and column
dimension at least N. On input, B
contains the other real symmetric matrix of
order N. Further, B is required to be
positive definite. Only the full upper
triangle of B need be supplied. On
output, the full upper triangle of B is
unaltered.

W   is a working precision real output one-
dimensional variable of dimension at least
N containing the eigenvalues for the real
symmetric generalized eigenproblem in
ascending order.

MATZ is an integer input variable set equal to
zero if only eigenvalues are desired;
otherwise it is set to any non-zero integer
for both eigenvalues and eigenvectors.

Z   is, if MATZ is non-zero, a working
precision real output two-dimensional
variable with row dimension NM and column
dimension at least N containing the
eigenvectors. The eigenvectors are
normalized so that $Z^T BZ = I$. If MATZ
is zero, Z is not referenced and can be a
dummy variable.

FV1,FV2 are working precision temporary one-
dimensional variables of dimension at least
N.

IERR is an integer output variable set equal to
an error completion code described in
section 2B. The normal completion code is
zero.

B. Error Conditions and Returns.

If N is greater than NM, the subroutine terminates
with IERR set equal to 10*N.

If the matrix B is not positive definite, the
subroutine terminates with IERR set to 7*N+1.

If more than 30 iterations are required to determine
an eigenvalue, the subroutine terminates with IERR set
equal to the index of the eigenvalue for which the
failure occurs. The eigenvalues in the W array should
be correct for indices 1,2,...,IERR-1, but no
eigenvectors are computed.

If all the eigenvalues are determined within 30
iterations, IERR is set to zero.

C. Applicability and Restrictions.

This subroutine can be used to find all the eigenvalues
and all the eigenvectors (if desired) for the real
symmetric generalized eigenproblem A*B*X = (LAMBDA)*X.

3. DISCUSSION OF METHOD AND ALGORITHM.

This subroutine calls the recommended sequence of subroutines
from EISPACK to find the eigenvalues and eigenvectors for
the real symmetric generalized eigenproblem
A*B*X = (LAMBDA)*X.

To find eigenvalues only, the sequence is the following.
REDUC2 - to reduce the generalized symmetric
          eigenproblem to the standard symmetric
          eigenproblem using Cholesky decomposition.
TRED1 - to reduce the real symmetric matrix of the
          standard problem to a symmetric tridiagonal
          matrix using orthogonal transformations.
TQLRAT - to determine the eigenvalues for the original
          problem from the symmetric tridiagonal matrix.

To find eigenvalues and eigenvectors, the sequence is the
following.
REDUC2 - to reduce the generalized symmetric
          eigenproblem to the standard symmetric
          eigenproblem using Cholesky decomposition.
TRED2 - to reduce the real symmetric matrix of the
          standard problem to a symmetric tridiagonal
          matrix using and accumulating orthogonal
          transformations.
TQL2   - to determine the eigenvalues and eigenvectors
          for the standard problem from the symmetric
          tridiagonal matrix.
REBAK - to backtransform the eigenvectors to those of
          the original problem.

4. REFERENCES.

1) Garbow, B.S. and Dongarra, J.J., EISPACK Path Chart,
April, 1974.

5. CHECKOUT.

A. Test Cases.

See the section discussing testing of the codes for
real symmetric generalized matrix systems.

B. Accuracy.

The accuracy of RSGAB can best be described in terms
of its role in those paths of EISPACK (1) which find
eigenvalues and eigenvectors of real symmetric
generalized matrix systems. In these paths, this
subroutine is numerically stable. This stability
contributes to the property of these paths that the
computed eigenvalues are the exact eigenvalues of a
system close to the original system and the computed
eigenvectors are close (but not necessarily equal) to
the eigenvectors of that system.

```
      SUBROUTINE RSGAB(NM,N,A,B,W,MATZ,Z,FV1,FV2,IERR)
C
      INTEGER N,NM,IERR,MATZ
      REAL A(NM,N),B(NM,N),W(N),Z(NM,N),FV1(N),FV2(N)
C
      IF (N .LE. NM) GO TO 10
      IERR = 10 * N
      GO TO 50
C
   10 CALL   REDUC2(NM,N,A,B,FV2,IERR)
      IF (IERR .NE. 0) GO TO 50
      IF (MATZ .NE. 0) GO TO 20
C     ********** FIND EIGENVALUES ONLY **********
      CALL   TRED1(NM,N,A,W,FV1,FV2)
      CALL   TQLRAT(N,W,FV2,IERR)
      GO TO 50
C     ********** FIND BOTH EIGENVALUES AND EIGENVECTORS **********
   20 CALL   TRED2(NM,N,A,W,FV1,Z)
      CALL   TQL2(NM,N,W,FV1,Z,IERR)
      IF (IERR .NE. 0) GO TO 50
      CALL   REBAK(NM,N,B,FV2,N,Z)
   50 RETURN
      END
```

NATS PROJECT

EIGENSYSTEM SUBROUTINE PACKAGE (EISPACK)

F311   RSGBA

A Fortran IV Driver Subroutine to Determine the Eigenvalues and
Eigenvectors for the Real Symmetric Generalized
Eigenproblem B*A*X = (LAMBDA)*X.

July, 1975

1. PURPOSE.

The Fortran IV subroutine RSGBA calls the recommended
sequence of subroutines from the eigensystem subroutine
package EISPACK to determine the eigenvalues and
eigenvectors (if desired) for the real symmetric generalized
eigenproblem B*A*X = (LAMBDA)*X.

2. USAGE.

A. Calling Sequence.

The SUBROUTINE statement is

SUBROUTINE   RSGBA(NM,N,A,B,W,MATZ,Z,FV1,FV2,IERR)

The parameters are discussed below and the
interpretation of working precision for various machines
is given in the section discussing certification.

NM   is an integer input variable set equal to
          the row dimension of the two-dimensional
          arrays A, B, and Z as specified in the
          DIMENSION statements for A, B, and Z in
          the calling program.

N,   is an integer input variable set equal to
          the order of the matrices A and B. N
          must not be greater than NM.

A   is a working precision real two-dimensional
          variable with row dimension NM and column
          dimension at least N. On input, A
          contains one of the the real symmetric
          matrices of order N that define the

eigenproblem whose eigenvalues and eigenvectors are to be found. Only the full upper triangle of A need be supplied. On output, the strict upper triangle of A is unaltered.

B   is a working precision real two-dimensional variable with row dimension NM and column dimension at least N. On input, B contains the other real symmetric matrix of order N. Further, B is required to be positive definite. Only the full upper triangle of B need be supplied. On output, the full upper triangle of B is unaltered.

W   is a working precision real output one-dimensional variable of dimension at least N containing the eigenvalues for the real symmetric generalized eigenproblem in ascending order.

MATZ   is an integer input variable set equal to zero if only eigenvalues are desired; otherwise it is set to any non-zero integer for both eigenvalues and eigenvectors.

Z   is, if MATZ is non-zero, a working precision real output two-dimensional variable with row dimension NM and column dimension at least N containing the eigenvectors. The eigenvectors are normalized so that $Z^T B Z = I$. If MATZ is zero, Z is not referenced and can be a dummy variable.

FV1,FV2 are working precision temporary one-dimensional variables of dimension at least N.

IERR   is an integer output variable set equal to an error completion code described in section 2B. The normal completion code is zero.

B. Error Conditions and Returns.

If N is greater than NM, the subroutine terminates with IERR set equal to 10*N.

If the matrix B is not positive definite, the subroutine terminates with IERR set to 7*N+1.

If more than 30 iterations are required to determine
an eigenvalue, the subroutine terminates with IERR set
equal to the index of the eigenvalue for which the
failure occurs. The eigenvalues in the W array should
be correct for indices 1,2,...,IERR-1, but no
eigenvectors are computed.

If all the eigenvalues are determined within 30
iterations, IERR is set to zero.

C. Applicability and Restrictions.

This subroutine can be used to find all the eigenvalues
and all the eigenvectors (if desired) for the real
symmetric generalized eigenproblem B*A*X = (LAMBDA)*X.

3. DISCUSSION OF METHOD AND ALGORITHM.

This subroutine calls the recommended sequence of subroutines
from EISPACK to find the eigenvalues and eigenvectors for
the real symmetric generalized eigenproblem
B*A*X = (LAMBDA)*X.

To find eigenvalues only, the sequence is the following.
    REDUC2 - to reduce the generalized symmetric
             eigenproblem to the standard symmetric
             eigenproblem using Cholesky decomposition.
    TRED1 - to reduce the real symmetric matrix of the
             standard problem to a symmetric tridiagonal
             matrix using orthogonal transformations.
    TQLRAT - to determine the eigenvalues for the original
             problem from the symmetric tridiagonal matrix.

To find eigenvalues and eigenvectors, the sequence is the
following.
    REDUC2 - to reduce the generalized symmetric
             eigenproblem to the standard symmetric
             eigenproblem using Cholesky decomposition.
    TRED2 - to reduce the real symmetric matrix of the
             standard problem to a symmetric tridiagonal
             matrix using and accumulating orthogonal
             transformations.
    TQL2   - to determine the eigenvalues and eigenvectors
             for the standard problem from the symmetric
             tridiagonal matrix.
    REBAKB - to backtransform the eigenvectors to those of
             the original problem.

4. REFERENCES.

    1) Garbow, B.S. and Dongarra, J.J., EISPACK Path Chart,
        April, 1974.

5. CHECKOUT.

    A. Test Cases.

        See the section discussing testing of the codes for
        real symmetric generalized matrix systems.

    B. Accuracy.

        The accuracy of RSGBA can best be described in terms
        of its role in those paths of EISPACK (1) which find
        eigenvalues and eigenvectors of real symmetric
        generalized matrix systems. In these paths, this
        subroutine is numerically stable. This stability
        contributes to the property of these paths that the
        computed eigenvalues are the exact eigenvalues of a
        system close to the original system and the computed
        eigenvectors are close (but not necessarily equal) to
        the eigenvectors of that system.

```
      SUBROUTINE RSGBA(NM,N,A,B,W,MATZ,Z,FV1,FV2,IERR)
C
      INTEGER N,NM,IERR,MATZ
      REAL A(NM,N),B(NM,N),W(N),Z(NM,N),FV1(N),FV2(N)
C
      IF (N .LE. NM) GO TO 10
      IERR = 10 * N
      GO TO 50
C
   10 CALL  REDUC2(NM,N,A,B,FV2,IERR)
      IF (IERR .NE. 0) GO TO 50
      IF (MATZ .NE. 0) GO TO 20
C     ********** FIND EIGENVALUES ONLY **********
      CALL  TRED1(NM,N,A,W,FV1,FV2)
      CALL  TQLRAT(N,W,FV2,IERR)
      GO TO 50
C     ********** FIND BOTH EIGENVALUES AND EIGENVECTORS **********
   20 CALL  TRED2(NM,N,A,W,FV1,Z)
      CALL  TQL2(NM,N,W,FV1,Z,IERR)
      IF (IERR .NE. 0) GO TO 50
      CALL  REBAKB(NM,N,B,FV2,N,Z)
   50 RETURN
      END
```

NATS PROJECT

EIGENSYSTEM SUBROUTINE PACKAGE (EISPACK)

F232 SVD

A Fortran IV Subroutine to Compute the Singular Value
Decomposition of an Arbitrary Real Rectangular Matrix.

July, 1975

1. PURPOSE.

The Fortran IV subroutine SVD computes the singular values
and complete orthogonal decomposition of a real rectangular
matrix A. A is decomposed into

$$U * DIAG(S) * V^T$$

with $U^T U = V^T V = I$. The diagonal elements of S are
the singular values of A, equal to the non-negative square
roots of the eigenvalues of $A^T A$.

2. USAGE.

A. Calling Sequence.

The SUBROUTINE statement is

SUBROUTINE SVD(NM,M,N,A,W,MATU,U,MATV,V,IERR,RV1)

The parameters are discussed below and the
interpretation of working precision for various machines
is given in the section discussing certification.

NM   is an integer input variable set equal to
the row dimension of the two-dimensional
arrays A and U (and V if MATV is
true) as specified in the DIMENSION
statements for A and U (and V) in the
calling program.

M   is an integer input variable set equal to
the number of rows of rectangular matrices
A and U. M must be not greater than NM.

N   is an integer input variable set equal to
             the number of columns of A and U and the
             order of the square matrix V. N must be
             not greater than NM.

A   is a working precision real input two-
             dimensional variable with row dimension NM
             and column dimension at least N which
             contains the matrix to be decomposed.

W   is a working precision real output one-
             dimensional variable of dimension at least
             N containing the singular values of A.

MATU   is a logical input variable set true if the
             matrix U is desired and set false
             otherwise.

U   is, if MATU is true, a working precision
             real output two-dimensional variable with
             row dimension NM and column dimension at
             least N. It contains orthogonal columns of
             the U matrix in the decomposition. If
             MATU is false, U is used as a temporary
             array.

MATV   is a logical input variable set true if the
             matrix V is desired and set false
             otherwise.

V   is, if MATV is true, a working precision
             real output two-dimensional variable with
             row dimension NM and column dimension at
             least N. It contains the orthogonal V
             matrix in the decomposition. If MATV is
             false, V is not referenced and can be a
             dummy (working precision) variable.

IERR   is an integer output variable set equal to
             an error completion code described in
             section 2B. The normal completion code is
             zero.

RV1   is a working precision real temporary one-
             dimensional variable of dimension at least
             N used to hold the off-diagonal elements of
             the bidiagonal form.

B. Error Conditions and Returns.

   If more than 30 iterations are required to determine a
   singular value, this subroutine terminates with IERR
   set to the index of the singular value for which the
   failure occurs. The singular values in the W array
   should be correct for indices IERR+1,IERR+2,...,N, as
   well as the corresponding columns of U and V.

   If all the singular values are determined within 30
   iterations, IERR is set to zero.

C. Applicability and Restrictions.

   The generalized inverse of A can be obtained from the
   decomposition in SVD by forming

$$V * DIAG(S^+) * U^T$$

   where each element of S^+ is the reciprocal of the
   corresponding element of S where non-zero and zero
   where S is zero. Some zero threshold would have to be
   employed (for example, the product of the square root of
   the machine precision and a norm of the matrix). Sample
   coding to perform this computation might be:

```
      DO 100 I = 1, N
         DO 100 J = 1, M
100      GENINV(I,J) = 0.0D0
      DO 300 K = 1, N
         IF (W(K) .LT. THRESH) GO TO 300
         DO 200 I = 1, N
            DO 200 J = 1, M
200         GENINV(I,J) = GENINV(I,J)+V(I,K)*U(J,K)/W(K)
      300 CONTINUE
C        GENINV IS THE GENERALIZED INVERSE MATRIX.
```

   Solutions of a system of homogeneous linear equations
   with coefficient matrix A can be obtained as those
   columns of V (or linear combinations of them) which
   correspond to zero elements of S.

   Either of U and V may coincide with A if desired.

3. DISCUSSION OF METHOD AND ALGORITHM.

The singular value decomposition $A = U * DIAG(S) * V^T$ is accomplished in two steps. A is first reduced to the bidiagonal form J by two sequences of Householder transformations, those on the left reducing columns of A, and those on the right reducing rows of A. Because the transformations are orthogonal, J has the same singular values as A, that is $J = G * DIAG(S) * H^T$. Further, if the product of the left transformations is denoted P and the product of the right transformations Q, so that $J = P^T * A * Q$, then $U = PG$ and $V = QH$.

The bidiagonal form J is then decomposed by a variant of the QR method applied to the symmetric tridiagonal matrix $J^T J$. (The singular values of J are the non-negative square roots of the eigenvalues of $J^T J$.) The essence of this method is a process whereby a sequence of symmetric tridiagonal matrices, unitarily similar to $J^T J$, is formed which converges to a diagonal matrix. The rate of convergence of this sequence is improved by shifting the origin at each iteration. Before the iterations for each eigenvalue, the symmetric tridiagonal matrix is checked for a possible splitting into submatrices. If a splitting occurs, only the lowermost submatrix participates in the next iteration. The left and right transformations used in each iteration are accumulated in the U and V arrays.

The origin shift at each iteration is an eigenvalue of the current lowermost 2x2 principal minor. Whenever the lowermost 1x1 principal submatrix finally splits from the rest of the matrix, its element is taken to be an eigenvalue of the original matrix and the algorithm proceeds with the remaining submatrix. This process is continued until the matrix has split completely into submatrices of order 1. The tolerances in the splitting tests are proportional to the relative machine precision.

This subroutine is a translation of the Algol procedure SVD written and discussed in detail by Golub and Reinsch (1).

4. REFERENCES.

1) Golub, G.H. and Reinsch, C., Singular Value
   Decomposition and Least Squares Solutions,
   Num. Math. 14,403-420 (1970). (Reprinted in Handbook for
   Automatic Computation, Volume II, Linear Algebra,
   J. H. Wilkinson - C. Reinsch, Contribution I/10, 134-151,
   Springer-Verlag, 1971.)

5. CHECKOUT.

   A. Test Cases.

      See the section discussing testing of the codes for
      singular value decomposition.

   B. Accuracy.

      The subroutine SVD is numerically stable (1); that is
      each computed singular value is exact for a matrix close
      to the original real rectangular matrix.

```
      SUBROUTINE SVD(NM,M,N,A,W,MATU,U,MATV,V,IERR,RV1)
C
      INTEGER I,J,K,L,M,N,II,I1,KK,K1,LL,L1,MN,NM,ITS,IERR
      REAL A(NM,N),W(N),U(NM,N),V(NM,N),RV1(N)
      REAL C,F,G,H,S,X,Y,Z,EPS,SCALE,MACHEP
      REAL SQRT,AMAX1,ABS,SIGN
      LOGICAL MATU,MATV
C
C     ********** MACHEP IS A MACHINE DEPENDENT PARAMETER SPECIFYING
C                THE RELATIVE PRECISION OF FLOATING POINT ARITHMETIC.
C
C                **********
      MACHEP = ?
C
      IERR = 0
C
      DO 100 I = 1, M
C
         DO 100 J = 1, N
            U(I,J) = A(I,J)
  100 CONTINUE
C     ********** HOUSEHOLDER REDUCTION TO BIDIAGONAL FORM **********
      G = 0.0
      SCALE = 0.0
      X = 0.0
C
      DO 300 I = 1, N
         L = I + 1
         RV1(I) = SCALE * G
         G = 0.0
         S = 0.0
         SCALE = 0.0
         IF (I .GT. M) GO TO 210
C
         DO 120 K = I, M
  120    SCALE = SCALE + ABS(U(K,I))
C
         IF (SCALE .EQ. 0.0) GO TO 210
C
         DO 130 K = I, M
            U(K,I) = U(K,I) / SCALE
            S = S + U(K,I)**2
  130    CONTINUE
C
         F = U(I,I)
         G = -SIGN(SQRT(S),F)
         H = F * G - S
         U(I,I) = F - G
         IF (I .EQ. N) GO TO 190
C
         DO 150 J = L, N
            S = 0.0
```

```
C
            DO 140 K = I, M
   140      S = S + U(K,I) * U(K,J)
C
            F = S / H
C
            DO 150 K = I, M
               U(K,J) = U(K,J) + F * U(K,I)
   150      CONTINUE
C
   190      DO 200 K = I, M
   200      U(K,I) = SCALE * U(K,I)
C
   210      W(I) = SCALE * G
            G = 0.0
            S = 0.0
            SCALE = 0.0
            IF (I .GT. M .OR. I .EQ. N) GO TO 290
C
            DO 220 K = L, N
   220      SCALE = SCALE + ABS(U(I,K))
C
            IF (SCALE .EQ. 0.0) GO TO 290
C
            DO 230 K = L, N
               U(I,K) = U(I,K) / SCALE
               S = S + U(I,K)**2
   230      CONTINUE
C
            F = U(I,L)
            G = -SIGN(SQRT(S),F)
            H = F * G - S
            U(I,L) = F - G
C
            DO 240 K = L, N
   240      RV1(K) = U(I,K) / H
C
            IF (I .EQ. M) GO TO 270
C
            DO 260 J = L, M
               S = 0.0
C
               DO 250 K = L, N
   250         S = S + U(J,K) * U(I,K)
C
               DO 260 K = L, N
                  U(J,K) = U(J,K) + S * RV1(K)
   260      CONTINUE
C
   270      DO 280 K = L, N
   280      U(I,K) = SCALE * U(I,K)
C
   290      X = AMAX1(X,ABS(W(I))+ABS(RV1(I)))
   300 CONTINUE
```

```
C     ********** ACCUMULATION OF RIGHT-HAND TRANSFORMATIONS **********
      IF (.NOT. MATV) GO TO 410
C     ********** FOR I=N STEP -1 UNTIL 1 DO -- **********
      DO 400 II = 1, N
         I = N + 1 - II
         IF (I .EQ. N) GO TO 390
         IF (G .EQ. 0.0) GO TO 360
C
         DO 320 J = L, N
C     ********** DOUBLE DIVISION AVOIDS POSSIBLE UNDERFLOW **********
  320    V(J,I) = (U(I,J) / U(I,L)) / G
C
         DO 350 J = L, N
            S = 0.0
C
            DO 340 K = L, N
  340       S = S + U(I,K) * V(K,J)
C
            DO 350 K = L, N
               V(K,J) = V(K,J) + S * V(K,I)
  350    CONTINUE
C
  360    DO 380 J = L, N
            V(I,J) = 0.0
            V(J,I) = 0.0
  380    CONTINUE
C
  390    V(I,I) = 1.0
         G = RV1(I)
         L = I
  400 CONTINUE
C     ********** ACCUMULATION OF LEFT-HAND TRANSFORMATIONS **********
  410 IF (.NOT. MATU) GO TO 510
C     **********FOR I=MIN(M,N) STEP -1 UNTIL 1 DO -- **********
      MN = N
      IF (M .LT. N) MN = M
C
      DO 500 II = 1, MN
         I = MN + 1 - II
         L = I + 1
         G = W(I)
         IF (I .EQ. N) GO TO 430
C
         DO 420 J = L, N
  420    U(I,J) = 0.0
C
  430    IF (G .EQ. 0.0) GO TO 475
         IF (I .EQ. MN) GO TO 460
C
         DO 450 J = L, N
            S = 0.0
C
            DO 440 K = L, M
  440       S = S + U(K,I) * U(K,J)
```

```
C         ********** DOUBLE DIVISION AVOIDS POSSIBLE UNDERFLOW **********
              F = (S / U(I,I)) / G
C
              DO 450 K = I, M
                 U(K,J) = U(K,J) + F * U(K,I)
  450         CONTINUE
C
  460         DO 470 J = I, M
  470         U(J,I) = U(J,I) / G
C
              GO TO 490
C
  475         DO 480 J = I, M
  480         U(J,I) = 0.0
C
  490         U(I,I) = U(I,I) + 1.0
  500      CONTINUE
C         ********** DIAGONALIZATION OF THE BIDIAGONAL FORM **********
  510 EPS = MACHEP * X
C         ********** FOR K=N STEP -1 UNTIL 1 DO -- **********
      DO 700 KK = 1, N
         K1 = N - KK
         K = K1 + 1
         ITS = 0
C         ********** TEST FOR SPLITTING.
C                    FOR L=K STEP -1 UNTIL 1 DO -- **********
  520    DO 530 LL = 1, K
            L1 = K - LL
            L = L1 + 1
            IF (ABS(RV1(L)) .LE. EPS) GO TO 565
C         ********** RV1(1) IS ALWAYS ZERO, SO THERE IS NO EXIT
C                    THROUGH THE BOTTOM OF THE LOOP **********
            IF (ABS(W(L1)) .LE. EPS) GO TO 540
  530    CONTINUE
C         ********** CANCELLATION OF RV1(L) IF L GREATER THAN 1 **********
  540    C = 0.0
         S = 1.0
C
         DO 560 I = L, K
            F = S * RV1(I)
            RV1(I) = C * RV1(I)
            IF (ABS(F) .LE. EPS) GO TO 565
            G = W(I)
            H = SQRT(F*F+G*G)
            W(I) = H
            C = G / H
            S = -F / H
            IF (.NOT. MATU) GO TO 560
```

```
C
          DO 550 J = 1, M
             Y = U(J,L1)
             Z = U(J,I)
             U(J,L1) = Y * C + Z * S
             U(J,I) = -Y * S + Z * C
  550     CONTINUE
C
  560    CONTINUE
C     ********** TEST FOR CONVERGENCE **********
  565    Z = W(K)
          IF (L .EQ. K) GO TO 650
C     ********** SHIFT FROM BOTTOM 2 BY 2 MINOR **********
          IF (ITS .EQ. 30) GO TO 1000
          ITS = ITS + 1
          X = W(L)
          Y = W(K1)
          G = RV1(K1)
          H = RV1(K)
          F = ((Y - Z) * (Y + Z) + (G - H) * (G + H)) / (2.0 * H * Y)
          G = SQRT(F*F+1.0)
          F = ((X - Z) * (X + Z) + H * (Y / (F + SIGN(G,F)) - H)) / X
C     ********** NEXT QR TRANSFORMATION **********
          C = 1.0
          S = 1.0
C
          DO 600 I1 = L, K1
             I = I1 + 1
             G = RV1(I)
             Y = W(I)
             H = S * G
             G = C * G
             Z = SQRT(F*F+H*H)
             RV1(I1) = Z
             C = F / Z
             S = H / Z
             F = X * C + G * S
             G = -X * S + G * C
             H = Y * S
             Y = Y * C
             IF (.NOT. MATV) GO TO 575
C
             DO 570 J = 1, N
                X = V(J,I1)
                Z = V(J,I)
                V(J,I1) = X * C + Z * S
                V(J,I) = -X * S + Z * C
  570        CONTINUE
C
  575        Z = SQRT(F*F+H*H)
             W(I1) = Z
```

274

```
C        ********** ROTATION CAN BE ARBITRARY IF Z IS ZERO **********
               IF (Z .EQ. 0.0) GO TO 580
               C = F / Z
               S = H / Z
   580         F = C * G + S * Y
               X = -S * G + C * Y
               IF (.NOT. MATU) GO TO 600
C
               DO 590 J = 1, M
                  Y = U(J,I1)
                  Z = U(J,I)
                  U(J,I1) = Y * C + Z * S
                  U(J,I) = -Y * S + Z * C
   590         CONTINUE
C
   600      CONTINUE
C
               RV1(L) = 0.0
               RV1(K) = F
               W(K) = X
               GO TO 520
C        ********** CONVERGENCE **********
   650      IF (Z .GE. 0.0) GO TO 700
C        ********** W(K) IS MADE NON-NEGATIVE **********
               W(K) = -Z
               IF (.NOT. MATV) GO TO 700
C
               DO 690 J = 1, N
   690         V(J,K) = -V(J,K)
C
   700 CONTINUE
C
         GO TO 1001
C        ********** SET ERROR -- NO CONVERGENCE TO A
C                   SINGULAR VALUE AFTER 30 ITERATIONS **********
  1000 IERR = K
  1001 RETURN
         END
```

NATS PROJECT

EIGENSYSTEM SUBROUTINE PACKAGE (EISPACK)

F223-2   TINVIT

A Fortran IV Subroutine to Determine Some Eigenvectors
of a Symmetric Tridiagonal Matrix.

May, 1972
July, 1975

1. PURPOSE.

The Fortran IV subroutine TINVIT determines those
eigenvectors of a symmetric tridiagonal matrix corresponding
to a set of ordered approximate eigenvalues, using inverse
iteration.

2. USAGE.

A. Calling Sequence.

The SUBROUTINE statement is

SUBROUTINE TINVIT(NM,N,D,E,E2,M,W,IND,Z,
                    IERR,RV1,RV2,RV3,RV4,RV6)

The parameters are discussed below and the
interpretation of working precision for various machines
is given in the section discussing certification.

NM   is an integer input variable set equal to
        the row dimension of the two-dimensional
        array Z as specified in the DIMENSION
        statement for Z in the calling program.

N   is an integer input variable set equal to
        the order of the matrix. N must be not
        greater than NM.

D   is a working precision real input one-
        dimensional variable of dimension at least
        N containing the diagonal elements of the
        symmetric tridiagonal matrix.

E   is a working precision real input one-
          dimensional variable of dimension at least
          N containing, in its last N-1 positions,
          the subdiagonal elements of the symmetric
          tridiagonal matrix. E(1) is arbitrary.

E2   is a working precision real input one-
          dimensional variable of dimension at least
          N containing, in its last N-1 positions,
          the squares of the corresponding elements of
          E with zeros corresponding to negligible
          elements of E. (The successive submatrices
          are located from the zeros of E2.) If
          MACHEP denotes the relative machine
          precision, then E(I) is considered
          negligible if it is not larger than the
          product of MACHEP and the sum of the
          magnitudes of D(I) and D(I-1). E2(1)
          should contain 0.0 if the eigenvalues are
          in ascending order and 2.0 if the
          eigenvalues are in descending order. If
          subroutine BISECT (F294) or TRIDIB (F237)
          has been used to determine the eigenvalues,
          their output E2 array is suitable for
          input to TINVIT.

M   is an integer input variable set equal to
          the number of specified eigenvalues for
          which the corresponding eigenvectors are to
          be determined.

W   is a working precision real input one-
          dimensional variable of dimension at least
          M containing the M specified eigenvalues
          of the symmetric tridiagonal matrix. The
          eigenvalues must be in either ascending or
          descending order in W. The ordering is
          required to insure the determination of
          independent orthogonal eigenvectors
          associated with close eigenvalues.

IND   is an integer input one-dimensional variable
          of dimension at least M containing the
          submatrix indices associated with the
          corresponding M eigenvalues in W.
          Eigenvalues belonging to the first submatrix
          have index 1, those belonging to the second
          submatrix have index 2, etc. If BISECT
          or TRIDIB has been used to determine the
          eigenvalues, their output IND array is
          suitable for input to TINVIT.

Z   is a working precision real output two-
            dimensional variable with row dimension   NM
            and column dimension at least   M.   It
            contains   M   orthonormal eigenvectors of the
            symmetric tridiagonal matrix corresponding
            to the   M   eigenvalues in   W.

IERR   is an integer output variable set equal to
            an error completion code described in
            section 2B.   The normal completion code is
            zero.

RV1,RV2,RV3
            are working precision real temporary one-
            dimensional variables of dimension at least
            N   used to store the main diagonal and the
            two adjacent diagonals of the triangular
            matrix produced in the inverse iteration
            process.

RV4,RV6 are working precision real temporary one-
            dimensional variables of dimension at least
            N.   RV4   holds the multipliers of the
            Gaussian elimination step in the inverse
            iteration process.   RV6   holds the
            approximate eigenvectors in this process.

B. Error Conditions and Returns.

    If more than   5   iterations are required to determine an
    eigenvector,   TINVIT   terminates the computation for
    that eigenvector and sets   IERR   to -R   where   R   is
    the index of the eigenvector.   If this failure occurs
    for more than one eigenvector, the last occurrence is
    recorded in   IERR.   The columns of   Z   corresponding to
    failures of the above sort are set to zero vectors.

    If all the eigenvectors are determined within   5
    iterations,   IERR   is set to zero.

C. Applicability and Restrictions.

    To determine some of the eigenvalues and eigenvectors of
    a full symmetric matrix,   TINVIT   should be preceded by
    TRED1 (F277)   to provide a suitable symmetric
    tridiagonal matrix for   BISECT (F294),   TRIDIB (F237),
    or   IMTQLV (F234)   which can then be used to determine
    the eigenvalues.   It should be followed by   TRBAK1
    (F279)   to back transform the eigenvectors from   TINVIT
    into those of the original matrix.

To determine some of the eigenvalues and eigenvectors of
a complex Hermitian matrix, TINVIT should be preceded
by HTRIDI (F284) to provide a suitable real symmetric
tridiagonal matrix for BISECT (F294), TRIDIB (F237),
or IMTQLV (F234). It should then be followed by
HTRIBK (F285) to back transform the eigenvectors from
TINVIT into those of the original matrix.

Some of the eigenvalues and eigenvectors of certain non-
symmetric tridiagonal matrices can be computed using the
combination of FIGI (F280), BISECT (F294) or TRIDIB
(F237), TINVIT, and BAKVEC (F281). See F280 for the
description of this special class of matrices. For
these matrices, TINVIT should be preceded by FIGI to
provide a suitable symmetric matrix for BISECT or
TRIDIB. It should then be followed by BAKVEC to back
transform the eigenvectors from TINVIT into those of
the original matrix.

The computation of the eigenvectors by inverse iteration
requires that the precision of the eigenvalues be
commensurate with small relative perturbations of the
order of MACHEP in the matrix elements. For most
symmetric tridiagonal matrices, it is enough that the
absolute error in the eigenvalues for which eigenvectors
are desired be approximately MACHEP times a norm of
the matrix. But some matrices require a smaller
absolute error, perhaps as small as MACHEP times the
eigenvalue of smallest magnitude.

3. DISCUSSION OF METHOD AND ALGORITHM.

The calculations proceed as follows. First, the E2 array
is inspected for the presence of a zero element defining a
submatrix. The eigenvalues belonging to this submatrix are
identified by their common submatrix index in IND.

The eigenvectors of the submatrix are then computed by
inverse iteration. First, the LU decomposition of the
submatrix with an approximate eigenvalue subtracted from its
diagonal elements is achieved by Gaussian elimination using
partial pivoting. The multipliers defining the lower
triangular matrix L are stored in the temporary array RV4
and the upper triangular matrix U is stored in the three
temporary arrays RV1, RV2, and RV3. Saving these
quantities in RV1, RV2, RV3, and RV4 avoids repeating
the LU decomposition if further iterations are required.
An approximate vector, stored in RV6, is computed starting
from an initial vector, and the norm of the approximate
vector is compared with a norm of the submatrix to determine
whether the growth is sufficient to accept it as an
eigenvector. If this vector is accepted, its Euclidean norm

is made 1. If the growth is not sufficient, this vector is used as the initial vector in computing the next approximate vector. This iteration process is repeated at most 5 times.

Eigenvectors computed in the above way corresponding to well-separated eigenvalues of this submatrix will be orthogonal. However, eigenvectors corresponding to close eigenvalues of this submatrix may not be satisfactorily orthogonal. Hence, to insure orthogonal eigenvectors, each approximate vector is made orthogonal to those previously computed eigenvectors whose eigenvalues are close to the current eigenvalue. If the orthogonalization process produces a zero vector, a column of the identity matrix is used as an initial vector for the next iteration.

Identical eigenvalues are perturbed slightly in an attempt to obtain independent eigenvectors. These perturbations are not recorded in the eigenvalue array W.

The above steps are repeated on each submatrix until all the eigenvectors are computed.

This subroutine is a subset (except for the resolution of non-convergent eigenvectors) of the Fortran subroutine TSTURM (F293), which is a translation of the Algol procedure TRISTURM written and discussed in detail by Peters and Wilkinson (1).

4. REFERENCES.

1) Peters, G. and Wilkinson, J.H., The Calculation of Specified Eigenvectors by Inverse Iteration, Handbook for Automatic Computation, Volume II, Linear Algebra, J. H. Wilkinson - C. Reinsch, Contribution II/18, 418-439, Springer-Verlag, 1971.

5. CHECKOUT.

A. Test Cases.

See the section discussing testing of the codes for complex Hermitian, real symmetric, real symmetric tridiagonal, and certain real non-symmetric tridiagonal matrices.

B. Accuracy.

The accuracy of TINVIT can best be described in terms
of its role in those paths of EISPACK which find
eigenvalues and eigenvectors of real symmetric matrices
and matrix systems. In these paths, this subroutine is
numerically stable (1). This stability contributes to
the property of these paths that the computed
eigenvalues are the exact eigenvalues of a matrix or
system close to the original matrix or system and the
computed eigenvectors are close (but not necessarily
equal) to the eigenvectors of that matrix or system.

```
      SUBROUTINE TINVIT(NM,N,D,E,E2,M,W,IND,Z,
     X                  IERR,RV1,RV2,RV3,RV4,RV6)
C
      INTEGER I,J,M,N,P,Q,R,S,II,IP,JJ,NM,ITS,TAG,IERR,GROUP
      REAL D(N),E(N),E2(N),W(M),Z(NM,M),
     X     RV1(N),RV2(N),RV3(N),RV4(N),RV6(N)
      REAL U,V,UK,XU,X0,X1,EPS2,EPS3,EPS4,NORM,ORDER,MACHEP
      REAL SQRT,ABS,FLOAT
      INTEGER IND(M)
C
C     ********** MACHEP IS A MACHINE DEPENDENT PARAMETER SPECIFYING
C                THE RELATIVE PRECISION OF FLOATING POINT ARITHMETIC.
C
C                **********
      MACHEP = ?
C
      IERR = 0
      IF (M .EQ. 0) GO TO 1001
      TAG = 0
      ORDER = 1.0 - E2(1)
      Q = 0
C     ********** ESTABLISH AND PROCESS NEXT SUBMATRIX **********
  100 P = Q + 1
C
      DO 120 Q = P, N
         IF (Q .EQ. N) GO TO 140
         IF (E2(Q+1) .EQ. 0.0) GO TO 140
  120 CONTINUE
C     ********** FIND VECTORS BY INVERSE ITERATION **********
  140 TAG = TAG + 1
      S = 0
C
      DO 920 R = 1, M
         IF (IND(R) .NE. TAG) GO TO 920
         ITS = 1
         X1 = W(R)
         IF (S .NE. 0) GO TO 510
C     ********** CHECK FOR ISOLATED ROOT **********
         XU = 1.0
         IF (P .NE. Q) GO TO 490
         RV6(P) = 1.0
         GO TO 870
  490    NORM = ABS(D(P))
         IP = P + 1
C
         DO 500 I = IP, Q
  500    NORM = NORM + ABS(D(I)) + ABS(E(I))
C     ********** EPS2 IS THE CRITERION FOR GROUPING,
C                EPS3 REPLACES ZERO PIVOTS AND EQUAL
C                ROOTS ARE MODIFIED BY EPS3,
C                EPS4 IS TAKEN VERY SMALL TO AVOID OVERFLOW **********
         EPS2 = 1.0E-3 * NORM
         EPS3 = MACHEP * NORM
         UK = FLOAT(Q-P+1)
```

282

```
          EPS4 = UK * EPS3
          UK = EPS4 / SQRT(UK)
          S = P
  505     GROUP = 0
          GO TO 520
C     ********** LOOK FOR CLOSE OR COINCIDENT ROOTS **********
  510     IF (ABS(X1-X0) .GE. EPS2) GO TO 505
          GROUP = GROUP + 1
          IF (ORDER * (X1 - X0) .LE. 0.0) X1 = X0 + ORDER * EPS3
C     ********** ELIMINATION WITH INTERCHANGES AND
C                    INITIALIZATION OF VECTOR **********
  520     V = 0.0
C
          DO 580 I = P, Q
             RV6(I) = UK
             IF (I .EQ. P) GO TO 560
             IF (ABS(E(I)) .LT. ABS(U)) GO TO 540
C     ********** WARNING -- A DIVIDE CHECK MAY OCCUR HERE IF
C          E2 ARRAY HAS NOT BEEN SPECIFIED CORRECTLY **********
             XU = U / E(I)
             RV4(I) = XU
             RV1(I-1) = E(I)
             RV2(I-1) = D(I) - X1
             RV3(I-1) = 0.0
             IF (I .NE. Q) RV3(I-1) = E(I+1)
             U = V - XU * RV2(I-1)
             V = -XU * RV3(I-1)
             GO TO 580
  540        XU = E(I) / U
             RV4(I) = XU
             RV1(I-1) = U
             RV2(I-1) = V
             RV3(I-1) = 0.0
  560        U = D(I) - X1 - XU * V
             IF (I .NE. Q) V = E(I+1)
  580     CONTINUE
C
          IF (U .EQ. 0.0) U = EPS3
          RV1(Q) = U
          RV2(Q) = 0.0
          RV3(Q) = 0.0
C     ********** BACK SUBSTITUTION
C                    FOR I=Q STEP -1 UNTIL P DO -- **********
  600     DO 620 II = P, Q
             I = P + Q - II
             RV6(I) = (RV6(I) - U * RV2(I) - V * RV3(I)) / RV1(I)
             V = U
             U = RV6(I)
  620     CONTINUE
C     ********** ORTHOGONALIZE WITH RESPECT TO PREVIOUS
C                    MEMBERS OF GROUP **********
          IF (GROUP .EQ. 0) GO TO 700
          J = R
```

```
C
         DO 680 JJ = 1, GROUP
  630       J = J - 1
            IF (IND(J) .NE. TAG) GO TO 630
            XU = 0.0
C
            DO 640 I = P, Q
  640       XU = XU + RV6(I) * Z(I,J)
C
            DO 660 I = P, Q
  660       RV6(I) = RV6(I) - XU * Z(I,J)
C
  680     CONTINUE
C
  700     NORM = 0.0
C
            DO 720 I = P, Q
  720       NORM = NORM + ABS(RV6(I))
C
            IF (NORM .GE. 1.0) GO TO 840
C     ********** FORWARD SUBSTITUTION **********
            IF (ITS .EQ. 5) GO TO 830
            IF (NORM .NE. 0.0) GO TO 740
            RV6(S) = EPS4
            S = S + 1
            IF (S .GT. Q) S = P
            GO TO 780
  740       XU = EPS4 / NORM
C
            DO 760 I = P, Q
  760       RV6(I) = RV6(I) * XU
C     ********** ELIMINATION OPERATIONS ON NEXT VECTOR
C               ITERATE **********
  780       DO 820 I = IP, Q
            U = RV6(I)
C     ********** IF RV1(I-1) .EQ. E(I), A ROW INTERCHANGE
C               WAS PERFORMED EARLIER IN THE
C               TRIANGULARIZATION PROCESS **********
            IF (RV1(I-1) .NE. E(I)) GO TO 800
            U = RV6(I-1)
            RV6(I-1) = RV6(I)
  800       RV6(I) = U - RV4(I) * RV6(I-1)
  820     CONTINUE
C
            ITS = ITS + 1
            GO TO 600
C     ********** SET ERROR -- NON-CONVERGED EIGENVECTOR **********
  830       IERR = -R
            XU = 0.0
            GO TO 870
C     ********** NORMALIZE SO THAT SUM OF SQUARES IS
C               1 AND EXPAND TO FULL ORDER **********
  840       U = 0.0
```

```
C
         DO 860 I = P, Q
  860    U = U + RV6(I)**2
C
         XU = 1.0 / SQRT(U)
C
  870    DO 880 I = 1, N
  880    Z(I,R) = 0.0
C
         DO 900 I = P, Q
  900    Z(I,R) = RV6(I) * XU
C
         X0 = X1
  920 CONTINUE
C
      IF (Q .LT. N) GO TO 100
 1001 RETURN
      END
```

NATS PROJECT

EIGENSYSTEM SUBROUTINE PACKAGE (EISPACK)

F235   TQLRAT

A Fortran IV Subroutine to Determine the Eigenvalues
of a Symmetric Tridiagonal Matrix.

July, 1975

1. PURPOSE.

The Fortran IV subroutine TQLRAT determines the eigenvalues
of a symmetric tridiagonal matrix using a rational variant of
the QL method.

2. USAGE.

A. Calling Sequence.

The SUBROUTINE statement is

SUBROUTINE TQLRAT(N,D,E2,IERR)

The parameters are discussed below and the
interpretation of working precision for various machines
is given in the section discussing certification.

N   is an integer input variable set equal to
            the order of the matrix.

D   is a working precision real one-dimensional
            variable of dimension at least N. On
            input, it contains the diagonal elements of
            the symmetric tridiagonal matrix. On
            output, it contains the eigenvalues of this
            matrix in ascending order.

E2   is a working precision real one-dimensional
            variable of dimension at least N. On
            input, the last N-1 positions in this
            array contain the squares of the subdiagonal
            elements of the symmetric tridiagonal
            matrix. E2(1) is arbitrary. Note that
            TQLRAT destroys E2.

IERR   is an integer output variable set equal to an error completion code described in section 2B. The normal completion code is zero.

B. Error Conditions and Returns.

If more than 30 iterations are required to determine an eigenvalue, TQLRAT terminates with IERR set to the index of the eigenvalue for which the failure occurs. The eigenvalues in the D array should be correct for indices 1,2,...,IERR-1. These eigenvalues are ordered but are not necessarily the smallest IERR-1 eigenvalues.

If all the eigenvalues are determined within 30 iterations, IERR is set to zero.

C. Applicability and Restrictions.

To determine the eigenvalues of a full symmetric matrix, TQLRAT should be preceded by TRED1 (F277) to provide a suitable symmetric tridiagonal matrix for TQLRAT.

To determine the eigenvalues of a complex Hermitian matrix, TQLRAT should be preceded by HTRIDI (F284) to provide a suitable real symmetric tridiagonal matrix for TQLRAT.

TQLRAT does not perform well on matrices whose successive row sums vary widely in magnitude and are not strictly increasing from the first to the last row. The subroutine IMTQL1 (F291) is not sensitive to such row sums and is therefore recommended for symmetric tridiagonal matrices whose structure is not known.

3. DISCUSSION OF METHOD AND ALGORITHM.

The eigenvalues are determined by a rational variant of the QL method. The essence of this method is a process whereby a sequence of symmetric tridiagonal matrices, unitarily similar to the original symmetric tridiagonal matrix, is formed which converges to a diagonal matrix. The rate of convergence of this sequence is improved by shifting the origin at each iteration. Before the iterations for each eigenvalue, the symmetric tridiagonal matrix is checked for a possible splitting into submatrices. If a splitting occurs, only the uppermost submatrix participates in the next iteration. The eigenvalues are ordered in ascending order as they are found.

The origin shift at each iteration is the eigenvalue of the current uppermost 2x2 principal minor closer to the first diagonal element of this minor. Whenever the uppermost 1x1 principal submatrix finally splits from the rest of the matrix, its element is taken to be an eigenvalue of the original matrix and the algorithm proceeds with the remaining submatrix. This process is continued until the matrix has split completely into submatrices of order 1. The tolerances in the splitting tests are proportional to the relative machine precision.

This subroutine is a translation of the Algol procedure TQLRAT written and discussed in detail by Reinsch (1). It is a rational variant of the subroutine TQL1 which is a translation of the Algol procedure TQL1 written and discussed in detail by Bowdler, Martin, Reinsch, and Wilkinson (2).

4. REFERENCES.

1) Reinsch, C.H., A Stable Rational QR Algorithm for the Computation of the Eigenvalues of an Hermitian, Tridiagonal Matrix, Math. Comp. 25,591-597 (1971). (Algorithm 464, Comm. ACM 16,689 (1973).)

2) Bowdler, H., Martin, R.S., Reinsch, C., and Wilkinson, J.H., The QR and QL Algorithms for Symmetric Matrices, Num. Math. 11,293-306 (1968). (Reprinted in Handbook for Automatic Computation, Volume II, Linear Algebra, J. H. Wilkinson - C. Reinsch, Contribution II/3, 227-240, Springer-Verlag, 1971.)

5. CHECKOUT.

A. Test Cases.

See the section discussing testing of the codes for complex Hermitian, real symmetric, real symmetric tridiagonal, and certain real non-symmetric tridiagonal matrices.

B. Accuracy.

The subroutine TQLRAT is numerically stable (1,2); that is, the computed eigenvalues are close to those of the original matrix. In addition, they are the exact eigenvalues of a matrix close to the original real symmetric tridiagonal matrix.

```
      SUBROUTINE TQLRAT(N,D,E2,IERR)
C
      INTEGER I,J,L,M,N,II,L1,MML,IERR
      REAL D(N),E2(N)
      REAL B,C,F,G,H,P,R,S,MACHEP
      REAL SQRT,ABS,SIGN
C
C     ********** MACHEP IS A MACHINE DEPENDENT PARAMETER SPECIFYING
C                THE RELATIVE PRECISION OF FLOATING POINT ARITHMETIC.
C
C                **********
      MACHEP = ?
C
      IERR = 0
      IF (N .EQ. 1) GO TO 1001
C
      DO 100 I = 2, N
  100 E2(I-1) = E2(I)
C
      F = 0.0
      B = 0.0
      E2(N) = 0.0
C
      DO 290 L = 1, N
         J = 0
         H = MACHEP * (ABS(D(L)) + SQRT(E2(L)))
         IF (B .GT. H) GO TO 105
         B = H
         C = B * B
C     ********** LOOK FOR SMALL SQUARED SUB-DIAGONAL ELEMENT **********
  105    DO 110 M = L, N
            IF (E2(M) .LE. C) GO TO 120
C     ********** E2(N) IS ALWAYS ZERO, SO THERE IS NO EXIT
C                THROUGH THE BOTTOM OF THE LOOP **********
  110    CONTINUE
C
  120    IF (M .EQ. L) GO TO 210
  130    IF (J .EQ. 30) GO TO 1000
         J = J + 1
C     ********** FORM SHIFT **********
         L1 = L + 1
         S = SQRT(E2(L))
         G = D(L)
         P = (D(L1) - G) / (2.0 * S)
         R = SQRT(P*P+1.0)
         D(L) = S / (P + SIGN(R,P))
         H = G - D(L)
C
         DO 140 I = L1, N
  140    D(I) = D(I) - H
C
         F = F + H
```

```
C        ********** RATIONAL QL TRANSFORMATION **********
         G = D(M)
         IF (G .EQ. 0.0) G = B
         H = G
         S = 0.0
         MML = M - L
C        ********** FOR I=M-1 STEP -1 UNTIL L DO -- **********
         DO 200 II = 1, MML
            I = M - II
            P = G * H
            R = P + E2(I)
            E2(I+1) = S * R
            S = E2(I) / R
            D(I+1) = H + S * (H + D(I))
            G = D(I) - E2(I) / G
            IF (G .EQ. 0.0) G = B
            H = G * P / R
  200    CONTINUE
C
         E2(L) = S * G
         D(L) = H
C        ********** GUARD AGAINST UNDERFLOW IN CONVERGENCE TEST **********
         IF (H .EQ. 0.0) GO TO 210
         IF (ABS(E2(L)) .LE. ABS(C/H)) GO TO 210
         E2(L) = H * E2(L)
         IF (E2(L) .NE. 0.0) GO TO 130
  210    P = D(L) + F
C        ********** ORDER EIGENVALUES **********
         IF (L .EQ. 1) GO TO 250
C        ********** FOR I=L STEP -1 UNTIL 2 DO -- **********
         DO 230 II = 2, L
            I = L + 2 - II
            IF (P .GE. D(I-1)) GO TO 270
            D(I) = D(I-1)
  230    CONTINUE
C
  250    I = 1
  270    D(I) = P
  290 CONTINUE
C
      GO TO 1001
C        ********** SET ERROR -- NO CONVERGENCE TO AN
C                   EIGENVALUE AFTER 30 ITERATIONS **********
 1000 IERR = L
 1001 RETURN
      END
```

NATS PROJECT

EIGENSYSTEM SUBROUTINE PACKAGE (EISPACK)

F290-2   TQL2

A Fortran IV Subroutine to Determine the Eigenvalues and
Eigenvectors of a Symmetric Tridiagonal Matrix.

May, 1972
July, 1975

1. PURPOSE.

The Fortran IV subroutine TQL2 determines the eigenvalues
and eigenvectors of a symmetric tridiagonal matrix. TQL2
uses the QL method to compute the eigenvalues and
accumulates the QL transformations to compute the
eigenvectors. The eigenvectors of a full symmetric matrix
can also be computed directly by TQL2, if TRED2 (F278) has
been used to reduce this matrix to tridiagonal form.

2. USAGE.

A. Calling Sequence.

The SUBROUTINE statement is

SUBROUTINE   TQL2(NM,N,D,E,Z,IERR)

The parameters are discussed below and the
interpretation of working precision for various machines
is given in the section discussing certification.

NM   is an integer input variable set equal to
          the row dimension of the two-dimensional
          array Z as specified in the DIMENSION
          statement for Z in the calling program.

N   is an integer input variable set equal to
          the order of the matrix. N must be not
          greater than NM.

D   is a working precision real one-dimensional
          variable of dimension at least N. On
          input, it contains the diagonal elements of
          the symmetric tridiagonal matrix. On
          output, it contains the eigenvalues of this
          matrix in ascending order.

E   is a working precision real one-dimensional
          variable of dimension at least N. On
          input, the last N-1 positions in this
          array contain the subdiagonal elements of
          the symmetric tridiagonal matrix. E(1) is
          arbitrary. Note that TQL2 destroys E.

Z   is a working precision real two-dimensional
          variable with row dimension NM and column
          dimension at least N. If the eigenvectors
          of the symmetric tridiagonal matrix are
          desired, then on input, Z contains the
          identity matrix of order N, and on output,
          contains the orthonormal eigenvectors of
          this tridiagonal matrix. If the
          eigenvectors of a full symmetric matrix are
          desired, then on input, Z contains the
          transformation matrix produced in TRED2
          which reduced the full matrix to tridiagonal
          form, and on output, contains the
          orthonormal eigenvectors of this full
          symmetric matrix.

IERR   is an integer output variable set equal to
          an error completion code described in
          section 2B. The normal completion code is
          zero.

B. Error Conditions and Returns.

If more than 30 iterations are required to determine
an eigenvalue, TQL2 terminates with IERR set to the
index of the eigenvalue for which the failure occurs.
The eigenvalues and eigenvectors in the D and Z
arrays should be correct for indices 1,2,...,IERR-1,
but the eigenvalues are unordered.

If all the eigenvalues are determined within 30
iterations, IERR is set to zero.

C. Applicability and Restrictions.

To determine the eigenvalues and eigenvectors of a full
symmetric matrix, TQL2 should be preceded by TRED2
(F278) to provide a suitable symmetric tridiagonal
matrix for TQL2.

To determine the eigenvalues and eigenvectors of a
complex Hermitian matrix, TQL2 should be preceded by
HTRIDI (F284) to provide a suitable real symmetric
tridiagonal matrix for TQL2, and the input array Z to
TQL2 should be initialized to the identity matrix.
TQL2 should then be followed by HTRIBK (F285) to back
transform the eigenvectors from TQL2 into those of the
original matrix.

TQL2 does not perform well on matrices whose successive
row sums vary widely in magnitude and are not strictly
increasing from the first to the last row. The
subroutine IMTQL2 (F292) is not sensitive to such row
sums and is therefore recommended for symmetric
tridiagonal matrices whose structure is not known.

3. DISCUSSION OF METHOD AND ALGORITHM.

The eigenvalues are determined by the QL method. The
essence of this method is a process whereby a sequence of
symmetric tridiagonal matrices, unitarily similar to the
original symmetric tridiagonal matrix, is formed which
converges to a diagonal matrix. The rate of convergence of
this sequence is improved by shifting the origin at each
iteration. Before the iterations for each eigenvalue, the
symmetric tridiagonal matrix is checked for a possible
splitting into submatrices. If a splitting occurs, only the
uppermost submatrix participates in the next iteration. The
similarity transformations used in each iteration are
accumulated in the Z array, producing the orthonormal
eigenvectors for the original matrix. Finally, the
eigenvalues are ordered in ascending order and the
eigenvectors are ordered consistently.

The origin shift at each iteration is the eigenvalue of the
current uppermost 2x2 principal minor closer to the first
diagonal element of this minor. Whenever the uppermost 1x1
principal submatrix finally splits from the rest of the
matrix, its element is taken to be an eigenvalue of the
original matrix and the algorithm proceeds with the remaining
submatrix. This process is continued until the matrix has
split completely into submatrices of order 1. The
tolerances in the splitting tests are proportional to the
relative machine precision.

This subroutine is a translation of the Algol procedure TQL2
written and discussed in detail by Bowdler, Martin, Reinsch,
and Wilkinson (1).

4. REFERENCES.

1) Bowdler, H., Martin, R.S., Reinsch, C., and
   Wilkinson, J.H., The QR and QL Algorithms for Symmetric
   Matrices, Num. Math. 11,293-306 (1968). (Reprinted in
   Handbook for Automatic Computation, Volume II, Linear
   Algebra, J. H. Wilkinson - C. Reinsch, Contribution II/3,
   227-240, Springer-Verlag, 1971.)

5. CHECKOUT.

   A. Test Cases.

   See the section discussing testing of the codes for
   complex Hermitian, real symmetric, real symmetric
   tridiagonal, and certain real non-symmetric
   tridiagonal matrices.

   B. Accuracy.

   The subroutine TQL2 is numerically stable (1); that
   is, the computed eigenvalues are close to those of the
   original matrix. In addition, they are the exact
   eigenvalues of a matrix close to the original real
   symmetric tridiagonal matrix and the computed
   eigenvectors are close (but not necessarily equal) to
   the eigenvectors of that matrix.

```
      SUBROUTINE TQL2(NM,N,D,E,Z,IERR)
C
      INTEGER I,J,K,L,M,N,II,L1,NM,MML,IERR
      REAL D(N),E(N),Z(NM,N)
      REAL B,C,F,G,H,P,R,S,MACHEP
      REAL SQRT,ABS,SIGN
C
C     ********** MACHEP IS A MACHINE DEPENDENT PARAMETER SPECIFYING
C                THE RELATIVE PRECISION OF FLOATING POINT ARITHMETIC.
C
C                **********
      MACHEP = ?
C
      IERR = 0
      IF (N .EQ. 1) GO TO 1001
C
      DO 100 I = 2, N
  100 E(I-1) = E(I)
C
      F = 0.0
      B = 0.0
      E(N) = 0.0
C
      DO 240 L = 1, N
         J = 0
         H = MACHEP * (ABS(D(L)) + ABS(E(L)))
         IF (B .LT. H) B = H
C     ********** LOOK FOR SMALL SUB-DIAGONAL ELEMENT **********
         DO 110 M = L, N
            IF (ABS(E(M)) .LE. B) GO TO 120
C     ********** E(N) IS ALWAYS ZERO, SO THERE IS NO EXIT
C                THROUGH THE BOTTOM OF THE LOOP **********
  110    CONTINUE
C
  120    IF (M .EQ. L) GO TO 220
  130    IF (J .EQ. 30) GO TO 1000
         J = J + 1
C     ********** FORM SHIFT **********
         L1 = L + 1
         G = D(L)
         P = (D(L1) - G) / (2.0 * E(L))
         R = SQRT(P*P+1.0)
         D(L) = E(L) / (P + SIGN(R,P))
         H = G - D(L)
C
         DO 140 I = L1, N
  140    D(I) = D(I) - H
C
         F = F + H
C     ********** QL TRANSFORMATION **********
         P = D(M)
         C = 1.0
         S = 0.0
         MML = M - L
```

```
C        ********** FOR I=M-1 STEP -1 UNTIL L DO -- **********
         DO 200 II = 1, MML
            I = M - II
            G = C * E(I)
            H = C * P
            IF (ABS(P) .LT. ABS(E(I))) GO TO 150
            C = E(I) / P
            R = SQRT(C*C+1.0)
            E(I+1) = S * P * R
            S = C / R
            C = 1.0 / R
            GO TO 160
  150       C = P / E(I)
            R = SQRT(C*C+1.0)
            E(I+1) = S * E(I) * R
            S = 1.0 / R
            C = C * S
  160       P = C * D(I) - S * G
            D(I+1) = H + S * (C * G + S * D(I))
C        ********** FORM VECTOR **********
            DO 180 K = 1, N
               H = Z(K,I+1)
               Z(K,I+1) = S * Z(K,I) + C * H
               Z(K,I) = C * Z(K,I) - S * H
  180       CONTINUE
C
  200    CONTINUE
C
         E(L) = S * P
         D(L) = C * P
         IF (ABS(E(L)) .GT. B) GO TO 130
  220    D(L) = D(L) + F
  240 CONTINUE
C     ********** ORDER EIGENVALUES AND EIGENVECTORS **********
      DO 300 II = 2, N
         I = II - 1
         K = I
         P = D(I)
C
         DO 260 J = II, N
            IF (D(J) .GE. P) GO TO 260
            K = J
            P = D(J)
  260    CONTINUE
C
         IF (K .EQ. I) GO TO 300
         D(K) = D(I)
         D(I) = P
C
         DO 280 J = 1, N
            P = Z(J,I)
            Z(J,I) = Z(J,K)
            Z(J,K) = P
  280    CONTINUE
```

```
C
  300 CONTINUE
C
      GO TO 1001
C     ********** SET ERROR -- NO CONVERGENCE TO AN
C                EIGENVALUE AFTER 30 ITERATIONS **********
 1000 IERR = L
 1001 RETURN
      END
```

NATS PROJECT.

EIGENSYSTEM SUBROUTINE PACKAGE (EISPACK)

F279-2   TRBAK1

A Fortran IV Subroutine to Back Transform the Eigenvectors
of that Symmetric Tridiagonal Matrix Determined by   TRED1.

May, 1972
July, 1975

1. PURPOSE.

The Fortran IV subroutine   TRBAK1   forms the eigenvectors of
a real symmetric matrix from the eigenvectors of that
symmetric tridiagonal matrix determined by   TRED1 (F277).

2. USAGE.

A. Calling Sequence.

The SUBROUTINE statement is

SUBROUTINE   TRBAK1(NM,N,A,E,M,Z)

The parameters are discussed below and the
interpretation of working precision for various machines
is given in the section discussing certification.

NM   is an integer input variable set equal to
            the row dimension of the two-dimensional
            arrays   A   and   Z   as specified in the
            DIMENSION statements for   A   and   Z   in the
            calling program.

N   is an integer input variable set equal to
            the order of the matrix.   N   must be not
            greater than   NM.

A   is a working precision real input two-
            dimensional variable with row dimension   NM
            and column dimension at least   N.   The
            strict lower triangle of   A   contains some
            information about the orthogonal
            transformations used in the reduction to the
            tridiagonal form.   The remaining upper part
            of the matrix is arbitrary.   See section 3
            of   F277   for the details.

E is a working precision real input one-
dimensional variable of dimension at least
N containing, in its last N-1 positions,
the subdiagonal elements of the tridiagonal
matrix. The element $E(1)$ is arbitrary.
These elements serve to provide the
remaining information about the orthogonal
transformations.

M is an integer input variable set equal to
the number of columns of Z to be back
transformed.

Z is a working precision real two-dimensional
variable with row dimension NM and column
dimension at least M. On input, the first
M columns of Z contain the eigenvectors
to be back transformed. On output, these
columns of Z contain the transformed
eigenvectors. The transformed eigenvectors
are orthonormal if the input eigenvectors
are orthonormal.

B. Error Conditions and Returns.

 None.

C. Applicability and Restrictions.

 This subroutine should be used in conjunction with the
subroutine TRED1 (F277).

3. DISCUSSION OF METHOD AND ALGORITHM.

 Suppose that the symmetric matrix C (say) has been reduced
to the tridiagonal symmetric matrix F by the similarity
transformation

$$F = Q^T CQ$$

where Q is a product of the orthogonal symmetric matrices
encoded in E and in the strict lower triangle of A. Then,
given an array Z of column vectors, TRBAK1 computes the
matrix product QZ. If the eigenvectors of F are columns
of the array Z, then TRBAK1 forms the eigenvectors of C
in their place. Since Q is orthogonal, vector Euclidean
norms are preserved.

This subroutine is a translation of the Algol procedure TRBAK1 written and discussed in detail by Martin, Reinsch, and Wilkinson (1).

4. REFERENCES.

1) Martin, R.S., Reinsch, C., and Wilkinson, J.H., Householder's Tridiagonalization of a Symmetric Matrix, Num. Math. 11,181-195 (1968). (Reprinted in Handbook for Automatic Computation, Volume II, Linear Algebra, J. H. Wilkinson - C. Reinsch, Contribution II/2, 212-226, Springer-Verlag, 1971.)

5. CHECKOUT.

A. Test Cases.

See the section discussing testing of the codes for real symmetric matrices.

B. Accuracy.

The accuracy of TRBAK1 can best be described in terms of its role in those paths of EISPACK which find eigenvalues and eigenvectors of real symmetric matrices and matrix systems. In these paths, this subroutine is numerically stable (1). This stability contributes to the property of these paths that the computed eigenvalues are the exact eigenvalues of a matrix or system close to the original matrix or system and the computed eigenvectors are close (but not necessarily equal) to the eigenvectors of that matrix or system.

```
      SUBROUTINE TRBAK1(NM,N,A,E,M,Z)
C
      INTEGER I,J,K,L,M,N,NM
      REAL A(NM,N),E(N),Z(NM,M)
      REAL S
C
      IF (M .EQ. 0) GO TO 200
      IF (N .EQ. 1) GO TO 200
C
      DO 140 I = 2, N
         L = I - 1
         IF (E(I) .EQ. 0.0) GO TO 140
C
         DO 130 J = 1, M
            S = 0.0
C
            DO 110 K = 1, L
  110       S = S + A(I,K) * Z(K,J)
C     ********** DIVISOR BELOW IS NEGATIVE OF H FORMED IN TRED1.
C               DOUBLE DIVISION AVOIDS POSSIBLE UNDERFLOW **********
            S = (S / A(I,L)) / E(I)
C
            DO 120 K = 1, L
  120       Z(K,J) = Z(K,J) + S * A(I,K)
C
  130    CONTINUE
C
  140 CONTINUE
C
  200 RETURN
      END
```

NATS PROJECT

EIGENSYSTEM SUBROUTINE PACKAGE (EISPACK)

F277-2   TRED1

A Fortran IV Subroutine to Reduce a Real Symmetric Matrix
to a Symmetric Tridiagonal Matrix Using
Orthogonal Transformations.

May, 1972
July, 1975

1. PURPOSE.

The Fortran IV subroutine TRED1 reduces a real symmetric
matrix to a symmetric tridiagonal matrix using orthogonal
similarity transformations. This reduced form is used by
other subroutines to find the eigenvalues and/or eigenvectors
of the original matrix. See section 2C for the specific
routines.

2. USAGE.

A. Calling Sequence.

The SUBROUTINE statement is

SUBROUTINE TRED1(NM,N,A,D,E,E2)

The parameters are discussed below and the
interpretation of working precision for various machines
is given in the section discussing certification.

NM   is an integer input variable set equal to
          the row dimension of the two-dimensional
          array A as specified in the DIMENSION
          statement for A in the calling program.

N   is an integer input variable set equal to
          the order of the matrix A. N must be not
          greater than NM.

A   is a working precision real two-dimensional
          variable with row dimension NM and column
          dimension at least N. On input, A
          contains the symmetric matrix of order N
          to be reduced to tridiagonal form. Only the
          full lower triangle of the matrix need be

supplied. On output, the strict lower
triangle of A contains information about
the orthogonal transformations used in the
reduction. The full upper triangle of A
is unaltered. See section 3 for the
details.

D   is a working precision real output one-
dimensional variable of dimension at least
N containing the diagonal elements of the
tridiagonal matrix.

E   is a working precision real output one-
dimensional variable of dimension at least
N containing, in its last N-1 positions,
the subdiagonal elements of the tridiagonal
matrix. The element E(1) is set to zero.

E2   is a working precision real output one-
dimensional variable of dimension at least
N containing, in its last N-1 positions,
the squares of the subdiagonal elements of
the tridiagonal matrix. The element E2(1)
is set to zero. E2 need not be distinct
from E (non-standard usage acceptable with
at least those compilers included in the
certification statement), in which case no
squares are returned.

B. Error Conditions and Returns.

None.

C. Applicability and Restrictions.

If all the eigenvalues of the original matrix are
desired, this subroutine should be followed by TQL1
(F289), IMTQL1 (F291), or TQLRAT (F235).

If some of the eigenvalues of the original matrix are
desired, this subroutine should be followed by BISECT
(F294) or TRIDIB (F237).

If some of the eigenvalues and eigenvectors of the
original matrix are desired, this subroutine should be
followed by TSTURM (F293), or by BISECT (F294) and
TINVIT (F223), or by TRIDIB (F237) and TINVIT, or by
IMTQLV (F234) and TINVIT, and then by TRBAK1 (F279).

If all the eigenvalues and eigenvectors of the original matrix are desired, subroutine TRED2 (F278) should be used rather than TRED1 to perform the tridiagonal reduction, and should be followed by TQL2 (F290) or IMTQL2 (F292).

If the matrix has elements of widely varying magnitudes, the smaller ones should be in the top left-hand corner.

3. DISCUSSION OF METHOD AND ALGORITHM.

The tridiagonal reduction is performed in the following way. Starting with J=N, the elements in the J-th row to the left of the diagonal are first scaled, to avoid possible underflow in the transformation that might result in severe departure from orthogonality. The sum of squares SIGMA of these scaled elements is next formed. Then, a vector U and a scalar

$$H = U^T U/2$$

define an operator

$$P = I - UU^T/H$$

which is orthogonal and symmetric and for which the similarity transformation PAP eliminates the elements in the J-th row of A to the left of the subdiagonal and the symmetrical elements in the J-th column.

The non-zero components of U are the elements of the J-th row to the left of the diagonal with the last of them augmented by the square root of SIGMA prefixed by the sign of the subdiagonal element. By storing the transformed subdiagonal element in E(J) and not overwriting the row elements eliminated in the transformation, full information about P is saved for later use in TRBAK1.

The transformation sets E2(J) equal to SIGMA and E(J) equal to the square root of SIGMA prefixed by sign opposite to that of the replaced subdiagonal element.

The above steps are repeated on further rows of the transformed A in reverse order until A is reduced to tridiagonal form; that is, repeated for J = N-1,N-2,...,3.

Only the elements in the lower triangle of A are accessed, and although the diagonal elements are modified in the algorithm, they are restored to their original contents by the end of the subroutine, thus preserving the full upper triangle of A.

This subroutine is a translation of the Algol procedure TRED1 written and discussed in detail by Martin, Reinsch, and Wilkinson (1).

4. REFERENCES.

1) Martin, R.S., Reinsch, C., and Wilkinson, J.H., Householder's Tridiagonalization of a Symmetric Matrix, Num. Math. 11,181-195 (1968). (Reprinted in Handbook for Automatic Computation, Volume II, Linear Algebra, J. H. Wilkinson - C. Reinsch, Contribution II/2, 212-226, Springer-Verlag, 1971.)

5. CHECKOUT.

A. Test Cases.

See the section discussing testing of the codes for real symmetric matrices.

B. Accuracy.

The accuracy of TRED1 can best be described in terms of its role in those paths of EISPACK which find eigenvalues and eigenvectors of real symmetric matrices and matrix systems. In these paths, this subroutine is numerically stable (1). This stability contributes to the property of these paths that the computed eigenvalues are the exact eigenvalues of a matrix or system close to the original matrix or system and the computed eigenvectors are close (but not necessarily equal) to the eigenvectors of that matrix or system.

```
      SUBROUTINE TRED1(NM,N,A,D,E,E2)
C
      INTEGER I,J,K,L,N,II,NM,JP1
      REAL A(NM,N),D(N),E(N),E2(N)
      REAL F,G,H,SCALE
      REAL SQRT,ABS,SIGN
C
      DO 100 I = 1, N
  100 D(I) = A(I,I)
C     ********** FOR I=N STEP -1 UNTIL 1 DO -- **********
      DO 300 II = 1, N
         I = N + 1 - II
         L = I - 1
         H = 0.0
         SCALE = 0.0
         IF (L .LT. 1) GO TO 130
C     ********** SCALE ROW (ALGOL TOL THEN NOT NEEDED) **********
      DO 120 K = 1, L
  120    SCALE = SCALE + ABS(A(I,K))
C
         IF (SCALE .NE. 0.0) GO TO 140
  130    E(I) = 0.0
         E2(I) = 0.0
         GO TO 290
C
  140    DO 150 K = 1, L
            A(I,K) = A(I,K) / SCALE
            H = H + A(I,K) * A(I,K)
  150    CONTINUE
C
         E2(I) = SCALE * SCALE * H
         F = A(I,L)
         G = -SIGN(SQRT(H),F)
         E(I) = SCALE * G
         H = H - F * G
         A(I,L) = F - G
         IF (L .EQ. 1) GO TO 270
         F = 0.0
C
         DO 240 J = 1, L
            G = 0.0
C     ********** FORM ELEMENT OF A*U **********
            DO 180 K = 1, J
  180          G = G + A(J,K) * A(I,K)
C
            JP1 = J + 1
            IF (L .LT. JP1) GO TO 220
C
            DO 200 K = JP1, L
  200          G = G + A(K,J) * A(I,K)
C     ********** FORM ELEMENT OF P **********
  220       E(J) = G / H
            F = F + E(J) * A(I,J)
  240    CONTINUE
```

```
C
         H = F / (H + H)
C     ********** FORM REDUCED A **********
         DO 260 J = 1, L
            F = A(I,J)
            G = E(J) - H * F
            E(J) = G
C
            DO 260 K = 1, J
               A(J,K) = A(J,K) - F * E(K) - G * A(I,K)
  260    CONTINUE
C
  270    DO 280 K = 1, L
  280    A(I,K) = SCALE * A(I,K)
C
  290    H = D(I)
         D(I) = A(I,I)
         A(I,I) = H
  300 CONTINUE
C
      RETURN
      END
```

NATS PROJECT

EIGENSYSTEM SUBROUTINE PACKAGE (EISPACK)

F278-2   TRED2

A Fortran IV Subroutine to Reduce a Real Symmetric Matrix
to a Symmetric Tridiagonal Matrix Accumulating the
Orthogonal Transformations.

May, 1972
July, 1975

1. PURPOSE.

The Fortran IV subroutine TRED2 reduces a real symmetric
matrix to a symmetric tridiagonal matrix using and
accumulating orthogonal similarity transformations. This
reduced form and the transformation matrix are used by
subroutine TQL2 (F290) or IMTQL2 (F292) to find the
eigenvalues and eigenvectors of the original matrix.

2. USAGE.

A. Calling Sequence.

The SUBROUTINE statement is

SUBROUTINE TRED2(NM,N,A,D,E,Z)

The parameters are discussed below and the
interpretation of working precision for various machines
is given in the section discussing certification.

NM   is an integer input variable set equal to
          the row dimension of the two-dimensional
          arrays A and Z as specified in the
          DIMENSION statements for A and Z in the
          calling program.

N   is an integer input variable set equal to
          the order of the matrix A. N must be not
          greater than NM.

A   is a working precision real input two-
         dimensional variable with row dimension NM
         and column dimension at least N.   A
         contains the symmetric matrix of order N
         to be reduced to tridiagonal form. Only the
         full lower triangle of the matrix need be
         supplied.

D   is a working precision real output one-
         dimensional variable of dimension at least
         N containing the diagonal elements of the
         tridiagonal matrix.

E   is a working precision real output one-
         dimensional variable of dimension at least
         N containing, in its last N-1 positions,
         the subdiagonal elements of the tridiagonal
         matrix. The element E(1) is set to zero.

Z   is a working precision real output two-
         dimensional variable with row dimension NM
         and column dimension at least N.   It
         contains the orthogonal transformation
         matrix produced in the reduction to the
         tridiagonal form.

B. Error Conditions and Returns.

   None.

C. Applicability and Restrictions.

   If all the eigenvalues and eigenvectors of the original
   matrix are desired, this subroutine should be followed
   by TQL2 (F290)   or   IMTQL2 (F292).

   If some other combination of eigenvalues and
   eigenvectors is desired, subroutine TRED1 (F277)
   should be used rather than TRED2 to perform the
   tridiagonal reduction.

   If the matrix has elements of widely varying magnitudes,
   the smaller ones should be in the top left-hand corner.

   Parameters A and Z need not be distinct.

3. DISCUSSION OF METHOD AND ALGORITHM.

The lower triangle of A is initially copied into Z and all subsequent operations are performed on Z.

The tridiagonal reduction is performed in the following way. Starting with J=N, the elements in the J-th row to the left of the diagonal are first scaled, to avoid possible underflow in the transformation that might result in severe departure from orthogonality. The sum of squares SIGMA of these scaled elements is next formed. Then, a vector U and a scalar

$$H = U^T U/2$$

define an operator

$$P = I - UU^T /H$$

which is orthogonal and symmetric and for which the similarity transformation PAP eliminates the elements in the J-th row of A to the left of the subdiagonal and the symmetrical elements in the J-th column.

The non-zero components of U are the elements of the J-th row to the left of the diagonal with the last of them augmented by the square root of SIGMA prefixed by the sign of the subdiagonal element. By storing the transformed subdiagonal element in E(J) and not overwriting the row elements eliminated in the transformation, full information about P is saved for later accumulation of transformations.

The transformation sets E(J) equal to the square root of SIGMA prefixed by sign opposite to that of the replaced subdiagonal element.

The above steps are repeated on further rows of the transformed A in reverse order until A is reduced to tridiagonal form; that is, repeated for J = N-1,N-2,...,3.

Finally, the orthogonal transformation matrix is accumulated in Z as the product of the N-2 operators defined in the tridiagonal reduction.

This subroutine is a translation of the Algol procedure TRED2 written and discussed in detail by Martin, Reinsch, and Wilkinson (1).

4. REFERENCES.

1) Martin, R.S., Reinsch, C., and Wilkinson, J.H.,
Householder's Tridiagonalization of a Symmetric Matrix,
Num. Math. 11,181-195 (1968). (Reprinted in Handbook for
Automatic Computation, Volume II, Linear Algebra,
J. H. Wilkinson - C. Reinsch, Contribution II/2, 212-226,
Springer-Verlag, 1971.)

5. CHECKOUT.

A. Test Cases.

See the section discussing testing of the codes for
real symmetric matrices.

B. Accuracy.

The accuracy of TRED2 can best be described in terms
of its role in those paths of EISPACK which find
eigenvalues and eigenvectors of real symmetric matrices
and matrix systems. In these paths, this subroutine is
numerically stable (1). This stability contributes to
the property of these paths that the computed
eigenvalues are the exact eigenvalues of a matrix or
system close to the original matrix or system and the
computed eigenvectors are close (but not necessarily
equal) to the eigenvectors of that matrix or system.

```
      SUBROUTINE TRED2(NM,N,A,D,E,Z)
C
      INTEGER I,J,K,L,N,II,NM,JP1
      REAL A(NM,N),D(N),E(N),Z(NM,N)
      REAL F,G,H,HH,SCALE
      REAL SQRT,ABS,SIGN
C
      DO 100 I = 1, N
C
         DO 100 J = 1, I
            Z(I,J) = A(I,J)
  100 CONTINUE
C
      IF (N .EQ. 1) GO TO 320
C     ********* FOR I=N STEP -1 UNTIL 2 DO -- **********
      DO 300 II = 2, N
         I = N + 2 - II
         L = I - 1
         H = 0.0
         SCALE = 0.0
         IF (L .LT. 2) GO TO 130
C     ********* SCALE ROW (ALGOL TOL THEN NOT NEEDED) **********
         DO 120 K = 1, L
  120    SCALE = SCALE + ABS(Z(I,K))
C
         IF (SCALE .NE. 0.0) GO TO 140
  130    E(I) = Z(I,L)
         GO TO 290
C
  140    DO 150 K = 1, L
            Z(I,K) = Z(I,K) / SCALE
            H = H + Z(I,K) * Z(I,K)
  150    CONTINUE
C
         F = Z(I,L)
         G = -SIGN(SQRT(H),F)
         E(I) = SCALE * G
         H = H - F * G
         Z(I,L) = F - G
         F = 0.0
C
         DO 240 J = 1, L
            Z(J,I) = Z(I,J) / H
            G = 0.0
C     ********* FORM ELEMENT OF A*U **********
            DO 180 K = 1, J
  180       G = G + Z(J,K) * Z(I,K)
C
            JP1 = J + 1
            IF (L .LT. JP1) GO TO 220
C
            DO 200 K = JP1, L
  200       G = G + Z(K,J) * Z(I,K)
```

312

```
C     ********** FORM ELEMENT OF P **********
  220         E(J) = G / H
              F = F + E(J) * Z(I,J)
  240     CONTINUE
C
          HH = F / (H + H)
C     ********** FORM REDUCED A **********
          DO 260 J = 1, L
              F = Z(I,J)
              G = E(J) - HH * F
              E(J) = G
C
              DO 260 K = 1, J
                  Z(J,K) = Z(J,K) - F * E(K) - G * Z(I,K)
  260     CONTINUE
C
  290     D(I) = H
  300 CONTINUE
C
  320 D(1) = 0.0
      E(1) = 0.0
C     ********** ACCUMULATION OF TRANSFORMATION MATRICES **********
      DO 500 I = 1, N
          L = I - 1
          IF (D(I) .EQ. 0.0) GO TO 380
C
          DO 360 J = 1, L
              G = 0.0
C
              DO 340 K = 1, L
  340             G = G + Z(I,K) * Z(K,J)
C
              DO 360 K = 1, L
                  Z(K,J) = Z(K,J) - G * Z(K,I)
  360     CONTINUE
C
  380     D(I) = Z(I,I)
          Z(I,I) = 1.0
          IF (L .LT. 1) GO TO 500
C
          DO 400 J = 1, L
              Z(I,J) = 0.0
              Z(J,I) = 0.0
  400     CONTINUE
C
  500 CONTINUE
C
      RETURN
      END
```

NATS PROJECT

EIGENSYSTEM SUBROUTINE PACKAGE (EISPACK)

F299-2 EISPAC

A Control Program for the Eigensystem Package
(F269 to F298 and F220 to F247).

May, 1972
July, 1975

1. PURPOSE.

The Fortran IV and OS/360-370 assembly language subroutine
EISPAC (together with its associated "keyword" entry points)
is designed to simplify the solution of the standard and
generalized matrix eigenproblems using the subroutines in the
eigensystem package (F269-F298, F220-F247). It thus may be
used to compute some or all of the eigenvalues, with or
without eigenvectors, of complex general, complex Hermitian,
real general, real symmetric, real symmetric tridiagonal,
certain real non-symmetric tridiagonal, and real symmetric
band matrices; and it may also be used to compute some or all
of the eigenvalues, with or without eigenvectors, for the
real symmetric generalized eigenproblem, or all of the
eigenvalues, with or without eigenvectors, for the real non-
symmetric generalized eigenproblem. EISPAC offers the
following advantages if you wish to solve an eigenproblem:

1. You describe the problem to EISPAC in simple,
   familiar terms.
2. Using your description, EISPAC automatically
   selects subroutines to solve your problem and
   executes them in the proper order and with parameters
   passed from one to another in the proper way. In
   general, EISPAC selects the sequence of subroutines
   in the eigensystem package which will solve your
   problem as rapidly as possible with reasonable
   assurance of stability in the calculations.
3. EISPAC loads each selected subroutine only as it is
   required, thus making available for data storage as
   much memory as possible. On the other hand, if
   sufficient memory is available, the subroutines used
   are retained in memory and are not reloaded when you
   repeatedly call EISPAC to solve the same problem.
   (See section 3 below.)
4. EISPAC allocates and frees any necessary auxiliary
   storage automatically.

5. Use of EISPAC minimizes the number of changes you must make to your program if you wish to solve a slight variation of your original problem or if you wish to take advantage of new methods when they are introduced.

6. EISPAC is called as a subroutine from your own driver program. Thus the matrix whose eigensystem is being computed may itself be the result of other computations in your program, and the computed eigensystem may conveniently be used in further calculations.

Thus EISPAC relieves you of having to develop a detailed knowledge of the applicability, efficiency, and calling sequences of the individual EISPACK subroutines.

2. USAGE.

A. Calling Sequence.

EISPAC employs variable length parameter lists and "keyword" parameters to simplify specification of your problem and to group related subparameters. An overview of the calls to EISPAC is given by the prototype calls below; specific calls for different classes of matrices are discussed in section 2.B.

The prototype call to EISPAC for the standard eigenproblem is:

CALL EISPAC (NM, N, MATRIX (...), BAND (...), VALUES (...), VECTOR (...), METHOD (...), ERROR (...), SUBR (...))

where

NM   is an integer variable which supplies the row (first) dimension of any two-dimensional arrays appearing in the call to EISPAC (as that dimension is specified in the DIMENSION statements for them in the calling program). For example, if your program contains arrays dimensioned: A(50,50), Z(50,50) which appear in the call to EISPAC, and the order of the eigenproblem being solved is 25, then NM = 50 and N = 25.

N   is an integer variable which supplies the order of the input matrix. N is checked to verify that it is neither greater than NM nor less than 1.

MATRIX, BAND, VALUES, VECTOR, METHOD, ERROR, SUBR are keyword parameters. They accept sets of subparameters which define the eigenproblem being solved. (These subparameters are discussed in detail in section 2.C below.) Keyword parameters not needed to specify a particular problem are omitted from the call to EISPAC; those appearing may appear in any order.

The prototype call to EISPAC for the generalized eigenproblem is:

    CALL EISPAC (NM, N, MATA (...), MATB (...), VALUES
    (...), VECTOR (...), ERROR (...), SUBR (...))

where MATA and MATB replace MATRIX as keyword parameters. Note: MATRIX and MATA are alternate forms of the same keyword and can be used interchangeably.

To use EISPAC, you must include a private library DD card for EISPACLB (the dynamic load library, see section 3 below) in the GO-step of your job. This card associates EISPACLB with the dataset where the load modules for EISPAC and the eigensystem package subroutines reside. If you are using a typical Fortran cataloged procedure, this card is:

    //GO.EISPACLB DD DISP=SHR,DSNAME=...

Similarly, if you are using the TSO time sharing system, you should execute the command:

    ALLOC FILE(EISPACLB) DATASET(...) SHR

before executing your program.

Finally, if you wish to use EISPAC from a PL/I (Checkout or Optimizer) program by means of the interlanguage communication facility, you should write a simple Fortran subroutine which is called from your PL/I program and which in turn calls EISPAC as described below. This is necessary because EISPAC makes certain (non-standard) assumptions about the Fortran environment of the program calling it which may not be satisfied

when the program is written in PL/I. The Fortran
program calling EISPAC should have as parameters the
variables to be passed to EISPAC; you should take care
that the vectors and arrays appear in DIMENSION
statements in it. Thus for the example concluding the
section on real symmetric matrices in section 2.B
below, the Fortran subroutine called by your PL/I
program should look like:

```
SUBROUTINE EISCAL (N, A, W, Z)
INTEGER N
REAL*8 A(N,N), W(N), Z(N,N)
CALL EISPAC (N, N, MATRIX ('REAL, A, 'SYMMETRIC'),
    VALUES (W), VECTOR (Z))
RETURN
END
```

This example assumes that the PL/I arrays corresponding
to the matrices A and Z are dimensioned exactly
NxN, and hence that the parameter NM can be replaced
by N. In the PL/I calling program, EISCAL would be
declared:

```
DCL EISCAL ENTRY (FIXED BINARY(31,0),
                  (*,*) FLOAT DECIMAL(16),
                  (*)   FLOAT DECIMAL(16),
                  (*,*) FLOAT DECIMAL(16))
                  OPTIONS (FORTRAN) EXTERNAL;
```

You must provide a DD card or allocation for FT06F001,
the standard Fortran output file, because Fortran
automatically tries to open it. This file should be
associated with the same dataset as the output from the
PL/I program, so that EISPAC error messages, if any,
appear with it. Finally, if you are using the PL/I
Checkout compiler, you need to specify the option
SIZE(-nK) to the execution step to reserve dynamic
storage for EISPAC; at a minimum n=14, and it must be
large enough to accommodate any temporary arrays that
are allocated. (An insufficiently large value of n
will result in either of the system completion codes 804
or 80A (see section 2.D).)

The use of EISPAC to solve various kinds of
eigenproblems is illustrated in the following section.
You may wish to read first the examples for the type of
matrix you have and then consult section 2.C for
further details about the keyword subparameters. (Note
that in these examples the continuation symbol which
must appear in column 6 of a Fortran continuation card
has been omitted.)

B. EISPAC Examples for Different Classes of Matrices.

Complex General Matrix
------- ------- ------

      The basic call, which finds all of the eigenvalues
(WR, WI) of the complex general matrix (AR, AI),
is:

    CALL EISPAC (NM, N, MATRIX ('COMPLEX', AR, AI),
       VALUES (WR, WI))

If you wish to find all of the eigenvectors
(ZR, ZI), add: VECTOR (ZR, ZI).

If you wish to find all of the eigenvalues and only
selected eigenvectors, add: VECTOR (ZR, ZI, MM, M,
SELECT).

If you prefer not to balance the matrix, add:
METHOD ('NO', 'BALANCE').

If you wish to use elementary instead of unitary
similarities, add: METHOD ('ELEMENTARY').

Thus a call to find all of the eigenvalues and some
of the eigenvectors of a complex general matrix is:

    CALL EISPAC (NM, N, MATRIX ('COMPLEX', AR, AI),
       VALUES (WR, WI), VECTOR (ZR, ZI, MM, M,
       SELECT))

Complex Hermitian Matrix
------- --------- ------

      Recall that a complex Hermitian matrix is a matrix
which is equal to its complex conjugate transpose.
If you wish to solve an eigenproblem for a complex
symmetric matrix (a matrix which is equal to its
transpose without conjugation), you must follow the
complex general matrix examples.

The basic call, which finds all of the eigenvalues
W of the complex Hermitian matrix (AR, AI), is:

    CALL EISPAC (NM, N, MATRIX ('COMPLEX', AR, AI,
      'HERMITIAN'), VALUES (W))

If the complex Hermitian matrix is packed into a single two-dimensional array, HP, substitute for MATRIX ('COMPLEX', AR, AI, 'HERMITIAN'): MATRIX ('COMPLEX', HP, HP, 'HERMITIAN', 'PACKED').

If you wish to find only the eigenvalues in the interval (RLB,RUB), substitute for VALUES (W) (see note 3): VALUES (W, MM, M, RLB, RUB).

Alternatively, if you wish to find exactly M eigenvalues, starting from the M11-th smallest one, substitute for VALUES (W): VALUES (W, M11, M). (See notes 1 and 3.)

If you wish to find the eigenvectors (ZR, ZI) corresponding to the eigenvalues found, add: VECTOR (ZR, ZI).

Thus a call to find a few eigenvalues and their corresponding eigenvectors of a complex Hermitian matrix is:

```
CALL EISPAC (NM, N, MATRIX ('COMPLEX', AR, AI,
    'HERMITIAN'), VALUES (W, MM, M, RLB, RUB),
    VECTOR (ZR, ZI))
```

Real General Matrix
---- ------- ------

The basic call, which finds all of the eigenvalues (WR, WI) of the real general matrix A, is:

```
CALL EISPAC (NM, N, MATRIX ('REAL', A), VALUES
    (WR, WI))
```

If you wish to find all of the eigenvectors ZP, add: VECTOR (ZP).

If you wish to find all of the eigenvalues and only selected eigenvectors, add: VECTOR (ZP, MM, M, SELECT).

If you prefer not to balance the matrix, add: METHOD ('NO', 'BALANCE').

If you wish to use orthogonal instead of elementary similarities for the reduction to upper Hessenberg form, add (see note 5): METHOD ('ORTHOGONAL').

Thus a call to find all of the eigenvalues of a
real general matrix without balancing and using
orthogonal similarities is:

    CALL EISPAC (NM, N, MATRIX ('REAL', A), VALUES
        (WR, WI), METHOD ('NO', 'BALANCE',
        'ORTHOGONAL'))

Real Non-Symmetric Tridiagonal Matrix
---- ------------- ----------- ------

The following examples apply only if the products
of corresponding off-diagonal elements of the
tridiagonal matrix all are non-negative. (Read
note 4 below for an additional restriction if you
wish to compute eigenvectors.) Otherwise the real
general matrix examples must be followed.

The basic call, which finds all of the eigenvalues
W of the real tridiagonal matrix UST, is:

    CALL EISPAC (NM, N, MATRIX ('REAL', UST,
        'TRIDIAGONAL'), VALUES (W))

If you wish to find only the eigenvalues in the
interval (RLB,RUB), substitute for VALUES (W)
(see note 3): VALUES (W, MM, M, RLB, RUB).

Alternatively, if you wish to find exactly M
eigenvalues, starting from the M11-th smallest
one, substitute for VALUES (W): VALUES (W, M11,
M). (See notes 1 and 3.)

If you wish to find the eigenvectors Z
corresponding to the eigenvalues found, add:
VECTOR (Z).

Thus a call to find exactly M eigenvalues,
starting from the M11-th smallest one, of a real
non-symmetric tridiagonal matrix is:

    CALL EISPAC (NM, N, MATRIX ('REAL', UST,
        'TRIDIAGONAL'), VALUES (W, M11, M))

Real Symmetric Matrix
---- --------- ------

The basic call, which finds all of the eigenvalues
W of the real symmetric matrix A, is (see note
2):

```
    CALL EISPAC (NM, N, MATRIX ('REAL', A,
        'SYMMETRIC'), VALUES (W))
```

If the real symmetric matrix is packed into a
single one-dimensional array, SP, substitute for
MATRIX ('REAL', A, 'SYMMETRIC'): MATRIX ('REAL',
SP, 'SYMMETRIC', 'PACKED').

If you wish to find only the eigenvalues in the
interval (RLB,RUB), substitute for VALUES (W)
(see note 3): VALUES (W, MM, M, RLB, RUB).

Alternatively, if you wish to find exactly M
eigenvalues, starting from the M11-th smallest
one, substitute for VALUES (W): VALUES (W, M11,
M). (See notes 1 and 3.)

If you wish to find the eigenvectors Z
corresponding to the eigenvalues found, add:
VECTOR (Z).

Thus a call to find all of the eigenvalues and
eigenvectors of a real symmetric matrix is:

```
    CALL EISPAC (NM, N, MATRIX ('REAL', A,
        'SYMMETRIC'), VALUES (W), VECTOR (Z))
```

Real Symmetric Tridiagonal Matrix
---- --------- ----------- ------

The basic call, which finds all of the eigenvalues
W of the real symmetric tridiagonal matrix ST, is
(see note 2):

```
    CALL EISPAC (NM, N, MATRIX ('REAL', ST,
        'SYMMETRIC', 'TRIDIAGONAL'), VALUES (W))
```

If you wish to find only the eigenvalues in the
interval (RLB,RUB), substitute for VALUES (W)
(see note 3): VALUES (W, MM, M, RLB, RUB).

Alternatively, if you wish to find exactly M
eigenvalues, starting from the M11-th smallest
one, substitute for VALUES (W): VALUES (W, M11,
M). (See notes 1 and 3.)

If you wish to find the eigenvectors Z
corresponding to the eigenvalues found, add:
VECTOR (Z).

Thus a call to find some of the eigenvalues of a
real symmetric tridiagonal matrix is:

```
CALL EISPAC (NM, N, MATRIX ('REAL', ST,
    'SYMMETRIC', 'TRIDIAGONAL'), VALUES (W, MM,
    M, RLB, RUB))
```

Real Symmetric Band Matrix

The basic call, which finds all of the eigenvalues
W of the real symmetric band matrix SB, is (see
notes 2 and 6):

```
CALL EISPAC (NM, N, MATRIX ('REAL', SB,
    'SYMMETRIC'), BAND (MB), VALUES (W))
```

If you wish to find only the eigenvalues in the
interval (RLB,RUB), substitute for VALUES (W)
(see note 3): VALUES (W, MM, M, RLB, RUB).

Alternatively, if you wish to find exactly M
eigenvalues, starting from the M11-th smallest
one, substitute for VALUES (W): VALUES (W, M11,
M). (See notes 1 and 3.)

If you wish to find the eigenvectors Z
corresponding to the eigenvalues found, add:
VECTOR (Z).

Thus a call to find some of the eigenvalues of a
real symmetric band matrix is:

```
CALL EISPAC (NM, N, MATRIX ('REAL', SB,
    'SYMMETRIC'), BAND (MB), VALUES (W, MM, M,
    RLB, RUB))
```

Generalized Real Symmetric Matrix Systems

There are three forms of the real symmetric
generalized eigenproblem that can be solved with
EISPAC: namely, the forms $Ax = (lambda)Bx$,
$ABx = (lambda)x$, and $BAx = (lambda)x$, where A
and B are both symmetric and B is positive
definite.

The basic call, which finds all of the eigenvalues
W of the real symmetric generalized system
Ax = (lambda)Bx, is (see notes 2 and 7):

```
CALL EISPAC (NM, N, MATA ('REAL', A,
    'SYMMETRIC'), MATB ('REAL', B, 'SYMMETRIC',
    'POSITIVE DEFINITE'), VALUES (W))
```

If you wish to find only the eigenvalues in the
interval (RLB,RUB), substitute for VALUES (W)
(see note 3): VALUES (W, MM, M, RLB, RUB).

Alternatively, if you wish to find exactly M
eigenvalues, starting from the M11-th smallest
one, substitute for VALUES (W): VALUES (W, M11,
M). (See notes 1 and 3.)

If you wish to find the eigenvectors Z
corresponding to the eigenvalues found, add:
VECTOR (Z).

If the problem is of the form ABx = (lambda)x or
BAx = (lambda)x, supply 'ABX=LX' or 'BAX=LX',
respectively, to MATB (in a position after the B
parameter).

Thus a call to find exactly M eigenvalues,
starting from the M11-th smallest one, and the
corresponding eigenvectors of the real symmetric
generalized system ABx = (lambda)x, is:

```
CALL EISPAC (NM, N, MATA ('REAL', A,
    'SYMMETRIC'), MATB ('REAL', B, 'SYMMETRIC',
    'POSITIVE DEFINITE', 'ABX=LX'), VALUES (W,
    M11, M), VECTOR (Z))
```

Generalized Real Non-Symmetric Matrix System
----------- ---- -------------- ------ ------

The basic call, which finds all of the eigenvalues
(ALPHAR/BETA, ALPHAI/BETA) for the real non-
symmetric generalized eigenproblem
Ax = (lambda)Bx, is (see note 8):

```
CALL EISPAC (NM, N, MATA ('REAL', A), MATB
    ('REAL', B), VALUES (ALPHAR, ALPHAI, BETA))
```

If you wish to find all of the eigenvectors, ZP,
of the system, add: VECTOR (ZP).

Thus a call to find all of the eigenvalues and
eigenvectors of a real non-symmetric generalized
system is:

```
CALL EISPAC (NM, N, MATA ('REAL', A), MATB
    ('REAL', B), VALUES (ALPHAR, ALPHAI, BETA),
    VECTOR (ZP))
```

C. Meanings of Keyword Subparameters.

Subparameters for MATRIX, MATA, and MATB:

'REAL'   specifies that the matrix whose eigensystem
            is to be computed is real. (See note 9.)

'COMPLEX'
            specifies that the matrix whose eigensystem
            is to be computed is complex. (See note
            9.)

AR, AI   are long precision real two-dimensional
            variables with row dimension NM and
            column dimension at least N. They supply,
            respectively, the real and imaginary parts
            of the complex matrix whose eigensystem is
            to be computed. In the non-Hermitian case,
            the information in the full AR and AI
            arrays specifies the matrix, and all of it
            is destroyed. In the Hermitian case, the
            information in the full lower triangle of
            AR and the strict lower triangle of AI
            specifies the matrix, and is destroyed as
            well as the diagonal of AI; the full upper
            triangle of AR and the strict upper
            triangle of AI are left unaltered.

A, B   are long precision real two-dimensional
            variables with row dimension NM and
            column dimension at least N. They supply
            the real matrices whose eigensystem is to
            be computed. (For the standard
            eigenproblem, only A is supplied.) In
            the non-symmetric case, the information in
            the full A and B arrays specifies the
            matrices, and all of it is destroyed. In
            the symmetric standard case, the
            information in the full lower triangle of
            A specifies the matrix; that in the strict
            lower triangle may be destroyed, and that
            in the full upper triangle is left

unaltered. In the symmetric generalized case, the information in the full upper triangles of A and B specifies the matrices; the full lower triangle of A and the strict lower triangle of B are destroyed, and the strict upper triangle of A and the full upper triangle of B are left unaltered.

UST is a long precision real two-dimensional variable with row dimension NM and column dimension at least 3. It supplies a real non-symmetric tridiagonal matrix whose subdiagonal elements are stored in the last N-1 positions of the first column, whose diagonal elements are stored in the second column, and whose superdiagonal elements are stored in the first N-1 positions of the third column. UST(1,1) and UST(N,3) are arbitrary. None of the information in UST is destroyed. The non-symmetric tridiagonal matrix supplied by UST must have the additional special property that the products of corresponding off-diagonal elements all are non-negative. (Read note 4 for an additional restriction on UST if eigenvectors are being computed.) Violation of these restrictions on UST causes an EISPAC execution phase error (see section 2.D below).

ST is a long precision real two-dimensional variable with row dimension NM and column dimension at least 2. It supplies a real symmetric tridiagonal matrix whose subdiagonal elements are stored in the last N-1 positions of the first column and whose diagonal elements are stored in the second column. ST(1,1) is arbitrary. The information in the subdiagonal (first column) only is destroyed.

HP is a long precision real two-dimensional variable with row dimension NM and column dimension at least N. On input, HP contains the lower triangle of a packed complex Hermitian matrix of order N whose eigensystem is to be computed. If the real part of the matrix is denoted by AR and the imaginary part by AI, then the full lower triangle of AR should be stored in the full lower triangle of HP, and the strict lower triangle of AI should be stored in the strict upper triangle of HP in transposed form. For example when N=4, HP should contain

```
( AR(1,1)    AI(2,1)    AI(3,1)    AI(4,1) )
( AR(2,1)    AR(2,2)    AI(3,2)    AI(4,2) )
( AR(3,1)    AR(3,2)    AR(3,3)    AI(4,3) )
( AR(4,1)    AR(4,2)    AR(4,3)    AR(4,4) ).
```

All of the information in HP is destroyed.

SP   is a long precision real one-dimensional variable with dimension at least $N*(N+1)/2$. It supplies the lower triangle of a real symmetric matrix A of order N, packed row-wise. For example when N=3, SP should contain

```
(A(1,1),A(2,1),A(2,2),A(3,1),A(3,2),A(3,3))
```

where the subscripts of each element refer to the row and column of the element in the standard two-dimensional representation. All of the information in SP is destroyed.

SB   is a long precision real two-dimensional variable with row dimension NM and column dimension at least MB. It supplies the lower triangle of a real symmetric matrix A of order N in band form with half bandwidth MB. The lowest subdiagonal of the matrix is stored in the last N+1-MB positions of the first column of SB, the next subdiagonal in the last N+2-MB positions of the second column, further diagonals similarly, and finally the principal diagonal in the N positions of the last column. Contents of storage locations not part of the matrix are arbitrary. For example, when N=5 and MB=3, SB should contain

```
(    *          *        A(1,1) )
(    *        A(2,1)      A(2,2) )
( A(3,1)      A(3,2)      A(3,3) )
( A(4,2)      A(4,3)      A(4,4) )
( A(5,3)      A(5,4)      A(5,5) ).
```

All of the information in SB is destroyed.

'HERMITIAN', 'SYMMETRIC', 'TRIDIAGONAL', 'POSITIVE DEFINITE', 'NEGATIVE DEFINITE', 'PACKED'
specify that the matrix whose eigensystem is to be found has the stated special property. (See also notes 1, 2, and 9.)

'ABX=LX', 'BAX=LX' (as subparameters for MATB) specify the corresponding variant of the real symmetric generalized eigenproblem.

Subparameter for BAND:

MB   is an integer variable which supplies the half bandwidth of a real symmetric band matrix. It is defined as the number of adjacent diagonals, including the principal diagonal, required to specify the non-zero portion of the lower triangle of the matrix.

Subparameters for VALUES:

WR, WI   are long precision real one-dimensional variables of dimension at least N. They receive, respectively, the real and imaginary parts of the N complex eigenvalues computed.

W   is a long precision real one-dimensional variable of dimension at least sufficient (N, MM, or M) to hold the eigenvalues. It receives the N (M) eigenvalues computed.

MM   is an integer variable which, when it is a subparameter to VALUES, supplies a maximum for the number of eigenvalues expected in the interval (RLB,RUB); more than MM eigenvalues in (RLB,RUB) is an error. The dimension of W, and the column dimension of ZR and ZI or Z if used, must be at least MM.

M   is an integer variable which, when it is a subparameter to VALUES, denotes the number of eigenvalues actually stored in W. It is supplied (in conjunction with M11) by the user if a specified number of eigenvalues is to be computed. It is set by the program, if an interval (RLB,RUB) has been specified, to the number of eigenvalues actually found.

RLB, RUB are long precision real variables which define an interval to be searched for eigenvalues. The eigenvalues found lie in the interval (RLB,RUB), which is closed on the left and open on the right; if RLB is not less than RUB, no eigenvalues are found. (RLB,RUB) must not contain more than MM eigenvalues.

M11 is an integer variable which, when it is a subparameter to VALUES, supplies the index of the smallest eigenvalue to be computed.

EPS1 is a long precision real variable which supplies an absolute error tolerance for the computed eigenvalues; if the input value of EPS1 is non-positive, a default value will be used. (See note 3.)

ALPHAR, ALPHAI, BETA
are .long precision real one-dimensional variables with dimension at least N which receive the complex eigenvalues for a real non-symmetric generalized eigenproblem. The real part of each eigenvalue is given by ALPHAR(I)/BETA(I) and the imaginary part by ALPHAI(I)/BETA(I). (See note 8.)

'LARGEST', 'SMALLEST'
specify that the M largest or smallest eigenvalues are to be computed if the rational QR method has been selected. In this case substitute for VALUES(W): VALUES (W, M, 'LARGEST') or VALUES (W, M, 'SMALLEST'), respectively. (See notes 1 and 9.)

Subparameters for VECTOR:

ZR, ZI are long precision real two-dimensional variables with row dimension NM and column dimension at least sufficient (N, MM, or M) to hold the eigenvectors. They receive, respectively, the real and imaginary parts of the N (M) eigenvectors computed.

ZP is a long precision real two-dimensional variable with row and column dimensions as described for ZR and ZI. It receives N (M) columns which represent eigenvectors of a real general matrix or matrix system. To conserve storage, these eigenvectors are stored in ZP in packed form:

corresponding to a real eigenvalue, one
column representing the real eigenvector is
stored; corresponding to a complex
conjugate pair of eigenvalues, two
consecutive columns representing the real
and imaginary parts of the eigenvector
corresponding to the first, or first
flagged (see SELECT below), of the pair
are stored. For example, suppose all of
the eigenvectors of a real general matrix
are being computed. If the K-th
eigenvalue is real (WI(K) = 0) then ZP(K)
is the corresponding eigenvector. If the
K-th and (K+1)-th eigenvalues are a
complex conjugate pair (with WI(K) .GT. 0)
then ZP(K) is the real part and ZP(K+1)
is the imaginary part of the eigenvector
corresponding to the K-th eigenvalue.
The conjugate of this vector is the
eigenvector for the conjugate eigenvalue.
(Example Fortran statements for unpacking
the eigenvectors may be found in section
2.3.2 of (6).)

Z is a long precision real two-dimensional
variable with row and column dimensions as
described for ZR and ZI. It receives
the N (M) eigenvectors computed. When
all of the eigenvectors of a real symmetric
(full) matrix or generalized matrix system
are being computed, the array A which
supplies the input matrix may be used for
Z; the eigenvectors then overwrite the
input matrix.

MM is an integer variable which, when it is a
subparameter to VECTOR, supplies the
maximum number of columns of ZR and ZI
or ZP which will be used. The column
dimension of ZR and ZI or ZP must be
at least MM.

M is an integer variable which, when it is a
subparameter to VECTOR, receives the
number of columns used to store
eigenvectors in ZR and ZI or ZP.

SELECT is a logical one-dimensional variable of
dimension at least N whose true elements
flag those eigenvalues of a real or complex
general matrix whose eigenvectors are to be
computed. If eigenvectors of a real
general matrix are being computed and both
of a pair of complex conjugate eigenvalues

are flagged, the second flag is set false
and only the eigenvector corresponding to
the first of the pair is computed. An
error results if MM is smaller than the
number of columns required to hold the
selected eigenvectors.

Subparameters for METHOD:

(See note 9 concerning alphanumeric
parameters.)

'ORTHOGONAL'
specifies that orthogonal similarities
(instead of elementary similarities) are to
be used to reduce a real general matrix to
upper Hessenberg form. Reduction by
orthogonal similarities is somewhat slower
than that by elementary similarities, but
in some cases it may improve the accuracy
of the computed eigensystem. In
particular, if you wish to calculate the
condition numbers for the computation of
the eigensystem of a matrix (see (3),
p. 199 and (4), pp. 86-89), you should use
the condition-number-preserving orthogonal
transformations.

'ELEMENTARY'
specifies that elementary similarities
(instead of unitary similarities) are to be
used on a complex general matrix (the LR
rather than the QR transformation).
Elementary similarities are somewhat faster
than unitary similarities, but in some
cases diminish the accuracy of the computed
(complex general) eigensystem.

'NO', 'BALANCE'
specifies that a real or complex general
matrix is not to be balanced before its
eigensystem is computed. In general,
balancing improves the accuracy of the
computed eigensystem and requires very
little additional computation time.

'RATQR' specifies that the rational QR method is
to be used to compute a few of the largest
or smallest eigenvalues. (See note 1.)

Subparameter for ERROR:

IERROR   is an integer variable which receives a
value indicating whether certain errors
occurred during the solution of the
eigensystem. See section 2.D below.

Subparameter for SUBR:

USUB   is a user-supplied subroutine with the
following parameter list:

USUB (SUBRNO, NM, N, AR, AI, WR, WI, ZR,
ZI, MM, M, RLB, RUB, EPS1, SELECT,
IDEF, SMLSTV, IERROR, LOW, UPP, BND,
D, E, E2, IND, INT, ORTR, SCALE, TAU,
ORTI, M11, NV, MB, BR, DL, ALPHAR,
ALPHAI, BETA).

The keyword parameter SUBR (USUB) may be
added to any EISPAC call. (Note that
USUB must be mentioned in an EXTERNAL
statement in the calling program.) USUB
will be called before execution begins and
after execution of each numbered routine in
the path determined by the parameters to
EISPAC and defined in the "EISPAC
Eigensystem Path Chart" (1); the number of
the routine (zero before execution begins)
is passed by the integer variable SUBRNO.
USUB may be used to examine intermediate
results, to obtain timing information,
etc.; its use is quite analogous to that of
the procedure "INFORM" described by
Rutishauser (5). For the meanings of the
parameters it receives, and appropriate
dimensions for those requiring them, see
(1), (2), and section 2.3.7 of (6).

Note 1: Computing a Few of the Largest or Smallest
Eigenvalues.

The recommended procedure for computing a few of
the extreme eigenvalues of a real symmetric or
complex Hermitian matrix is by appropriate
specification of the subparameters M11 and M to
VALUES. Alternatively, the rational QR method
may be employed, although it has proven less stable
numerically. If the rational QR method is
selected and you know that the matrix is positive
(negative) definite, you may indicate so by adding
the subparameter 'POSITIVE DEFINITE' ('NEGATIVE
DEFINITE') to MATRIX, e.g.,

> MATRIX ('REAL', ST, 'SYMMETRIC',
> 'TRIDIAGONAL', 'POSITIVE DEFINITE'), METHOD
> ('RATQR'), VALUES (W, M, 'SMALLEST').

Computational economy results only when the largest
(smallest) eigenvalues of a negative (positive)
definite matrix are sought.

Note that subparameter W to VALUES must be of
dimension at least N, if the rational QR method
is used, even though only M eigenvalues are
requested.

Note 2: 'HERMITIAN' for Real Matrices.

For a real matrix, 'HERMITIAN' and 'SYMMETRIC'
are synonymous.

Note 3: EPS1 as a Subparameter to VALUES.

EPS1 is a long precision real variable which
supplies an absolute error tolerance for the
computed eigenvalues when only a few eigenvalues
(or a few eigenvalues and their corresponding
eigenvectors) are being calculated for the standard
or generalized real symmetric problems; or for the
non-symmetric generalized problem where all
eigenvalues and possibly eigenvectors are being
found. If the input value of EPS1 is non-
positive, a suitable default value, which is
related to the machine precision and the norm of
the matrix, is used in place of EPS1; this same
default is used if EPS1 is not supplied to
EISPAC. The input value, if any, of EPS1 is not
altered when the default value is employed;
however, for the standard problem only, the (last)
default value used may be examined by means of a
user subroutine supplied as the subparameter to
SUBR (see above). To supply EPS1 to EISPAC,
substitute for the recommended call to VALUES:
VALUES (W, MM, M, RLB, RUB, EPS1) or VALUES
(ALPHAR, ALPHAI, BETA, EPS1) as appropriate.

If eigenvalues only (no eigenvectors) are being
computed, EPS1 may be used to control the trade-
off between computation time and absolute accuracy
of the computed eigenvalues, if less (or more)
accuracy than that given by the default value of
EPS1 is required.

If eigenvalues and their corresponding eigenvectors are being computed, extreme care must be taken in choosing a value for EPS1 other than the default, since if EPS1 is too large, the eigenvectors may be poor because the eigenvalues are not sufficiently accurate; whereas if EPS1 is smaller than necessary for convergence, the additional accuracy of the computed eigenvalues will not increase the accuracy of the eigenvectors. For further discussion, or in case of difficulty, see section 2.3.3 of (6), and also the NATS subroutine documents for F223 TINVIT, F294 BISECT, F237 TRIDIB, and F239 QZIT (2).

Note 4: Class of Non-Symmetric Tridiagonal Matrices for which Eigenvectors may be Found.

The class of real non-symmetric tridiagonal matrices for which eigenvectors can be computed is somewhat more restricted than that for which eigenvalues can be found. For the eigenvector computation to be successful, not only must the products of corresponding off-diagonal elements all be non-negative, but also when such a product is zero, the corresponding off-diagonal elements must both be zero.

Note 5: 'UNITARY' for Real Matrices.

For a real matrix, 'UNITARY' and 'ORTHOGONAL' are synonymous.

Note 6: Symmetric Band Matrices of Half Bandwidth 2.

If MB is specified as 2 for a real symmetric band matrix, EISPAC selects the same subroutines as if 'TRIDIAGONAL' had been specified as a subparameter to MATRIX.

Note 7: Generalized Problem Matrix Subparameters.

As discussed earlier, for a problem to be classified "Real Symmetric Generalized", the A and B input matrices must each be symmetric with B positive definite. Unless 'SYMMETRIC' is specified as a subparameter to MATA and both 'SYMMETRIC' and 'POSITIVE DEFINITE' are specified as subparameters to MATB, EISPAC will select a path corresponding to the real non-symmetric generalized case instead (and assume storage of the full A and B matrices).

Note 8: Eigenvalues for the Non-Symmetric Generalized Problem.

The divisions ALPHAR(I)/BETA(I) and ALPHAI(I)/BETA(I) to obtain the real and imaginary parts of the eigenvalues for the real non-symmetric generalized problem are left to the user. The arrays ALPHAR, ALPHAI, and BETA themselves are returned instead, because they have more information than the quotients when B (or both A and B) is nearly singular. Indeed, if B is singular, at least one element of BETA will be zero and division dare not be attempted.

Note 9: Negation and Abbreviation of Alphanumeric Subparameters.

Any alphanumeric subparameter (e.g., 'BALANCE') is negated if its immediately preceding subparameter is 'NO', 'NON', or 'NOT'. Similarly, the subparameters 'YES', 'IS', 'USE', and 'DO' act as identity alphanumeric subparameters. These conventions are useful when you desire to use a single EISPAC call to compute the eigensystem of a matrix which sometimes is to be balanced and sometimes not, say, since the subparameter 'NO' or 'YES' may be an alphanumeric variable.

Any alphanumeric subparameter may be abbreviated by enough of its initial letters to unambiguously distinguish it from all other alphanumeric subparameters. For protection against ambiguities arising from the future introduction of new alphanumeric subparameters, you should use at least three (perhaps four) letter abbreviations when they exist. The alphanumeric subparameters currently in use are listed below (synonyms are separated by commas, antonyms by hyphens):

```
'DO', 'IS', 'USE', 'YES'
'NO', 'NON', 'NOT'
'REAL' - 'COMPLEX'
'HERMITIAN' - 'GENERAL' (see note 2)
'SYMMETRIC' - 'GENERAL'
'TRIDIAGONAL' - 'FULL'
'POSITIVE DEFINITE'
'NEGATIVE DEFINITE'
'BALANCE'
'ORTHOGONAL' - 'ELEMENTARY'
'UNITARY' - 'ELEMENTARY' (see note 5)
'AX=LBX', 'AZ=WBZ'
'ABX=LX', 'ABZ=WZ'
'BAX=LX', 'BAZ=WZ'
'LARGEST' - 'SMALLEST'.
```

As a final example illustrating these concepts, suppose you wish to compute the eigenvalues and eigenvectors of an order N real general matrix without balancing and using orthogonal transformations, with retrieval of the error indicator and calls to a user subroutine, in a program with variables dimensioned: A(100,100), WR(100), WI(100), Z(100,100). Then two of several possible calls are:

```
CALL EISPAC (100, N, MATRIX ('REAL', A), VALUES
    (WR, WI), VECTOR (Z), METHOD ('ORTHOGONAL',
    'NO', 'BALANCE'), ERROR (IERROR), SUBR
    (USUB))

CALL EISPAC (100, N, MATRIX ('NOT', 'COMPLEX',
    A), METHOD ('USE', 'ORTHOG', 'NO', 'NO',
    'NO', 'BALAN'), VALUES (WR, WI), VECTOR (Z),
    SUBR (USUB), ERROR (IERROR))
```

(Recall in the last example that keyword parameters can appear in any order in the third parameter position and beyond.)

D. Error Conditions and Returns.

Three types of errors can occur in EISPAC: "decision phase" errors, "execution phase" errors, and "linkage" errors. (See section 3 below.) Decision phase errors arise when EISPAC detects a mistake or inconsistency in the form of the parameters it receives. Execution phase errors are those which it detects during the execution of the eigensystem-package subroutines themselves. Decision phase errors always result in a message describing the error and the further message "EXECUTION CONTINUING" or "EXECUTION TERMINATED" and the appropriate action. Execution phase errors always result in a message describing the error and termination of execution, unless the ERROR keyword was supplied (see below).

Linkage errors may occur either during the decision or execution phases and always cause termination of execution. Linkage error 00 arises when the internal file name EISPACLB has not been associated with a dataset via a DD card or ALLOC command. Linkage error 01 arises when such an association has been made but a requested subroutine or phase of EISPAC cannot be found in the associated dataset. In this case, check that it contains the required eigensystem-package subroutines and the phases of EISPAC. (See sections 3 and 5 below.)

You may modify the behavior of EISPAC when an
execution phase error is detected by supplying the
ERROR keyword. When it is supplied, its subparameter
IERROR is set to a value characterizing the error and
return is made to the calling program (i.e., execution
is not terminated). Furthermore, you may suppress the
printing of the error message by setting IERROR to the
value -755 870 989 before calling EISPAC.

A non-zero value of IERROR on return from EISPAC
indicates that an execution phase error has occurred.
If IERROR is positive, the computation has been
abandoned, and few, if any, useful results have been
produced. However, if IERROR is negative, the
computation has been continued despite the error(s) and
some meaningful results have been produced; use of the
ERROR keyword thus permits you to recover these
results. The values IERROR may assume and their
significance are discussed below. (See also (2) and
(6).)

Value of IERROR	Error Msg. No.	Significance
0	None	No execution phase errors occurred.
I	00	The calculation of the I-th eigenvalue failed to converge. If the eigensystem of a real or complex general matrix or for a non-symmetric generalized problem was being computed, eigenvalues I+1,I+2,...,N should be correct; otherwise, eigenvalues 1,2,...,I-1 should be correct.
N+I	01	For a real non-symmetric tridiagonal matrix, $A(I,1)*A(I-1,3)$ .LT. 0, violating the restriction discussed above. No useful results are produced.
2*N+I	02	For the eigenvectors of a real non-symmetric tridiagonal matrix, $A(I,1)$ and $A(I-1,3)$ violated the restriction of note 4, above. All eigenvalues, but no eigenvectors, are correct.

3*N+1	03	Either: (1) Parameter MM specified insufficient storage to hold all of the eigenvalues in the interval (RLB,RUB). The only useful result is M, which contains the number of eigenvalues which lie in the interval. Or: (2) It is not possible to compute exactly M eigenvalues (starting from the Mll-th) because of exact multiplicity at index Mll. No useful results are produced.
3*N+2	04	It is not possible to compute exactly M eigenvalues (starting from the Mll-th) because of exact multiplicity at index Mll+M-1. No useful results are produced.
4*N+I	None	Not used in EISPAC.
5*N+I	05	The M largest or smallest eigenvalues were being computed by the rational QR method and the I-th eigenvalue failed to converge. All eigenvalues probably have some accuracy, but no stronger statement can be made.
6*N+1	06	The M largest or smallest eigenvalues were being computed by the rational QR method, the matrix was specified negative or positive definite, but the computation suggests it may not be; try again omitting the definiteness specification. No useful results are produced.
7*N+1	07	The eigensystem for a real symmetric generalized problem was being computed and the matrix supplied to MATB was not positive definite. No useful results are produced.
-I	50	The calculation of one or more eigenvectors including the I-th failed to converge. All eigenvalues and the non-zero eigenvectors are correct.

-(N+I)	None	Both error 50 above and error 52 below occurred.
-(2*N+I)	52	Parameter MM specified insufficient columns to hold the selected eigenvectors. All eigenvalues and the first MM columns of (ZR, ZI) or Z are correct.
-(3*N+I)	None	This error predicts that error 02 above will occur. It will not normally be returned from EISPAC but may be observed when the user subroutine is employed.

In addition to the above errors which are diagnosed by EISPAC, other errors may produce System/360-370 completion codes (SCC). The most commonly produced completion codes and their meanings in conjunction with EISPAC are the following:

> 804 There was not enough storage to dynamically load a requested subroutine. Provide more storage (region), reduce the size of the eigenproblem being solved, or choose a path which requires less temporary storage (see (1) and (6)). The minimum storage requirement for EISPAC is approximately 22,000 (decimal) bytes on System/360-370.

> 606 Same as SCC804 above.

> 80A There was not enough storage to allocate a temporary vector or matrix. See suggestions under SCC804 above.

E. Applicability and Restrictions.

EISPAC is applicable to the solution of the standard and generalized eigensystem problems for the classes of matrices for which examples are given above. For further details on applicability, see (6), or consult the "EISPAC Eigensystem Path Chart" (1) to determine which subroutines are used in the path of interest and then the NATS subroutine documents (2) for those subroutines.

3. DISCUSSION OF METHOD AND ALGORITHM.

EISPAC consists of three major parts, the parameter-
interpreter phase, the decision phase, and the execution
phase, which are co-ordinated by a supervisor. The
supervisor employs brief assembly language routines to count
the number of subparameters supplied to each of the keywords
and the number of parameters supplied to EISPAC itself. It
then loads the parameter-interpreter phase dynamically and
passes the parameter information to it.

The parameter-interpreter phase analyzes the parameters,
checks them for consistency, supplies defaults for omitted
optional parameters, and produces a characterization of the
problem they specify. It returns this characterization and a
standardized list of parameters to the supervisor.

If errors have been detected in the parameter-interpreter
phase, the supervisor loads an error message module
dynamically which prints error messages and which may
terminate execution. Otherwise, the supervisor loads a
decision phase appropriate to the problem being solved and
passes the characterization to it. The decision phase
determines the "path", or sequence, of eigensystem-package
subroutines and auxiliary actions (e.g., temporary storage
allocations) needed to solve the specified eigenproblem. It
then returns a representation of this path to the supervisor.

The supervisor then calls the execution phase, which
interprets the representation of the path (and information
about order of execution) to load dynamically the required
eigensystem subroutines and to allocate and free needed
temporary storage. (Loading, allocating, and freeing are
performed by operating system requests contained in brief
assembly language routines.) When execution is complete, or
as soon as a fatal error occurs, the execution phase returns
to the supervisor. If execution phase errors have occurred
and error messages are to be printed (see section 2.D
above), the supervisor loads the error message module
dynamically and prints them; execution terminates or
continues as described above. When execution continues, the
supervisor returns the results of the computation to the
calling program.

Certain economies of execution are possible when EISPAC is
called repeatedly to solve the same eigenproblem. After the
first execution of the path for the problem, usable copies of
the eigensystem-package subroutines for it may remain in
memory (if sufficient storage is available), and if so they
are reused without being reloaded on subsequent executions of
the path.

The design and implementation of EISPAC are highly modular, so that additional subroutines and paths can be added relatively easily and with only a minimum of disturbance to existing paths. This modular design of EISPAC and the philosophy behind it are discussed in detail in (7).

4. REFERENCES.

1) Boyle, J.M., Hauser, C.H., and Rothaar, H.R., EISPAC Eigensystem Package Path Chart, Release 2, Argonne National Laboratory, Applied Mathematics Division, February, 1975.

2) NATS Project, Eigensystem Subroutine Package (EISPACK), Subroutines F269 to F298 and F220 to F247.

3) Wilkinson, J.H. and Reinsch, C., Handbook for Automatic Computation, Volume II, Linear Algebra, Springer-Verlag, (1971).

4) Wilkinson, J.H., The Algebraic Eigenvalue Problem, Oxford, Clarendon Press (1965).

5) Rutishauser, H., Interference With an Algol-Procedure, Annual Review in Automatic Programming, Vol. 2 (R. Goodman, Ed.), Pergamon Press, (1961).

6) This publication. (Reference retained to resolve User Guide pointers, thus enabling compatibility with distributed documentation.)

7) Boyle, J.M. and Grau, A.A., Modular Design of a User-Oriented Control Program for EISPACK, Applied Mathematics Division Technical Memorandum No. 242, Argonne National Laboratory, Argonne, Illinois 60439, November 1973.

5. PROGRAM STATISTICS.

A. Additional Entry Point Names in EISPAC.

The entry point names listed below are entry point names in the part of EISPAC loaded with your program. Your program must not include other subroutines or functions having any of these names:

BAND, COREEP, EERMEP, EIDFEP, EISPAC, ERROR, FIDFEP, LINKEP, MATA, MATB, MATRIX, METHOD, SUBR, SUPVEP, VALUES, VECTOR.

In addition, the other phases of EISPAC contain entry
points with the names DGNHEP, DGSHEP, DIDFEP, DSNHEP,
EGNHEP, EGSHEP, ERMSEP, ERSEP, ESNHEP, FIDFEP, IBCMEP,
IBCOM#, ICHREP, INTREP, and LKUPEP. These entry points
will not, however, conflict with those in your program,
since these phases are loaded dynamically.

B. Common Storage.

None.

C. Space Requirements.

The parts of EISPAC loaded with your program
(subroutine EISPAC and the supervisor) require
2738 (HEX) = 10040 (DECIMAL) bytes under FORTRAN H,
OPT=2, Release 21.7 of OS/360. However, EISPAC
requires an additional amount of storage for the
dynamically loaded subroutines and the temporary arrays
some of them require. At a minimum, this requirement is
2EA0 (HEX) = 11936 (DECIMAL) bytes for the parameter-
interpreter phase of EISPAC. During execution, up to
3100 (HEX) = 12544 (DECIMAL) bytes are required for the
appropriate execution phase of EISPAC and a typical
EISPACK subroutine, plus whatever additional storage is
needed for dynamically allocated temporary arrays. See
(1) and (2) for further information for estimating this
dynamically-determined amount of storage.

6. CHECKOUT.

A. Test Cases.

EISPAC has been tested on the same matrices as have the
separate EISPACK subroutines. See Section 3 --
"VALIDATION OF EISPACK".

B. Accuracy.

The accuracy of EISPAC depends directly upon the
subroutines used from the EISPACK package (2).
Consult the path chart (1) to learn which subroutines
have been selected, and then reference the separate
accuracy statements that apply to these subroutines.

REFERENCES

1. Wilkinson, J. H. and Reinsch, C., Handbook for Automatic Computation, Volume II, Linear Algebra, Part 2, Springer-Verlag, New York, Heidelberg, Berlin, 1971.

2. Wilkinson, J. H., The Algebraic Eigenvalue Problem, Clarendon Press, Oxford, 1965.

3. Boyle, J. M., Cody, W. J., Cowell, W. R., Garbow, B. S., Ikebe, Y., Moler, C. B., and Smith, B. T., NATS, A Collaborative Effort to Certify and Disseminate Mathematical Software, Proceedings 1972 National ACM Conference, Volume II, Association for Computing Machinery, New York, 1972, pp. 630-635.

4. Smith, B. T., The NATS Project, A National Activity to Test Software, SHARE SSD 228, October, 1972, item C-5732, pp. 35-42.

5. Smith, B. T., Boyle, J. M., Cody, W. J., The NATS Approach to Quality Software, Software for Numerical Mathematics, D. J. Evans, ed., Academic Press, London, New York, 1974, pp. 393-405.

6. Boyle, J. M. and Grau, A. A., Modular Design of a User-Oriented Control Program for EISPACK, Technical Memorandum No. 242, Applied Mathematics Division, Argonne National Laboratory, 1973.

7. Garbow, B. S., EISPACK - A Package of Matrix Eigensystem Routines, Computer Physics Communications, North-Holland, Amsterdam, Vol. 7, 1974, pp. 179-184.

8. Moler, C. B. and Stewart, G. W., An Algorithm for Generalized Matrix
    Eigenvalue Problems, SIAM Journal of Numerical Analysis, Vol. 10,
    1973, pp. 241-256.

9. Ward, R. C., An Extension of the QZ Algorithm for Solving the Generalized
    Matrix Eigenvalue Problem, Technical Note NASA TN D-7305, National
    Aeronautics and Space Administration, Washington, 1973.

10. Smith, B. T., Boyle, J. M., Dongarra, J. J., Garbow, B. S., Ikebe, Y.,
    Klema, V. C., and Moler, C. B., Matrix Eigensystem Routines - EISPACK
    Guide, Lecture Notes in Computer Science, Vol. 6, Second Edition,
    Springer-Verlag, New York, Heidelberg, Berlin, 1976.